Mini

By the same author

VW BEETLE
A Celebration

THE MAHARAJAH'S BOX
An Imperial Story of Conspiracy, Love and a Guru's Prophecy

FENIAN FIRE
The British Government Plot to Assassinate Queen Victoria

PHYLLOXERA
How Wine Was Saved for the World

BAND OF BRIGANDS
The Extraordinary Story of the First Men in Tanks

Mini

An Intimate Biography

by Christy Campbell

Published by Virgin Books 2009
2 4 6 8 10 9 7 5 3 1

First published in Great Britain in 2009 by
Virgin Books
Random House, 20 Vauxhall Bridge Road,
London SW1V 2SA

www.virginbooks.com
www.rbooks.co.uk

Addresses for companies within The Random House Group Limited
can be found at: www.randomhouse.co.uk/offices.htm

The Random House Group Limited Reg. No. 954009

A CIP catalogue record for this book
is available from the British Library

Hardback ISBN 9781905264629

The Random House Group Limited supports The Forest Stewardship
Council [FSC], the leading international forest certification organisation.
All our titles that are printed on Greenpeace-approved FSC-certified
paper carry the FSC logo. Our paper procurement policy can be found
at www.rbooks.co.uk/environment

Mixed Sources

Product group from well-managed
forests and other controlled sources
www.fsc.org Cert no. TT-COC-2139
© 1996 Forest Stewardship Council

Typeset by Palimpsest Book Production Limited,
Grangemouth, Stirlingshire

Printed and bound in Great Britain by
CPI Mackays, Chatham ME5 8TD

For Joe

Contents

Contents

Preface: First Car, First Love	1
Acknowledgements	5
Author's Note	7
Foreword	11
1 A Mini Funeral and Three Weddings	13
2 War Baby	19
3 The Big Sell	27
4 Think Small	35
5 Badge Engineers	43
6 Style Council	59
7 Pop Goes the Motor Car	65
8 The Monster We Love	71
9 Market Research Is Bunk	75
10 Sputnik	83
11 Look at Us, We're Poor	95
12 Getaway People	101
13 City Car	107
14 Room at the Top	113
15 Bit More Steam	119
16 Conspicuous Thrift	133
17 Mini Scandal	141
18 Mini Converts	147
19 Sunday Night at the London Palladium	153
20 'Sixties Sexpot	161
21 Third Time Unlucky	169
22 Mini Troubles	173
23 Turin Car	177
24 Not So SuperMini	183
25 Mini Heartbreak	193
26 Mid-Life Crisis	199
27 Cooper Reborn	217
28 Second Coming	235
29 Are We Nearly There Yet?	243
30 MINI	255
Mini Timeline	269
Appendix: 50 Mini Facts	281
Index	287
Picture Credits	295

Mini Maestro: Sir Alec Issigonis, who in 1957–9 inspired a small team of
engineers to create the British Motor Corporation's baby car – which would be
known pretty soon thereafter as the 'Mini'. It was a towering achievement.

First Car, First Love

Five and a half million Minis. That's how many were made and anyone who has ever encountered a Mini has something to tell you about it. So that would be about fifty million stories.

'I had one of those'; 'my dad had one of those'. Mention Minis and sensible people go dewy-eyed. The memories, you see. I wonder where the old girl is now? First kiss, first love, first car.

Of course it was temperamental. Of course it let you down. But it was fabulous. That is why the Mini always gets you.

This is the portrait of a fifty-year-old. It's about being alive and kicking some time in the second half of the twentieth century. It's about the one inanimate object that people find it possible to have deep and meaningful relationships with – a motor car. It's about a special sort of motor car that you could just about afford to keep going and that always cheered you up at the very thought that it was yours. It still does.

If you didn't have one, your friend did. The funny friend who was always up for it – the one who had the special sticky-out wheels, who knew how to get into the party you weren't invited to – but which was way too far to get to. But you got there. And you got there in a Mini.

The man who conceived it was aged exactly fifty when he started putting it together – and in 2009 it is fifty years since his baby gurgled into life.

But unlike the human participants in some Friends Reunited autumnal romance, mechanical things have the ability to regenerate. Real Minis, proper Minis, were made from 1959 to 2000.

When it first went on sale half a century ago, this iconic

machine, the creation of an eccentric, homosexual engineering genius, stunned everybody with its technical innovation and sheer charm. There was a bigger surprise – it was Made in England. Perhaps it needed an outsider, a foreign (Issigonis was half Greek, half German) designer to make it happen. His creation became nothing less than a symbol of national renewal. Along with the Spitfire fighter aircraft of two decades before, the Mini was Britain's most uncompromising twentieth-century statement of individuality. For forty-one years the production line churned on regardless amidst cultural upheaval, industrial dingdong and a revolution in consumer aspirations. And it should not be forgotten that for many thousands of Brits of a certain age, the Mini was not some swinging style statement. It was the car that Mum and Dad had, the family car, the small people mover in which they were taken to school or went on holiday.

The curtain nearly came down so very often – but there was something about that machine and its place in the national psyche that kept it ever young while generations of Mini lovers came and went. Then it bowed out to make way for a different act – MINI.

It went on for so long – while so much changed around it. Like those Japanese soldiers on a remote Pacific island who didn't know the war had ended, it just went on doing what it did until it seemed like time to surrender.

It was swinging in the 'sixties and stodgy in the 'seventies. It was pert in the 'eighties and retro in the 'nineties. It just about made it to the 'noughties. As a brand it was priceless but nobody was quite sure what to do with it. Then along came somebody who did.

When the Mini was young the world loved cars. When the Mini was old the love affair was fading. It wasn't the Mini's fault. The automobile and all its works – anti-urban, socially atomising, death-dealing, child-killing, nature-destroying – had become a parody of what had once seemed an optimistic future of mass mobility. It still needed semi-pornographic images of mastery and submission to pull jaded buyers to bloated, irrelevant machines. In late 2008 the US auto industry came out with its hands up. Was there ever a Good Car? someone asked. There was. It was the Mini.

This could be an essay in mid-life, mid-century nostalgia. It is very tempting to linger around the point a half-century ago when the brick dust of two world wars was at last blown off the Edwardian china by all things fab. There will be some of that – and the inevitable parade of whiskery celebrities whose swinging credentials were enhanced by association with the little car. There will be outings to Carnaby Street and Bayswater mews. But we will soon be motoring on.

What fifty years of the Mini is really about is the story of an idea. It is that making things and consuming things both bring responsibility. Get it right and the resulting relationship can engender immense human happiness. And of all man-made things, motor cars can trigger the most intense passions. Only a few of them can do that. The Mini is one. Some would say it is the only one.

Yeah so it breaks and never works properly. Yeah so it feels like you're constantly about to die. Yeah so the bigger vehicles think they can bully you. Yeah well, who cares when you look so gosh darn cool!

Mini blogger, spring 2008

Are there any hot girls who own Minis?
I've only ever seen a woman driving a Mini once . . . do HOT girls drive Minis?
any help anyone . . .

Mini lonely-heart, autumn 2008

Acknowledgements

More than mini-thanks are due to the individuals and institutions who have helped me along this journey. But it was their affection for the Mini that opened the door. To start at the beginning I must thank my father, the archetypal Mini-Dad of the 'sixties and 'seventies, for letting me drive his cars. Without the encouragement at the time of Jonathan Wood (whose 2005 biography of the great designer proved a lodestar) and the late Tony Dawson, then of British Leyland, I would never have ventured in pilgrimage to Edgbaston thirty years ago to interview Sir Alec Issigonis himself and to whom the world owes thanks.

In no order of Mini-preference I must gratefully acknowledge the contributions and help of Paddy Hopkirk, Sir Stirling Moss, Mrs Joanna Barlow, Mrs Marilyn Foreman, Richard Bacchus, Jan Valentino, Prof Dale Harrow, Gillian Bardsley, Geoff Upex, Natalie Churchill (and all members of the Upavon Mini Drivers club), Dr Alex Moulton, Janey Bain, Mary Quant, Gert Hildebrand, Sarah Bauer, Manuel Werner, Stephanie Guttenberger, Ray Wert, Gillian Marston, Wanda Polanksi, Abigail Humphries, Miguel Plano, Miedalo Miedalo, Boo Long, the Virgin team, Ed Faulkner, Sophia Brown, Kelly Falconer, Hugo de Klee, and at Curtis Brown, Felicity Blunt and my agent Vivienne Schuster. Thanks also to the librarians and system managers at the British Library, the National Archives and the British Motor Industry Heritage Trust. I thank my wife Clare Campbell and my children, Katy, Maria and Joe for putting up with months of Mini-monomania. To those many Mini-forum posters around the world, I am grateful for sharing their thoughts and Mini-memories. Where archival material, textual or pictorial, is used without direct accreditation after anguished attempts to locate the originator, I ask for forgiveness, and shall duly acknowledge as a matter of course and when possible.

Author's Note

The Mini is fifty – happy birthday! There are lots of us who have seen you grow up. I knew your dad – well, sort of. When you were twenty and I was twenty-something, I came to see you as a youthful journalist on a mission to interview Sir Alec Issigonis, the celebrity car designer, in fact Britain's only one. I drove from London to Brum in my student-bought car, a Morris Minor series MM convertible, built three years before I was born. Alexander Arnold Constantine Issigonis had designed the Minor during the war.

But that was not the only thing that had got me interested in Sir Alec (he'd been knighted in 1969) and his cars. It was Mini business that had brought me on this brisk spring day to leafy Westbourne Gardens, Edgbaston. I was a child of the 'fifties – like the Mini. I loved them from the very start. Aged eight, I knew the difference between the crinkly-grilled 'Austin Seven' and the 'Morris Mini-Minor'. In shabby, post-austerity London – quite suddenly all these cheeky little cars appeared driven by people determined to be with-it. 'The in-car as different as the people in it' said the ad on TV.

Once, when my father's Morris Minor broke down on the way to a family funeral, we were given a lift by a stranger in a Mini Cooper. He wore a tweed hat, sheepskin car-coat and string-back driving gloves. He attacked the twisting country lanes like Paddy Hopkirk on the way down from the mountains into Monte. I was in heaven. My father bought a Mini (an ordinary one – a Cooper would not have been his style). I think he did it to impress me. It was the most uncompromisingly 'modern' thing he ever did. In fact he bought a succession of them and even lent the latest to me as I grew up – for forays in search of beer and girls.

A north London friend had one, done over in purple Dulux. We took it to the Isle of Wight pop festival in 1969. At college

I had a Hooray Henry friend – 'Crasher' – the son of a Conservative MP. He had a brand-new, orange Mini 1275GT in which we would drive very fast to the Clermont Club in London. I thought it was fabulous.

On the Mini's twentieth birthday I went in pilgrimage to Edgbaston, Birmingham, to interview its then seventy-three-year-old creator for the just-launched *Thoroughbred & Classic Cars* magazine. Sir Alec was opinionated, peppery and boastful. 'All cars today are so boring,' he announced with a disparaging wave.

'Do you know Margaret and Tony?' he asked. I did not, but that did not seem to diminish me in his eyes. In his retirement twilight he would receive all sorts of people like me who were genuinely enthusiastic about him and his cars. And the true Mini adept, Lord Snowdon himself, was due to visit soon after me – to make a twentieth-anniversary portrait of the great designer for *Vogue*. Sir Alec was frail, but alert. He demolished the reputations of both rivals and collaborators in a camp wave of his hand. Martinis were served (very dry) and the remarks became more waspish. Some are recorded in the narrative that follows.

A fire was burning in the grate. On the mantelpiece was a silver model of the first Mini, inscribed the 'launching of the Sputnik 26 August 1959'. The house was single-storey and modernist in style but had a tweedy Edwardian comfort as befitted its inhabitant. The drawing room was spacious and ordered, with a table at one end strewn with sketches and plans, and a study dominated by the world's largest Meccano set. He had received it eight years earlier as a retirement present from the British Leyland Motor Corporation. There were plenty of books, P G Wodehouse especially and the detective fiction he adored – plus a venerable edition of *Wind in the Willows*. Mr Toad, wearing cap, motoring dust coat, goggles and gauntlets, blinked triumphantly from the spine. Issigonis was aged two when the boastful, motor-car-loving amphibian was first created.

In his spacious garage was a steam-powered Mini prototype

and something equally strange, the 'gearless Mini' with constantly variable transmission. I was astonished.

It was 3 May 1979, election day. The papers were full of pictures of Mrs Margaret Thatcher, leader of the Conservative Party. Was he a supporter? He would not reveal his intentions when he went off to the voting station – in a Mini.

But the old ways of doing things were crumbling (like the rust-eaten front wings of the 1949 Minor in which I had arrived in Britain's motor city). You could sense it – after the political turmoil of the winter just passed. British industry, as exemplified by the nationalised British Leyland at Longbridge not so far up the road from where we were sitting, was about to get a massive kick up the production line. The fate of the brilliant little car was shackled to a state-owned Stegosaurus, the management and workforce of which had writhed and thrashed through the decade about to end and which would continue to change in a series of corporate upheavals. But the Mini pottered on – because there was never enough investment money to replace it properly. And it had found a base of loyalists from Omagh to Osaka who would just go on and on buying it. They would continue doing so for an astonishing further twenty-one years.

Sir Alec died in 1988. What would he have thought of his baby's survival for so long? He would have been immensely proud of course but I suspect he would have been surprised too. He himself produced a successor design, but it was never put into production. It was something that clearly saddened him greatly. As his biographer wrote not too long after the Mini's fortieth birthday: 'The Mini was one link in the chain of his personal creative progression. He never doubted that he would find a better way, and like the Minor, the Mini must one day belong to the past. That is not what happened.'

Well, now the classic Mini does belong to the past – my past and that of millions like me. It broke our hearts – but we love it still.

Mini legs: As miniskirt originator Mary Quant declared in 1967: 'Once only the rich set the fashion. Now it was the inexpensive little dress seen on the girl in the high street.' Thus it was with an inexpensive little car.

Foreword

In 1965 Jean Shrimpton gave me a lift in her maroon Mini; I was almost speechless at the honour of being driven by the toppest of top models in the chicest of cars, and sat in admiring envy until she dropped me off at Earl's Court, where I shared a flat with three others. I was a model, too, but very much a beginner; I travelled by tube, lugging my huge model bag, which contained wigs and shoes, gloves and belts, jewellery, make-up and Carmen rollers.

Then came a stroke of luck; a wonderful photographer called Crispian Woodgate found he couldn't pay back £120 I had lent him (we were all as poor as rats in those days, but happy as kings). Would I accept his Mini instead? I would. It was grey with a yellow interior . . . but wait! After a thorough scrubbing inside and out it turned out to be pale blue under the grime and the nicotine. To start it, you turned a key then pressed a switch on the floor. The dip switch was next to the clutch on the ground, which could introduce dazzling moments during my elaborate double de-clutching on corners at night. The doors opened by pulling down on a piece of string. I suppose she went at 70 mph with the accelerator pedal floored. The interior was sparse, tinny but spacious in a titchy way. Friends could cram in, three in the back and one beside me, and London was at our feet, almost literally as ground clearance was about two inches. Heaven it was in that dawn to be alive – to be a model in the heart of the fashion world, in the hottest city on the planet, in the coolest, grooviest car ever made.

Joanna Lumley

CHAPTER 1

A Mini Funeral and Three Weddings

Single 23yr old Male, owner of 2 [classic] Minis wants to meet a female of similar interests between 18 and 30. Must like drives out and understand that one of my Minis requires a lot of attention being restored. Pref local to the Manchester area.

Mini lonely-heart, 2008

The Northavon Mini club was in deepest mourning. There is a line from a popular poem that provides comfort in such times: 'You can turn your back on tomorrow and live yesterday or you can be happy for tomorrow because of yesterday.' But the mood at this particular funeral was not happy for tomorrow. An impostor had taken the loved one's place.

All this was about a motor car. On the afternoon of 4 October 2000, production of the 'Mini' had ceased at the mighty factory at Longbridge outside Birmingham after over four decades. A great British institution had passed away. There had been no funerary rites, no lying in state. Instead a blousy old Matt Monro song from the swinging 'sixties had been played and evergreen pop singer Lulu had sat in the passenger seat as Mr Geoff Powell, Mini production-line supervisor (known within the plant as 'Mr Mini'), ceremonially drove the last one off the line. Executives from the MG Rover car company looked on, joined by Herr Professor Werner Sämann of the Bavarian Motor Works, now owners of the Mini patrimony.

It was a red Cooper Sport. Actually the last car to be built was a blue one, completed some days before. However, a red car was chosen as 'more appropriate' and had spent a week being specially burnished for its big day. Meanwhile, as everyone knew, the BMW motor works of Munich, Bavaria, had developed a 'replacement'. They called it MINI. There had been plenty of press exposure and real-life versions were promised to appear later that month at the Birmingham Motor Show. But already the purists were up in arms. What was coming was a 'bloated pastiche'. This had not been a dynastic succession. This had been an assassination.

Down in the West Country, as in many other places across Britain and the wider world, there was deep anguish. Members of the Northavon Mini Drivers club were not going to see their beloved car pass away unmourned.

Club founder Natalie Curtis celebrated her twenty-eighth birthday on the day the Mini 'died'. She did so in an unusual way. As she recalled:

> When we found out that production was going to end, I suppose we felt that it couldn't really be happening – that the Mini would go on for ever.
>
> That afternoon we went round Bristol in a little convoy, about a dozen of us, going slow like we were following a hearse. We'd made little crosses and wreaths saying RIP Mini. We wore black armbands. We stopped outside the main Rover dealer and held a two-minute silence. Afterwards we held a wake. We were all very serious about it.

Some people might think Natalie was eccentric. They might describe her and her fellow Mini lovers as 'anoraks' or 'nerds' – and conclude that they had taken their enthusiasm for an inanimate object too far. But Minis get people that way.

'People love Minis,' she had told a reporter at the time of the funeral. 'Their owners even give them names and many believe they have their own little personalities – they are much more than just a normal car.' She could not 'imagine driving anything else', she said. 'The Mini is a British institution and it's hard to believe it has now gone. It may be a small car but it has played a large part in the history of this country.' Of the new MINI she was deeply suspicious.

Natalie had owned eight Minis since she had been a teenager – and 'loved them all'. She'd got her first when she was eighteen 'off a friend's dad' for seventy-five quid. It was teal blue, M reg. She'd got through several more as a student (of window-dressing – 'I've always had an eye for style'). Once a back wheel fell off when she and two friends were coming back from a party. 'We managed to push it home.' Mini memories are at their most memorable when they involve some banal letting-down that is then triumphantly overcome. Perhaps it's the ease of getting out of such scrapes that make Minis so forgivable.

Natalie had founded the club in 1994 – membership grew steadily then it had sort of run out of steam after the old Mini passed away. In 2004 it started up again on a new tide of Mini love and love for life. In 2008 it was booming.

Seven years on since that mournful black-armbanded day and Natalie was now Natalie Churchill. Her husband, Darren, was a mobile-phone salesman. They had met through the Mini club. He drove a blue MINI. Nevertheless their relationship had prospered.

On a cold autumn night in 2008 outside a pub in the suburbs of Bristol, Minidom had come to stretch out and relax. In the car park a 'seventies Clubman nestled besides a rather nice Equinox special edition. A green early 'sixties Traveller cosied up to a bright yellow Mk II. A Mini Mayfair sprinkled some Thatcher-era yuppie nostalgia on the proceedings. Several late-model BMW MINIs looked on forlornly as if they would like to join the party.

Inside the barn-like pub, the Northavon Mini club sipped lager and lemonade. They were late-twenty-somethings with a smattering of grandparents. Young children played with model Minis and Mini puzzles as their parents talked of Mini celebrations past and yet to come. Romances had been made here. After the funeral, there had been two Mini marriages.

There were Natalie and Darren. Then there had been Jenny and Dominic. As Dominic recalled:

> We met through the Mini club . . . there was a Mini procession at our wedding in 2002. So it was natural we should go on honeymoon in Layla, my 1979 Mini pickup. We went camping in Dorset and threw everything in the back of her. We went up a hill slowly, slowly, and overtook an articulated lorry. Coming down the other side the brakes just weren't there. There was smoke pouring out of them. I steered into the kerb and we stopped OK. The brakes cooled down and were working fine again. It was a fabulous honeymoon. Actually three couples we know met through Minis . . .

Then there were Charlotte and Ryan, who were planning their forthcoming 2009 wedding to coincide with the Mini fiftieth celebrations in Birmingham. That was real Mini love perhaps but nobody here thought it was over the top. This lot were the happiest, most normal car owners it was possible to imagine.

Mini attraction: Sue Cuff, Miss Great Britain, compels all eyes to observe the excitements of the Mini 1275 GT's Dunlop Denovo 'runflat' tyres in a 1975 publicity shot. The Mini's own sensual attractions (or lack of them) were always the stuff of excitable comment.

ration, sweets, clothing, bread – for year after austere year. Meat went on being rationed until summer 1954. Anything the nation made, especially motor cars, was for shipping overseas to earn dollars. There were scant domestic luxuries – it was 'export or die', so people were told. They'd got fed up hearing it.

What people wanted was cars. They wanted new ones. In the post-war years, most of the things plugging along the nation's war-coarsened highways looked ancient – dingy veterans revived from their wartime slumber. And to get things started again, in 1945 British carmakers had just put back into production what they had been making in 1939. Most new cars were bound for export anyway. Steel allocation in the still-wartime-style control economy were made according to a manufacturer's overseas order book.

Hence the crop of startlingly styled, mid-century motors with supposedly Yank-pleasing names like Triumph 'Mayflower' and Austin 'Atlantic' that fleetingly appeared at the time. The Americans couldn't believe that cars could have engines so small. Actually what they really liked were trad British sports cars with wire wheels and long bonnets like the, beloved-of-Californians, MG Midget TC.

Owning a new car was hugely aspirational – if you could find one to buy in the first place. You had to sign a legal covenant that you wouldn't sell it for at least two years. It was all dead dodgy. The second-hand motor trade, operating off myriad bombsites, took on the Brylcreemed mantle of the wartime spiv. Any sort of car was a thing of wonder.

Belfast-born Mini-legend-to-be Paddy Hopkirk, a young adult in the early 'fifties, remembered: 'Driving to Bangor to meet student friends – we'd walk up and down and just endlessly examine each other's cars, whatever they were. When someone came to your house for dinner, you asked about their car, you went outside and took a look at it. It didn't matter how old it was or what it was, it was a car.'

Lesley Hornby, born in 1949 in Neasden, north-west London,

would remember: 'We were the first family in our street to have a car. Then quite suddenly from being no cars in the road it was full of them – quite posh ones too.' By the time Miss Hornby became Twiggy in 1966 she could afford any sort of car she liked. She liked Minis.

At Longbridge, Birmingham, the home of the Austin car company, a mighty new factory had been built on the site of a wartime airfield. First the admin block, known as the 'Kremlin', had arisen in 1948. Then came Car Assembly Building 1, 'the greatest and most modern car plant in the world'. It was the wonder of the age, capable of producing 2,000 units of the top-selling Austin A40 every week – if it could get the steel.

The beastly Germans had gone back into their bombed-out factories and put some curious things into production. The Volkswagen for one (aided by British Army engineers). And wartime plane makers Heinkel and Messerschmitt had reopened for business, making sewing machines and invalid carriages. Before long they would be making something the British would call 'bubble cars'.

Lack of petrol and basic materials had kindled a similar ingenuity in Britain. In 1949 Laurie Bond of the Bond Aircraft and Engineering Co. (Blackpool) Ltd introduced the three-wheeled Bond 'Mk A' – a kind of fairground dodgem fitted with a 125cc engine, lacking virtually all refinements and with no rear suspension whatsoever.

It would, however, go for miles. A letter to the *Yorkshire Post* from a Bond owner read: 'I have just got to London from Preston with the wife, the dog, and the weekend luggage . . . 200 miles at an average 31.4 mph. It cost us 2 gallons of petrol and 7 penny worth of oil . . . total four shillings and nine pence.' Mr Bond called his frugal creation the 'Minicar'.

Mr T L Williams, owner of the Reliant Motor Company of Tamworth, Staffs, put four seats in a three-wheel, cut-down delivery van with an Austin Seven engine. It was called the 'Reliant Regal Mk 1'. It was almost as crude as the Minicar.

These were what might be described as 'microcars', downsized individual transporters which had always bubbled up in the aftermath of wars and in time of scarcity. What people really wanted was a proper car – with four wheels, recognisable as something two persons wide by two persons long. But until such things came along they would put up with anything. Buying 'foreign' was no answer. Import duty remained at a prohibitive thirty-three and a third per cent of the wholesale price (and that was before purchase tax). Only the very rich or the very eccentric bothered.

But amid the gloom there had been a few splashes of light. A year after the end of the war, the newly formed Council of Industrial Design staged an exhibition called 'Britain Can Make It' at the V&A Museum in London. The title of course worked on several levels. But if the nation was really to pull through – what was this? A washing machine, an oilcan, a filing cabinet, an electric kettle, pottery, socks – it didn't amount to much – but almost one and a half million people queued for hours and paid 3d to see the unimaginable luxuries within. Things that one day they might be able to buy. Only model motor cars were featured; real ones were for export only. Times were hard but the mood was optimistic. Things could only get better.

In 1948 over half a million people had flocked to the first post-war Motor Show, held at Earl's Court, London, where three brand-new British stunners appeared, the Morris Minor MM (with a pre-war engine), the Land Rover and the Jaguar XK120.

Two years later the post-war Labour government's last hurrah had been the Festival of Britain, which blew a whiff of alien modernism along the decaying wharves of the Thames before folding up its tents in autumn 1951. Much of the festival's 'contemporary' design flavour would linger into the 'fifties and beyond – although the arrival of Mr Churchill's Conservatives, back in power in late 1951, somewhat slowed the stampede of the 'deciding classes' towards super-modernity.

Minor success: Morris series MM convertible of 1949. Issigonis's cleverly engineered and beautifully packaged wartime creation, the Morris Minor, would be the quintessential British car of the 'fifties.

But there was a political consensus in Britain on left and right that the epoch-making task of modernisation would be heralded by ever wider private car ownership. The working class would be truly enfranchised as they turned from lumpen producers into self-mobile consumers – just as Henry Ford's 'gasoline buggy' had liberated post-WWI rural America from the tedium of life on the farm. Who dare stand in their way?

The *private* car was just that – a matter of personal choice to buy and self-responsibility to keep running. But of course it needed public space in the form of roads (which all agreed must be free at the point of use) and parking lots. All those fusty old market towns and cathedral cities – they were in for a shake-up. And the dozy old railways. A few eccentrics had started to complain about noise, air pollution, safety and the sheer amount of metal trying to navigate the cronky urban fabric. They were spoilsports. The loudest voices were those shouting Buy more, buy more stuff, buy more cars!

The Suez fracas would turn out to be a hiccup in the march of the motor car. The oil was turned on again after four months. It wasn't quite apocalypse at the petrol pumps but the political and cultural shock was extreme. Meanwhile there had been a brief revival of the minicars that had appeared post-war – but this time a strange froth of alien bubbles sucked in from Germany and Italy. Could not British manufacturers do better?

In November 1956 *Motor* magazine published a stern editorial called 'Miniature Motoring'. It proclaimed: 'Everyone must now consider how they can best serve the national interest by using a minimum of petrol . . . our motor cars have got to be small . . . there can never be sufficient room on the roads of this island for hordes of vehicles equal in size to the present transatlantic automobile.'

The article was prescient and it was true. But in the absence of a political regime ready to impose 'sensible' cars on the masses, free-market forces must do the downsizing. The same editorial saw the technical task ahead clearly: 'On the other hand the battle to produce the greatest possible passenger accommodation on the shortest possible wheelbase means saving every inch on the dimensions of the power unit and this will give the clever designer great scope when it comes to tucking away the cylinder block.'

But where in the land was a company with the required industrial muscle combined with the will to take big risks in engineering and marketing? There was such a company, itself not long forged by market forces into what was in fact by far the biggest single car producer in Britain. Its headquarters were at Longbridge, Birmingham. Its chairman was Sir Leonard Lord, a 'foul-mouthed, hard-driving production man', in one description, 'a born businessman and a great production engineer' in another. It was called the British Motor Corporation. It employed a talented if somewhat eccentric chief designer called Alec Issigonis. He was known to motor-industry insiders as the creator of Britain's most successful post-war car, the Morris Minor.

A lot later, Alec Issigonis liked to say that it was the bubble-car boom that did it, driving his boss, the patriotic Sir Leonard, to pronounce one day in late 1956: 'God damn these bloody awful bubble cars. We must drive them off the streets by designing a proper miniature car.'

It was the beginning of something small.

CHAPTER 3

The Big Sell

Mini road rage 1
I was driving [in my classic Mini] home from work, went to go to the exit as u do and a black BMW MINI cut me up then slammed his brakes on for no reason at all – so I gave him a bit of a horn as u would and at the traffic lights I had my window down and so did he and he shouted 'get a real MINI u c***!' . . .

Mini-forum posting, November 2008

America in the 'fifties, land of the free, land of the automobile, was on a surging economic wave. The transition from wartime to peacetime production had been very rapid. In make-do-and-mend Britain, affluence was just beginning to burst out all over although the pace was far too slow for some.

In the US former war industries now churned out the material goods for the richest and most technologically advanced society in history. It meant lots of big, shiny automobiles. Still-rationed Britons observed it longingly through movies and magazines (not quite yet on TV – but it was coming). The whiff of remade affluence was blowing across the Atlantic. It smelled like a new car.

The new prosperity must surely be welcomed. It would create a just society without the apparent need (as in post-war Britain) for state-imposed redistribution. But there were doubters. In Harvard, Mass., a Canadian-born economics professor called John Kenneth Galbraith was drafting his soon-to-be-famous tract –

The Affluent Society – while a twenty-something graduate of the same university's law school called Ralph Nader was beginning to get cross about US carmakers' perceived indifference to safety.

When it was published in 1958, Professor Galbraith's book was pounced on by British cultural and political commentators. As the old 'working class' was being shown the promised land of washing machines and package holidays on newborn commercial television, this analysis of 'modern consumer demand' was very timely. Especially its analysis of the power of advertising to create 'new wants which the consumer did not previously possess', as the professor put it. The paradox was that every effort to increase production to satiate those wants 'brought with it a raising of the level of consumption which itself increases want'.

Americans had been going on about this sort of thing ever since an eccentric economist called Thorstein Veblen had published his *Theory of the Leisure Class* sixty years earlier. He had coined the phrase 'conspicuous consumption'. Everyone sought perceptible status, that was the human condition, he suggested. But in developed industrial societies, status was shown by the *futility*, rather than the usefulness, of what was being consumed.

Such things must be clearly expensive and at the same time manifestly wasteful. That is what made them desirable. Meanwhile the lower classes were not out to overthrow the upper class but instead strived to climb until they too might wallow in absurdity. By which time the original lot had moved on to something else.

It might have been a prescription for the twentieth-century auto industry. It was why cars always grew bigger. Why argue with what the public wanted? At its millennial apogee, the process would climax with 'Chelsea tractors' at British school gates and America's toxic sport-ute love affair, which in the end would bring Detroit to its knees. Manufacturers had loved conspicuous consumption all along. Big cars made big profits.

The greatest component in the cost of sale, labour, was more or less the same whatever the size of the end product.

But as interesting as why cars got bigger is why they (periodically) got *smaller*. Besides spikes in the price of fuel, the amount of roadspace and periodic government intervention, there is a cycle in the history of the automobile when a bunch of rationalists (normally, but not always, city-based) suddenly turn against conspicuous consumption and go for the most austere thing possible. It happened in Britain in the late 'fifties and in the US two decades later with the Iranian revolution and the 'second oil-price shock' (it's always the Middle East). It began to happen again in the late 'noughties.

Detroit's mid-century automobile makers with their yearly programme of 'new' models were the paradigm of creating want without end. But underneath, while the sheet metal and chrome surfaces of cars changed each year, the mechanics remained the same for years, sometimes decades, to facilitate the economies of scale required by mass production. Automotive designers (they were called 'stylists') were merely there to pimp the ride. Some of them seemed to know it. The fêted French-born industrial designer, Raymond Loewy (otherwise a stern critic of Detroit's follies), once famously said: 'Good design is an upwards sales curve.' Loewy had set up a London design studio in 1936.

He recognised the inherent conservatism of consumers – even when goaded to buy by a parade of fashionable novelty. He formulated his famous 'Most Advanced Yet Acceptable' principle to express the fact that product designs are not simply bounded by functional constraints but by the social expectations that determine their market acceptance.

'The adult public's taste is not necessarily ready to accept the logical solutions to their requirements if the solution implies too vast a departure from what they have been conditioned into accepting as the norm,' he said. Make something really New! and the mass market would shun it.

Academics and government took a huge interest in the concept of the consumer as TV advertising became the driver of a new social and economic order. A new science (it was actually invented in the 'twenties) called 'market research' became massively energised. All sorts of theorists piled in. In a famous treatise called *The Strategy of Desire*, a Vienna-born psychoanalyst called Ernest Dichter used Freudian techniques to analyse the dynamics of what he called 'the Pyscho-Economic' age – and particularly why Americans bought motor cars. Convertibles attracted them into the showroom because they represented a man's mistress, but they ended up buying a sedan – representing a 'wife'. A hardtop meanwhile was a convenient union of the two.

The failure of the 1957 Ford Edsel to attract buyers had been ascribed anecdotally to the fact that its front-end chromework resembled female genitalia. There were crude jokes aplenty. All that was true, said Dr Dichter – but of course 'rational' market research had failed to pick it up in the design phase. His brand of deep psycho probing would have done.

Were cars phallic or feminine? They seemed to be both. According to Dr Dichter they were 'containers' and thus 'female' – inspiring men to want to 'thrust forward and control them'. Hence rounded shapes with female body cues were good for sales. Confusingly perhaps he decided that cars with small bonnets showed lack of 'penetrating power' and would thus fail to attract male buyers.

Others took such 'motivational' market research forward, looking especially at how ordinary Americans, the older generation at least, had been raised on frontier ideals of thrift and self-reliance. Wartime movies had further encouraged Americans to 'consume wisely' for the general good, just as they had done in rationed Britain. Women meanwhile were perceived by the researchers as ever more powerful in deciding what a family bought, including motor cars, having gained new political authority in the context of good 'consumership' in the time of austerity. The day might come when they actually bought cars themselves, rather than leaned on their husbands to get something 'sensible'.

But austerity was over. The American public must be be reconditioned to spend and consume more and more. A deep psychological understanding of their needs and desires was the key and Dr Dichter was there to help. He identified how a young man passing that rite of passage of buying a first car might feel 'anxious' if what he bought was too luxurious or powerful. He must be re-educated – to buy without fear – *beyond his means* if necessary. Indeed America's route to prosperity lay where 'a man contemplating buying a second or even a third car' should do so without any feeling of guilt whatsoever. Conspicuous consumption was now a patriotic act.

In America the automobile had long since led the way down this seductive used-car-lot-lined road. The war had merely been an interruption. A book called *Consumer Engineering, a New Technique for Prosperity*, published in the mid-'thirties, had been hugely influential, shamelessly explaining how automobile buyers could be lured into showrooms to replace an existing vehicle that was perfectly mechanically sound. 'Planned obsolescence', designing something so that it would rapidly go out of date, was the conjuring trick. A new car took two years to develop. It might stay in production for five years (with some styling tweaks and add-ons) before its tooling wore out. A car that lasted longer? That was ridiculous.

But there was more to it than that. How do the mass of people come to concur that such a look is fashionable? How do they agree that a particular style has become outmoded? Female fashion had been doing this stuff for years. But with something as complex and seemingly durable as an automobile, how would potential consumers react when there was a *genuine* technological step-change?

All that research in the 'fifties had identified an interesting section of modern society. They were called the 'early adopters'. A later generation might call them 'trendies'. They were the greeters of the dawning age of mass affluence – the getaway people, those toned, tanned, glamorous adventurers who have inhabited every advertisement anyone has ever seen from the dawn of time.

They dared to be different – and didn't it make you envious how good they looked doing it. We all wanted to be like them. And once we were – those people we so admired had effortlessly moved on to something else. They understood intuitively what we were desperate to know. What to smoke, what to wear, what to drink, what to listen to, what to drive, what was really cool. These people knew. They understood the power of *brands*.

In most cases, however, what these early adopters were non-chalantly consuming was exclusive and expensive. Its very novelty made it so. Never mind, said the marketing theorists of the 'fifties, the so-called 'trickle-down' effect would ensure that – if only the wealthy could afford the product right now – in a little while the price would have fallen enough for the general mass to be able to buy in. That is, if what was on offer was not so startlingly innovative that the lumpen herd would be frightened away.

It was patriotic to consume. It was patriotic for automotive designers to push consumption forward in a wave of newness whether it was real or illusory.

But Britain was different, wasn't it? Such ideas were increasingly the currency of political and cultural discussion in Britain, where 'motivational researchers' were popping up all over the place – and admen of the new TV age sought out the early adopters as the stormtroopers of tomorrow.

Rising prosperity brought something else. Consumers had rights. Rather than merely subsist, they were free to choose, and how they chose defined their feeling of self-worth. It wasn't necessarily about size and glitz – in fact it was the opposite. To be an 'early adopter' was to show your true status.

In 1957 the hyperactive social busybody Michael Young (who had written the Labour election manifesto of 1945) founded the Consumers' Association with its magazine *Which?* to guide the grazing middle classes through the new abundance. He presciently wrote: 'Politics will become less and less the politics of production, and more and more the politics of consumption.' The consumer was not bovine but a rational creature capable of rational choice – as long as there were well-thinking organisations like the one he chaired to nudge them in the right direction.

You've never had it so small: PM Harold Macmillan takes the wheel at the 1959 Motor Show. 'You're better off under the Conservatives' was that year's election-winning slogan – and the proof was owning a £500 BMC minicar.

The same year the Prime Minister, Harold Macmillan, famously declared: 'Go around the country . . . and you will see a state of prosperity such as we have never had in my lifetime . . . most of our people have never had it so good.' That was visible enough in the tide of shiny new cars, chrome-laden Vauxhalls, Ford Zodiacs and jukeboxy Austins. But the patrician premier had added in his 1957 speech: 'What we need is restraint and commonsense – restraint in the demands we make and common-sense on how we spend our income.'

So don't consume too conspicuously, the British were told. That would be vulgar.

CHAPTER 4

Think Small

When I was a lad . . . my mum had a little red Traveller, I
loved it . . . all the wood and all . . .

Mini memory, 2008

The British loved motor cars as much as anyone else. But unlike
America, where all those Freudian autosexual interpretations
might indeed be true, Britons saw cars as an expression of *class*.
If you were middle-class and had a car to use for leisure it was
to take Mother to the coast or to potter around the English
shires, taking in cathedrals in some Shell-film-unit, John
Betjeman fantasy. It was called 'motoring'. The working class
didn't have cars – not yet.

To actually get somewhere you went by train, all the way if
necessary down those funny little branch lines that set a steam-
age Victorian tableau in every crevice of the land. Not-long-since-
nationalised British Railways employed half a million workers.

Meanwhile lots of little car dealerships had tentatively re-
occupied their pre-war stalls – pitching their all-British wares
to an all-British male customer base. They were bound by tribal
loyalty to old school, wartime regiment and, for some arcane
reason, 'marque' of motor car.

Like the *Daily Telegraph*'s fantasy character J. Bonington
Jagworth – defender of 'the basic right of every motorist to drive
as fast as he pleases, how he pleases and over what or whom he
pleases'. And Britain was indeed the land of the free – on the
roads anyway. No breath test, no seat belts, no road-worthiness

test, no obligatory crash helmets, no parking meters. When the first motorways arrived, there was not even a speed limit.

Mr Jagworth and his like would enjoy downing a pint or two in a Tudorbethan roadhouse before heading uncertainly home to Mrs Jagworth in a 'Cyclops' Rover. His car was his mobile castle. When during the Suez fuel crisis compulsory car-sharing was briefly proposed, the *Motor* recognised the impossibility of changing attitudes: 'It is of very little use to tell such motorists they must use public transport or share the car with their neighbour.'

Post-war productions had put the clock back to more gracious days, Jags, Rollers, Lagondas, Bentleys, Daimlers, etc. for those in possession of gravel drives – and Rover 90s, Austin Herefords, Standard Vanguards, Morris Oxfords, Wolseley 4/50s and Ford Pilots for the resurgent middle class. The fastback Jowett Javelin, launched in 1947, was very radical in mechanics and styling. Its begetter was a talented ex-MG man called Gerald Palmer. For gilded youths and fighter pilots who had not yet come down to earth there was a trickle of MG TCs (most went to America). For the common man it was a bike, a motorcycle combination, an old banger or take the bus.

With scarcely a single car to sell on the home market, the mighty Austin of Longbridge, Birmingham, advertised the elusive A40 (its first and most important post-war machine) as the acme of long-lived solidity. 'That's why so many gallant old Austins are still carrying on and why the exciting new Austins are earning so much credit for Britain overseas,' said a cheerful ad of 1949. But you couldn't buy one in Britain. Actually there were so many gallant old warriors still carrying on regardless because there was as yet no MOT test to run them off the road. You could get one from a railway-arch car dealer for a fiver.

The true automotive icon of 'fifties Britain was the Morris Minor. It had been a long time in the making. And its originator was born a long way from England – in Smyrna (Izmir), Turkey, where he was christened Alexander Arnold Constantine, names drawn from his Greek ancestry and the regard that his father, a British-national proprietor of an engineering concern, felt for Britain.

Issigonis was eight years old in October 1914 when the Ottoman empire came into the war on what would turn out to be the losing side. The Issigonis family had eventually been rescued by the Royal Navy when in 1922 Smyrna was being fought over by Greeks and Turks. 'There was a deep gratitude imbued into him and a respect for the [British] Establishment,' according to Alex Moulton, Issigonis's collaborator.

His father died in 1922. He enrolled at Battersea Technical College, where he failed his mathematics exams three times. He would share a home with his formidable Bavarian-born mother until her death in 1972. Issigonis never married. There was plenty of gossip within the motor industry and beyond that he was a homosexual.

In the 'thirties many of his ideas had found expression in the design and construction of a hillclimb and sprint car called the 'Lightweight Special' – constructed of plywood laminated in aluminium sheet with an advanced rubber-based suspension. With this machine he showed that he could create a complete car, a skill he would apply first to the Morris Minor and then the Mini. He would subsequently claim, a little too loudly for some, to be the *only* begetter of both iconic machines. A distinguished biographer described him as 'Arrigonis – incapable of according praise or credit to his colleagues'.

In 1936 he applied for a job at Morris Motors of Cowley. The founder and chairman was William Morris, now Lord Nuffield. The applicant had a funny name, Greek apparently, and lived with his mother, a German lady. Mr Issigonis was given a job by the Chief Engineer, Robert Boyle, and the appointment was approved by the Morris General Manager, Leonard Lord (who would row with Nuffield and defect to arch-rival Austin within two years).

Mr Boyle, who had been sent on an eye-opening tour of Detroit by Lord, saw things in the then fashionable American way of designing cars in discrete components, steering, suspension, chassis, with engineers toiling over their given area, the whole thing being brought together at the end by someone called a 'stylist'.

Mr Issigonis set up house with his mother at Abingdon to work on designing suspension systems for a new car to have a chassisless, monocoque body, the Series M Morris 10, due to be launched at the 1939 Motor Show. He was aided by an assistant, younger by six years, called William John 'Jack' Daniels, Oxford-born, who had begun his motor-industry career as a fifteen-year-old engineering apprentice with MG. Together they created a new independent front suspension, incorporating rack-and-pinion steering, an advanced feature for the time.

There was no 1939 Motor Show. Private cars vanished from the road. It was war work now. Issigonis and Daniels laboured at blacked-out Cowley, producing designs for the War Office and Ministry of Supply. A design for an airborne 'landcart' reached prototype stage. An amphibious version known as the Gosling, with tiny wheels, tiller steering and a one-cyl Villiers outboard motor, was trialled on the ornamental lake at Blenheim Palace. Issigonis himself tested it in the choppy waters of Bideford Bay off the Devon Coast, towed behind a Royal Navy motor gunboat.

Daniels worked on the big end of things – the experimental Argosy tracked amphibian – and on the development of the suspension for a monstrous self-propelled gun called the 'Tortoise'. It used the system employed on German armoured vehicles called the 'torsion bar'.

By 1944 it looked pretty clear that the war would be won. It would be back to making motor cars. Semi-officially Issigonis had begun doodling away at an idea two years earlier, not just for the suspension of a small car but the whole thing.

What was emerging was a four-seater in a downsized, USthemed body, all curves and with a vee windscreen and head-lamps neatly incorporated into the front grille. Alec Issigonis would later cheerfully admit to the 'Chevrolet' influence – which extended to the interior, especially the original dash treatment with its chrome mouldings. Jack Daniels worked on the detail design and the advanced, yet simple suspension. Daniels, fresh from his Ministry of Supply work, set up rigs to stress-test the car's torsion-bar front suspension, determined that the vehicle would stand up to colonial conditions. Disappointed not to achieve a full 100,000 test cycles without breaking any bars, he instigated a hardening process that resulted in the bars safely doing half a million cycles. The fourteen-inch wheels were a complete novelty.

The draughtsman, Reg Job, did body studies while chief engineer A V Oak kept things in order. Issigonis meanwhile had more or less a completely free hand in designing a technically advanced vehicle with safe handling and the maximum interior space for a given overall size. The project was codenamed 'Mosquito' (a luxury version was outlined called the 'Wolseley Wasp').

The car progressed under its three-man design and engineering team until a road-going prototype was ready at the end of 1943. But the proportions looked wrong. The prototype was physically cut down the middle and the halves moved outwards to widen it by four inches – at which point Issigonis was satisfied with the proportions. Nuffield himself was dubious. He could never remember the designer's name – it was 'Issy-wissy' or 'that foreign chap'.

When he eventually saw the prototype, the boss was horrified. He thought it 'looked like a poached egg'. Nor was the Morris sales director, Donald Harrison, terribly keen. Bigger cars made bigger profits and were easier to sell abroad. When the Nuffield chief executive, the former Royal Flying Corps pilot and motoring writer, Miles Thomas, who had backed the wartime work on the new small car, left Nuffield in 1947 it looked as if the Mosquito might be swatted at birth. But Thomas's replacement, Reginald Hanks, a company man since the 1920s, liked what he saw. Work continued.

In spite of the ensemble work in the Mosquito's creation, Issigonis was sure of his place as the car's single auteur. 'I designed the whole car myself, even the little knob that opens the glove box – and the door handles,' he would say.

It was always intended to be an economy car. Issigonis had at first considered a flat-four horizontally opposed engine of Lilliputian capacity to attract the lowest tax rate – but it soon became clear it would need too much development. It was Miles Thomas (armed with a technical report by Issigonis) who in 1947 made a deposition to the Treasury that the way cars were taxed on horsepower was a millstone for designers and exporters. And they were duly persuaded. It was replaced by a flat-rate 'road fund' tax of £10. But the engine for the new car would be a pre-war relic, the 918cc side valve from the Morris Eight – 'a terrible old thing' as Issigonis described it, dropped into the state-of-the-art shell with its advanced suspension and rack-and-pinion steering.

In spite of its venerable (but reliable) power plant, the new machine was an astonishingly innovative package for its time – the most advanced small car possibly in the world. Its road holding and handling were revelatory – yet it was basically simple and cheap to manufacture and maintain.

To appease the salesmen the minimalist interior was tarted up a bit, and the name was changed by a board decision to be a direct echo from William Morris's glory days – the Morris Minor.

The new car's debut came in late October at the 1948 Earl's Court Motor Show, a puddle of light in the post-war gloom. Milling crowds gawped at the unobtainable. Virtually everything on display was for export only.

But this small car just might be really within reach. And its degree of innovation fitted a post-war world of jet planes and atomic piles. 'A triumph of British design' said *The Autocar*. Unitary construction, ingenious suspension and 'harmonious good looks' disguised the cranky old engine. It was a modern marvel. The Minor was yours for £358 10s 7d. There was no heater, even as an extra. And it had a single wiper blade. Top speed was 62 mph.

The Minor was a hit. The 'big baby', as a motoring journal called it, was instantly popular. There was a clamour to get hold of one. A four-door joined the two-door and soft-top tourer in 1950 with, horror of horrors, headlamps now raised in the front wing fairings. It was to meet new automobile construction-and-use regulations in the State of California, a vital export market. The auto auteur Issigonis hated what had been done to his creation. He never forgave the perpetrators.

The Greek-born designer, after some gentle press attention, was now a bit of a celebrity. He loved the fact of the car's popular success. Perhaps he could go further with an even more innovative but affordable machine. He told Gerald Palmer (who had come from Jowett and had styled Nuffield's MG Magnette and Riley Pathfinder) of his ambitions. Issigonis wanted to create something smaller and cheaper than the Minor, a car for the deserving masses. He called it his 'charwoman's car'.

CHAPTER 5

Badge Engineers

Twenty-year-old female would like to meet a male, who
loves Tweety [my Mini] and who has a little Mini companion
for her. Has to be caring, and occasionally romantic . . .
Has to like snuggly nights in, and trips to the pub, and
tinkering with Minis is a plus point! I am never happy
unless I am covered in Mini engine oil!!!

Mini lonely heart, 2009

Alec Issigonis would get his chance to make a car for everyman,
but not quite yet. In 1952 the British Motor Corporation (BMC)
had been formed with the merger of two venerable companies
dating back to the pioneer days of motoring, Nuffield (which
grouped Morris, MG, Wolseley and Riley) with its clutch of
factories strung across the Midlands from Coventry to Abingdon
and venerable headquarters at Cowley, Oxford – and the more
monolithic Austin of Longbridge, Birmingham.

The first chairman was Lord Nuffield (William Morris) but he
was replaced in August 1952 by Austin's mercurial Leonard Lord
– who continued as chairman until his sixty-fifth birthday in
1961. In the year of Suez he had handed over, in theory at least,
the responsibilities of managing director to his deputy, the
Austin veteran, George Harriman.

Labour unions also merged to become the BMC Joint Shop
Stewards Committee. Its Longbridge-based convener was the UK
Communist Party's organiser for the motor industry. His approach
to labour relations was as primitive as the management's.

In the corporate shakedown, it was the Austin strand of things that came out on top. The power lay at Longbridge. All new car designs were coded 'ADO' from 'Austin Drawing Office' although there was a design centre at Cowley. There were defections and grumpiness as Cowley was hollowed out, although an independent design operation kept some of the old Nuffield flame burning. One of its guardians was Gerald Palmer, who was made chief engineer of the new BMC, a very significant job.

The first thing to do with the corporation's slammed-together model range was to sort them as market offerings before all those 'marques' even came into it. On the eve of the merger, Austin had already launched something at the bottom, the A30, a chubbily endearing little car described at its launch as 'the new Austin Seven'.

The original styling was actually done by an American on assignment from the Raymond Loewy studio; his name was Holden R Koto. Two Austin engineers got it into production. It was the company's answer to the then rival Morris Minor. The A30's newly designed A-series four-cylinder engine of 803 cc was state-of-the-art for the time and admirably fuel-efficient. In developed form it would stay in production for almost four decades.

Leonard Lord's post-merger masterplan called for three basic engines that would power an entire range of cars, and these duly appeared as the A, B and six-cylinder C series engines in capacities from 850 cc to three litres. Morris-originated engines, gearboxes and axles were to be phased out. There were rumours for years that many such components were dumped in an Oxfordshire lake.

The Austin-developed A-series engine went into the Morris Minor Series II in 1952. Riley and Wolseley variants appeared on a modified Minor chassis with 1.5-litre B-series engines. Meanwhile the Minor remained far and away BMC's most popular car, chugging on with styling tweaks, four-door, estate (the half-timbered Traveller), pick-up and van versions. In October 1956 the 948cc-engine Minor 1000 made its debut. Production increased year on year and it went above six figures in 1957, when 106,680 were made.

BMC's engines and running gear were pretty soon standardised but the baroque portfolio of 'marques' carried on. It was called 'badge engineering', bunging a bit of scrollwork or a different grille on the basic body shape. BMC dealerships perpetuated the strange myth of brand exclusivity and class snobberies. It was like 'houses' at some fantasy minor public school, Morris, Austin, Wolseley, Riley. It was as if consumer choice depended on which car your father had aspired to in 1932. Actually it did.

But instead of no choice at all or the artificial abundance of badge engineering, the amount of real choice for car buyers was ever widening. As the 'fifties wore on, wartime-inspired prejudice against foreign cars was fading – although import duty was still an eye-watering thirty-three and a third per cent.

A funny-looking beetle-shaped car was puttering around British roads but you had to be brave to get behind the wheel. In the byways of Surrey, drivers of Volkswagens were greeted by Heil Hitler salutes from diehard Germanophobes.

The VW story is well known but worth reprising. The smashed production line at KdF-Stadt (Strength-through-Joy-Town – soon to be renamed Wolfsburg) was captured by the Americans in 1945. It was offered to representatives from the car industries of the victorious Western allies. All rejected it. Lord Nuffield could see no advantage in having a production line in continental Europe – especially one so close to the Soviet control zone. What about making the car in Britain or anywhere else for that matter? The British industrialist Lord Rootes said the car 'is quite unattractive to the average motor-car buyer, is too ugly and too noisy'. The men from Ford concluded the car was 'not worth a damn'. So production had restarted in Germany, directed by a major of the Royal Electrical and Mechanical Engineers, at first to provide some utilitarian wheels for the use of the occupiers and the Deutsche Post. Pretty soon after that, you could buy them.

Some British servicemen brought their VW Beetles home when they were demobilised. A KdF-Wagen was exhibited in Oxford Street, London in summer 1946 as part of an exhibition on the Control Commission for Germany that included a tableau comparing British and German food rations and pots and pans made from Wehrmacht helmets.

The show was very popular. That weird car at its heart was either especially intriguing or completely laughable. The UK's first official Volkswagen importer, Colborne Garages of Ripley, near Guildford, Surrey, ran up the VW flag in 1949 (it's been flying ever since). The 'car of which you may be proud' said the first UK sales brochure. The VW buyer was rational yet he kicked against the mainstream. He was an 'early adopter'.

Just two VWs were sold in the US the same year. But it was the beginning of a story that would influence global car culture for decades to come. Sales in the US climbed steadily but unspec-tacularly through the 'fifties. The VW assault was aided by a 25-cent D-Mark, a unified dealer network, the effective slogan 'service first and sales second' (which delivered what it promised), and German government tax incentives for exporters.

The Labour MP and economic busybody Douglas Jay, on a trip to the US in 1955, observed nothing less than: 'A tragedy which I regret as much as anyone else – while British car sales in the United States went down by 25 per cent, in a year of American boom, Volkswagen actually trebled their sales in the same year and now sell more than the whole British industry put together.'

'Why?' he was asked in Parliament in February 1956 in a set-piece debate on the British motor industry. 'I asked that ques-tion of innumerable people throughout the United States,' he replied. 'They said the answer was that the British motor industry was not making the effort that it should, because it was so easy to sell in this country.'

So British carmakers found it just too easy to sell at home. The story of the Morris Minor (2,658 sold in 1949 in the USA as opposed to just 2 VWs) was the exemplar. The Minor had been an initial hit among transatlantic reviewers – 'this little English roller-skate rides like a Detroit cushion and gets 40 miles out of a gallon of gas' wrote one – but sales of what was optimistically dubbed the 'family man's MG' rapidly withered through lack of service back-up and a reputation for poor electrics.

In 1956, just 463 Morris Minors were sold to adventurous US customers compared with an astonishing 55,000 VWs. The 1000 revamp of 1957 bounced sales up again but even at peak they represented a tenth of what the rival from Wolfsburg was selling. The chance to make the Morris Minor a world car in a way the Beetle became was thrown away.

But the real VW take-off in America was still to come. In 1959 an ambitious car salesman called Carl H. Hahn (he'd end up as chairman emeritus of the biggest carmaker in the world) set up a dedicated marketing operation in New Jersey. A Madison Avenue adman called William Bernbach was hired to promote the brand. Mr Bernbach's slogan was minimal in content and execution. It was brilliant: 'Think small.'

And Americans (some of them) did. Over 150,000 VWs were shipped that year. As a fan of the famous 1959 campaign wrote later: 'Bill Bernbach and his merry men [at the Doyle Dane Bernbach ad agency] positioned Volkswagen as a protest against the vulgarity of Detroit cars in those days, thereby making the Beetle a cult with those Americans who eschewed conspicuous consumption.'

Meanwhile other once-warlike Teutonic enterprises were finding their way back on to the paths of peace. Some reconstructed Germans were thinking very small. In 1953 collaboration between an engineer called Fritz Fend, Dipl.-Ing., and his former employer Prof. Willy Messerschmitt resulted in the Messerschmitt KR175, what was called a 'Kabinenroller' (cabin scooter), with a 175cc two-stroke engine, two front and one rear wheels, handlebar steering and a fighter aircraft-style 'bubble' canopy. The developed 'Tiger' with 425 cc had astonishing performance on four wheels.

In spite of the martial sternness of their styling, there was a slight absurdity about them, as if a swarm of tiny fighter planes was trying to redress the aerial disappointments of 1940.

The same year the recrudescent BMW company of Munich, Bavaria (which had made vast quantities of aero engines, using slave labour, for the Luftwaffe), bought the rights to a strange machine designed by a Milanese refrigerator manufacturer. They put their 297cc motorcycle engine into it. It went on sale as the BMW Isetta 300 (versions were also built in France and Brazil). That front-loading passenger door was so that it could be parked sideways on – handy in cities.

Bubble boom: The BMW version of the Isetta (the creation of an Italian washing machine company) and others like it set post-war Germany on the move and at the same time infuriated BMC boss Leonard Lord who in 1956 demanded something be done to drive them off Britain's roads.

In 1954 the Le Corbusier-bespectacled, ex-bomber-builder Ernst Heinkel came up with a similar machine, 'Der Kabine', also with a large front opening door, powered by a 175cc four-stroke engine. BMW sued for patent infringement and Heinkel sold the rights to Dundalk Engineering in Ireland who, having assembled a few, smartly sold the rights on to Trojan of Croydon, south London. The bubble-car market was in a right old froth.

In faraway Japan (which might have been on the moon as far as British car buyers were concerned), they were making so-called *keijidosha* (light automobiles or 'kei cars') – limited by government regulation to tiny dimensions and motorcycle-sized engines. They were still making them (although the size and power constraints had increased) five decades later.

But frugal-minded car buyers didn't have to think quite so small. The choice of new-wave European 'economy cars', as they were being called, went way beyond the Beetle. And, like the VW, although they looked laughably minimal, technically they were extremely advanced.

The Citroën 2CV, dating from 1948, for example, had all-round fully independent suspension, front-wheel drive with an air-cooled flat twin engine. The Swedish Saab 92 of 1949 had a water-cooled, two-cylinder, two-stroke driving the front wheels. It was mounted transversely, a hugely innovative idea. The fast-back Saab had aircraft-derived monocoque construction with exemplary aerodynamics. The French had more solutions. The Renault 4CV of 1946 was a highly compact rear-engined four-door, designed clandestinely during the German occupation. It was powered by a 748cc engine coupled to a three-speed manual transmission. Soon it would be the most popular car in France. From 1949 it was assembled from imported parts in Acton, west London and Hino Motors of Japan began licensed manufacture in 1952.

The 4CV's intended replacement was the Dauphine of 1956, heavier and longer but with an uprated version of the same engine mounted in the rear of an elegantly bulbous body pitched at perceived American taste. Queen Elizabeth II was presented with one on her state visit to France (actually it had been assembled in Acton) in 1957; it was pale blue with whitewall tyres. It ended up, reportedly, at Balmoral.

The Dauphine was exotic and pretty in a gamine sort of way. It was taken up excitedly by the progressive classes in Britain and California but became notorious for being terribly slow, quick to rust and possessed of a general talent for letting you down. The dealer network proved hopeless. More often than not it wouldn't start. The 'Dauphine débâcle' turned Middle America off Euro-auto-rationalism for a generation. A battery-powered version was briefly sold in the US.

In Italy the Fiat 500 Topolino (Little Mouse) of 1936 vintage had gone back into production in 1945. Ten years later the astonishingly modernist Fiat 600 came out of the Lingotto factory in Turin, the work of Dante Giacosa, the company's leading design engineer. The little car could accommodate four adults in a vehicle only 3.28 metres in length and 1.39 metres wide.

To perform the apparent conjuring trick, Signor Giacosa integrated the four-cylinder 633cc engine with gearbox and final drive into a tiny volume of space at the rear end of a unitary-construction steel body. The result combined exemplary fuel economy with the ability to fit into Apennine hill villages or pocket-sized urban spaces. Two years later the design solution for the 600 became the inspiration for the still-smaller 500cc Nuova Cinquecento.

Dante Giacosa would win the Compasso d'Oro prize for the 500, the super-prestigious award for Italian industrial design founded in 1954. Other winners in that decade would include Gio Ponti, furniture maker Vico Magistretti and Giovanni Battista 'Pinin' Farina, stellar names in mid-century Italian architectural and product design, which right then was on a path of global conquest.

Italian style: Roberto Giolito, designer of the reborn Fiat 500 (with a certain amount of input from MINI-styler, Frank Stephenson) is pictured at Milan Design Week 2007 with an original Fiat Nuova Cinquecento created fifty years earlier by Dante Giacosa. Italian car design of the late 'fifties was seen as the pinnacle of innovative cool. Then, to general astonishment, BMC seized the crown.

Manufacturers, many of them small family-based operations that were willing to take risks with innovative designs, were much more driven than hidebound Brits to develop new, attractive products that could be marketed worldwide. Italian automobile 'stylists' set up shop around Milan and Turin as if they were fashion couture houses.

Pininfarina (in 1961 his family surname was changed by presidential decree from Farina to Pininfarina to match that of the company) is the one name from the period that perhaps retains the most immediate recognition. Born in Turin in 1893, his nickname 'Pinin' ('smallest' in Piedmontese dialect) was earned by being the tenth of eleven brothers. He formed Carrozzeria

Pininfarina in 1930. His work for Ferrari from the early 'fifties made this otherwise niche activity world famous; his son Sergio and son-in-law Renzo Carli took over much of the work as the world's big carmakers came calling.

It was the French however who really lit a flame under mid-century modern automotive design – at the Paris Salon de l'Auto with the unveiling at 9.30 a.m. on 6 October 1955 of the Citroën DS 19. It was one of the most compelling automotive designs ever. To the amazed crowds who surged round the Citroën stand in the Grand Palais, it seemed to have fallen from the heavens. Press and public were 'stupefied' it was reported. *Paris Match* magazine put the DS on the cover with the curvaceous Italian film actress Gina Lollobrigida at the steering wheel. And guess what, its stylist was an Italian.

Flaminio Bertoni came from Como in northern Italy. Before his work in industrial design, he was a sculptor. He had made his commercial career in France with the Citroën company and was said to have styled the clay model for the front-wheel-drive Traction Avant of 1934 in a single night. That iconic machine would stay in production for two decades. In 1935 Bertoni started working on the Citroën TPV (Toute Petite Voiture), a kind of motorised cart to get French farmers moving around a bit. It emerged after the war as the 2CV. Light and spacious with front-wheel drive and simple, flexible suspension, the 2CV was admired on its debut for its functional attributes, but the public was less entranced by its agricultural provenance. Initial orders were slow.

But it was the DS that was Bertoni's real masterpiece – sharing the credits (as in the case of the Traction and the 2CV) with the automotive engineer André Lefèbvre.

Citroën boss Pierre Boulanger had conceived it a decade earlier as the 'world's best, most beautiful, most comfortable and most advanced car, a masterpiece, to show the world and the American car factories in particular, that Citroën and France could develop the ultimate vehicle'.

Now, there was a statement. It showed too how much a motor industry reflected national machismo as European countries blinked out of the still-settling dust of the war years.

The long-gestating project was originally called the VGD (Voiture de Grande Diffusion – 'mass-market vehicle') but it emerged as something that, it seemed, only élite super-modernists might consider as a practical means of transport.

Of which, France at the time seemed to have plenty. Minutes after its formal unveiling in the Grand Palais, scores of the cars were driven out of the factory gates and into the Paris traffic. By 09.45 that morning, Citroën had taken 749 orders, and by the end of the day, 12,000.

The DS was years ahead of any other car of the time, with a multiplicity of innovations – the hydro-pneumatic suspension and dual-circuit braking systems especially – and a plethora of man-made materials in the seats and carpeting. These were especially beloved of Lefèbvre – 'one of the first Frenchmen in a nylon shirt and his office and home were filled with plastic bags, nylon stockings and artificial materials'. Every detail was ahead of the curve – when Lefèbvre asked for a single-spoke steering wheel, Bertoni designed one as a monobloc piece of sculpture.

After the DS it was hard for competitors not to look utterly pedestrian. At the Earl's Court Motor Show a week after the excitements in Paris, Leonard Lord found himself confronted by the motoring journalist Laurence Pomeroy 'who suggested to the BMC Chairman that it was high time he progressed from cart-springs and built something a little more interesting. Lord replied, "You bloody well tell us what to build and we'll build it." Then and there he commissioned from Pomeroy his ideas for a competitive European car.'

The result was what Pomeroy named the 'Maximin', a rear-engined four-seater developed for BMC by engineering consultants English Racing Automobiles of Dunstable. A single prototype was actually built. It was horrible-looking.

But with France swooning over the DS's very promise of the future, the march of the modernists on the other side of the Channel had hardly begun. British buyers were not at all sure about the French dream-machine – even if the ones assembled in Slough were finished without all that nylon (hide upholstery and wool carpets for conservative Brits). In the decade to come, the new Citroën was to sell less than half the numbers of the old Traction Avant, which had been assembled at the company's Slough plant since 1945 and long enjoyed an enlightened UK following. But something had to be done. BMC's products looked stuck in the past as continental Europe soared onwards into the space-age future.

It was not just a matter of the unadventurous mechanicals of the corporation's products that required attention, the styling of its entire range was in need of a radical updating. Even the Morris Minor was not immune.

After the judgement of Paris (Peugeot also showed an Italian job at the 1955 salon, the Farina-styled 403), a whiff of Italy seemed just the thing for stodgy British carmakers to catch the fashion wave. Alma Cogan sang 'Mambo Italiano' and Gaggia espresso machines were frothing out the cappuccino. 'Vince' of Carnaby Street was selling the much sought-after Italian look in clothes to young men who were not necessarily homosexual. There was a positive rush to get over the Alps.

Standard-Triumph, for example, turned to the comparatively young Giovanni Michelotti for the facelift of their Vanguard (it emerged in 1956 as the Ensign) – and he set to, styling a new mid-size machine that would emerge in spring 1959 as the Triumph Herald.

There had been a dose of cosmopolitanism at Longbridge for many years. Chief stylist was the veteran Ricardo 'Dick' Burzi, Argentine-born of a French mother, whom Lord (Herbert) Austin had recruited from Lancia as long before as 1929. He designed the flying-A badge that graced post-war Longbridge productions.

Burzi had Anglicised somewhat the US-styled A30. And he did the very English county set, the Devon, Dorset, Hereford, Hampshire and Somerset that were the company's plumply bodied staples in the export-or-die post-war years. He was also responsible for the completely over-the-top A90 Atlantic. In the management culture of the time, Burzi would confess that his role as stylist was subservient to those of engineer and marketing man. In Lord's prescription it was the production engineer who was king – 'build bloody good cars and they well sell themselves,' he was fond of saying.

After the Loewy-influenced A30/35, Longbridge's transatlantic styling flirtation had continued with an agreement in 1952 to make a strange thing called the Metropolitan, badged as a Nash or Rambler in the US, where it was to be sold as a compact aimed at those rationalists who might buy such a small (by US standards) car. It got up to forty miles per gallon, and began as an entrepreneurial wheeze by one William Flajole, an independent designer who approached European carmakers, including Fiat and Standard-Triumph, to build his un-American dream.

According to his daughter: 'My dad thought people were moving to the suburbs and there was a need for a second car, for the woman to drive.' In the end a deal was struck with Austin, who would build the car at Longbridge. All of them went to America, with scant mention of their made-in-Birmingham provenance in the Nash- or Hudson-branded marketing. They consistently outsold the export Morris Minor. In 1957 the strange vehicles were offered on sale in the UK. They looked ridiculous – but even so a curious cult following would come to surround the mini-Yank made in Brum. They were about as authentic as an Elvis impersonator.

Burzi had been responsible for the bulbous, chrome-laden Austin A40/50 Cambridge and Austin A90 Westminster that would run from 1955 to 1959. But by now the Detroit high style was losing its appeal. To the progressive classes in Britain, Ford and Vauxhall productions and the mid-size BMC me-toos were beginning to look more vulgar than desirable. With no recognisable style of its own emerging, BMC was running out of options. Like everyone else it seemed, the corporation looked to Italy for salvation.

The recovery of Europe's carmakers from war was now manifestly complete. The protectionism that had nurtured reborn national industries and precarious trade balances was also on the road to being scaled back (although it would take another three decades to disappear completely). In June 1956 politicians of every European country of consequence (apart from the United Kingdom) had come together in Brussels at a conference to begin the process leading to the formation of the Common Market and the Treaty of Rome, signed in March 1957.

Whether it was the new glamour of Europe or one of those famous exhortations by HRH Duke of Edinburgh for British industry to get 'with it' (and do other things besides) that inspired the next move is debatable. There is a story told that in December 1955 the duke was visiting Longbridge and was shown the Austin drawing office. Various clay models and concept drawings were perused. The duke said, or so it is reported: 'Sir Leonard, I think you ought to have another look at things because I am not sure these are up to the foreign competition.'

The next day the BMC boss summoned Battista Farina from Turin, so the story went. 'He flew in one morning and went away with an £84,000 contract.'

The first commission was for a small car, the planned-for A35 replacement, codenamed 'ADO8'. Launched in 1958 it was known as the A40 Farina (Futura in Norway and Sweden – where the name had been claimed by a brand of porridge). It was straight-edged (sold as 'the car with square corners') with a cut-off back, cool and different-looking although mechanically conventional with a 948cc A-series engine at the front, driving the rear wheels.

The launch ad copy had come a long way from that of ten

years before extolling sturdy longevity: 'Brilliant in appearance and performance, and styled by Farina of Italy,' drooled the copywriters, 'the new Austin A40 . . . starts a new trend in motoring fashion.'

The London design establishment loved the A40 – just as they swooned over Olivetti typewriters and Harry Bertoia chairs. Soon the cool little Austin would establish itself as a proto-global car, with kits of components sent for final assembly in Australia, New Zealand, Mexico, South Africa, Holland, Belgium and Ireland. In the USA it was advertised as 'The Gayest Economy Sedan Ever'.

The Italian Innocenti company of Lambrate, Milan (maker of Lambretta scooters since 1946), began building them under licence in 1960. BMC were looking for a hedge against British non-entry into the Common Market – an increasingly portentous political issue. An A40 'Countryman' version with a split tail followed in 1961. There was no badge-engineered 'Morris' version.

The really big impact of the Farina connection came in 1958–9 when the floor pans, engines, suspension systems, brakes, electrics and switch gear of the original A55 generation were rebodied in Farina-styled sheet steel and chromework. It was the A40 upsized, crisp, straight-edged with jet-age fins at the rear. The first generation of the mid-sized, unitary-construction Farinas was introduced with the Wolseley 15/60 in December 1958.

The look would be extended across all those BMC badges. They looked especially sleek and prosperous. They fitted the times.

Suez had been a warning, but the petrol had been turned on again within six months. Cars were getting bigger again. The fuel famine had already, however, had a deep effect of which the public and the press were not even vaguely aware. In the belly of the Longbridge beast a baby had been conceived, which was already slouching towards the car showrooms to be born. It had all happened in a bit of a rush.

CHAPTER 6

Style Council

You could say that the Mini appeared when the planets were aligned just right for a small car of revolutionary design to succeed. There was a kind of fever in Britain at the beginning of the 'sixties, a sense of social churn. Popular culture was beginning to drive art, music and designed objects, including motor cars, towards a mass audience. Along came the Mini. Its timing was perfect.

It spoke of efficiency and optimism for the future. It was designed for need and said simply and convincingly I'm fit for purpose. Its outward shape implied just enough power, just enough room. And it went on doing so for years. It was a tremendous achievement . . .

Professor Dale Harrow, Head of Department of Vehicle
Design, Royal College of Art, November 2008

In Italy car designers were given gold medals by the state. They were hailed like renaissance princes of style. Their names were global signifiers of taste and prestige. In Britain car designers were regarded as jumped-up draughtsmen.

A 1956 survey of the state of British design said this about the motor industry: 'There is no established source of trained body engineers. The usual method is to provide them from the drawing office. They earn a salary of £1,000–1,500. The work of the body engineer is often marred by the fashionable styling twists insisted upon by the sales manager. The artistic judgment of the managing director is often decisive.' That was exactly how it was. Especially at BMC.

- Which is not to say that the cultural élite in Britain were not as design-aware as they were in Italy or France. They were, except they were much more neurotic about it. It was to do with *class*. It was also to do with a much more complex relationship with all things American.

In the export-or-die years it was clear that British manufacturers must be competitive in design as well as in price and quality. The Council of Industrial Design (later the Design Council) had been behind those 'prosperity is round the corner'-style statements like Britain Can Make it and the Festival of 1951. Now its job was to spur both manufacturers and consumers along to actually *consume*. The world's first Design Centre was opened in the Haymarket in London. The design-conscious Duke of Edinburgh cut the ribbon in April 1956.

The council pushed an approved list of products. Younger critics attacked its prescription that well-wrought objects, a bit like wooden toys for children, could be morally improving for grown-ups. They mocked the idea that 'good taste' could somehow be sprinkled on the advancing poor like some 'aesthetic charity'. But this was indeed the council's function. If Britain was to be truly modernised the working class must be lured out of their grimy slums and pigeon lofts.

To chivvy mass taste along, the BBC deliberately used Council-approved products to deck out its studio sets. The judges for *Come Dancing* sat in trendy Robin Day chairs. Gritty dramas were played out in starkly modernist interiors. The curtains draped behind newsreaders came from Heal's. The working class didn't care or didn't notice.

Although the Council sought to influence design in big public undertakings such as the nationalised railways or municipal housing, the bulk of mainstream British manufacturers in fact ignored their strictures. Especially Midlands carmakers who did not want to be lectured by a bunch of London arty-farties otherwise fussing over the design of spoons. They were real men, who had come up the hard way. They were body engineers – not 'stylists'. There was not an art-school graduate among them.

So Britain's most important consumer manufacturing industry, motor cars, had ideas about design contrary to the London establishment. They would go their own way. There was another big problem for British design purists – America.

The British cultural establishment was deeply suspicious of all things transatlantic. Manufacturing companies of the period remained devoid of consumer psychologists and motivational Freudians. But to ordinary people, especially the young, American stuff was fantastic. Why should anyone care if Detroit's dream makers were 'consciously and deliberately designing sexual symbols into automobiles, like penile hood ornaments, bosom-like bumper bullets, and vaginal grilles', as a controversial US book of the time (*The Insolent Chariots*, 1958) claimed. Why couldn't British carmakers give everyone a treat and do the same?

The hugely influential 'pop' artist Richard Hamilton lectured the Institute of Contemporary Arts in late 1959 on the transatlantic peril – although he himself like other artists of the period was half in love with it. 'During the last ten years market and motivation research have been the most vital influence on leading industrialists' approach to design,' he said. The artist was speaking of America, where all this had served to diminish the role of the individual designer. This was a bad thing because: 'As in any art, the most valued products will be those which emerge from a strong personal conviction and these are often the products which succeed in a competitive market . . .'

Richard Hamilton, godfather of so much that was to come in British pop culture, might have been describing the goings-on right then in unfashionable Brum, where a *very individual designer* indeed had by a series of accidents been given the task of producing a tiny motor car for mass production.

But change was coming. The lower orders were getting richer

– and they had 'taste' too, even if it was pretty awful. The Design Council chairman, Sir Gordon Russell (otherwise a worthy crafter of Cotswold-made furniture), introduced the annual report in November 1959 thus:

> Today Britain is building up through the welfare state a new kind of civilization made possible by scientific discovery and technological development ... this challenge presents industry with splendid opportunities, for the rise in working-class incomes coupled with a heightened popular interest in design opens up a new kind of market, a market with perhaps fewer prejudices and inhibitions than the great middle-class market of pre-war days.

But wouldn't pandering to this new kind of market just swamp the place with American-cloned products? The style would later be called 'populuxe'. Among the super-trendy early adopters it was nowhere when compared with the new design gods of Italy and Scandinavia, but it had its own irresistible dynamic. You could see it already on British roads in the two-tone chariots made by the US-owned subsidiaries.

Ford had made a considered move in 1950. The portentous Consul and Zephyr of that year had been styled in Dearborn, Michigan, as much as in Dagenham, Essex. The British public adored them. Raymond Loewy did the 1949 Hillman Minx for Rootes, while the chrome-laden 1952 Vauxhall Wyvern made in Luton, Beds., looked like a scaled-down Buick. Its jukebox looks went well with leopard-skin seat covers and Diana Dors. As George Walker, head of styling at Ford USA, told *Popular Mechanics* magazine in 1959: 'The American public is aggressive, it's moving upward all the time ... and that means bigness. When the American workingman gets a little money he wants a bigger house and he wants a bigger car.'

As did the British working class. And what did they really care about good design? On their day they could be as stylish as anybody. They adored American stuff – especially the young. They wanted jeans, rock and roll, and chewing gum. Those amazing cars tootling round country roads leading to US air bases in East Anglia were like something from another world – a world that they wanted to be part of. So why not let them?

The British cultural commentator Reyner Banham saw no reason why not. As he wrote: 'The products of Detroit are symbols of the war between the generations. Young people like them – where their elders do not.' And he recognised that, in their very flamboyance, Detroit's 'insolent chariots' obeyed 'a language of visual design not based on subjective good taste but in objective research into consumer preferences'. Give the people what they wanted.

Such thinking was part of a youthful rumble coming from the art schools and those deep thinkers loafing around in coffee bars. As Banham exhorted at the time: 'Progressive people, the people who are going to make social action, have got somehow to ride with the culture of the working class as it exists now.' Soon enough it would be called 'pop'. As Mary Quant remembered: 'Young people started to make their own fun and their own life, and they changed everything – food, dance, music, furniture, theatre, film, art, photography and fashion. Most of this came out of the art schools.'

As austerity retreated it was beginning to prove irresistible anyway. It was both a letting-go of all that wartime restriction and a simple demographic. The proportion of that newly discovered tribe 'teenagers' was approaching 10 per cent of the population and their spending power was rising exponentially.

As the financially enfranchised youth of the 'fifties entered young adulthood, a new kind of madness gripped them, motor-lust. Everywhere in the developed world it was on the motor car that personal ambitions were focused. For a young man in search of a bird-puller, a motorbike wasn't enough. And the age of car buyers was falling. Anything to get mobile, to polish, to love, to get away from the dreary parental hutch, to chase girls in or make them come to you. Anything on wheels would do.

CHAPTER 7

Pop Goes the Motor Car

The [choice of] getaway car was vital . . . If you're in the City of London, and you're doing a small safe, then you'd want a Mini . . . But if you're doing a big safe, you'd want a larger car with a big boot to carry around the oxyacetylene torch. Freddie Forman liked to use Austin Westminsters or the Princess. You could get more people in them . . .

Bruce Reynolds (planner of the Great Train Robbery)

To survive in this bold new era of choice, brands and consumer empowerment, British manufacturers had also to encourage a continual stream of novelty and embrace the new mix of fashion, industry and entertainment. As Mary Quant would write, a decade later: 'Once only the rich set the fashion. Now it was the inexpensive little dress seen on the girl in the high street.' Thus it was with inexpensive little cars.

Automotive design was also moving to the pop end of things. The idea that a motor car could be a fashion object and not a half-timbered house made somehow mobile was taking hold in Britain. The handful of Detroit's jukebox excesses that were imported meanwhile were only for suddenly enriched pop idols or pools winners.

Britain's automotive transition had come in a series of jerks, technical and cultural. The first had been to do with the way private cars were taxed. Abandoning the old horsepower tax had given designers much more freedom. Which way would the design of British cars go – solid and traditional or flashy downsized-Yanks? They got bigger, chubbier and greedier. Their technology remained entirely conventional. Against the new wave of cool, urban-friendly products from Europe they had begun, by the late 'fifties, to look positively baroque.

In one corner of the Midlands however, a small group of innovators had been thinking very differently. With the Morris Minor launched, the urge of its orginator to experiment seemed unstoppable. How to get more passenger room in the same overall length? 'Compactness' became an obsession. The solution, thought Alec Issigonis, was to turn the engine *sideways* to power the front wheels through drive-shaft joints. Work on a front-wheel-drive experimental Minor ticked over with no imperative from above to actually put something so radical into production.

Then in 1952 came the Austin merger. Cowley was suddenly an outstation of imperial Longbridge. Vic Oak retired and Issigonis also headed for door – for the tiny but upmarket Alvis company, with a commission to design a new 'sporting family car'. With its big V8 engine it was hardly a small car but it was certainly innovative with a rubber suspension conceived by an independent engineer and inventor called Alex Moulton.

A single prototype was built and proved exceptionally fast. But the Alvis company (their main business was now armoured cars and rotary aero engines for military aircraft) could not remotely afford to put it into full-scale production. Eventually the prototype car and all its engineering drawings were destroyed.

Issigonis got the call in December 1955. It was Leonard Lord, hectoring, cajoling but beguiling too. Think of the opportunities – come back to us, he said to the prodigal, come and be one of the big boys. Not Cowley this time, but at the heart of things – Longbridge.

There was a vacancy. Gerald Palmer, the incumbent engineering director, had been sacked after a car he had been associated with got a bad review in the motoring press. And Alec Issigonis did go back to the big time. His title would be assistant engineering director.

His elderly mother was reluctant to leave Oxford so Issigonis lived midweek at a Birmingham hotel. He would return to the flat in Linkside Avenue, north Oxford at the end of the working week, popping in on Cowley and taking up a barstool at the favoured Trout pub at Godstow on a Sunday lunchtime for a Worthington E and to chainsmoke Wills Gold Flake cigarettes.

He brought two engineers from Alvis with him to Longbridge, Chris Kingham and John Sheppard. Jack Daniels at Cowley soon came into the fold. Left behind at the Oxford factory was the part-built, prototype front-wheel-drive Minor that Daniels had completed. Registered TFC 717, it became his regular transport. The road holding was exceptionally good. He chose to commute from Oxford to Birmingham in it, parking it with a certain flamboyance in the directors' car park. It was noticed.

Thus in the midst of Longbridge's corporate orthodoxy there existed from early 1956 a cell of freethinkers. They were not 'mavericks', they were too schooled in conventional engineering for that, but, as product design went in the mid-'fifties, they were pretty much ahead of their time.

Alex Moulton for example, born in 1920, and independently wealthy. As a schoolboy he'd shown a propensity for engineering by restoring a Locomobile steam car on the family estate. A Victorian ancestor had a century before acquired the licence from the American Charles Goodyear to make vulcanised rubber and thus founded the Moulton fortune. He also established the factory on the banks of the River Avon, not too far from the fine Jacobean house, 'The Hall', within which big chapters of the Mini story (and that of other small-wheeled means of transport) would come to be written for decades to come.

After Marlborough, King's College, Cambridge, and a wartime

apprenticeship with the Bristol Aeroplane Company (where he worked on high-powered radial aero engines), he returned to the family firm, Spencer Moulton, trying out the uses of rubber for vehicle suspension. He devised an experimental rubber-sprung set-up on a Morris Minor. It was built and showed great promise. The Alvis work was another result.

In 1956 Moulton sold the factory to Avon Rubber and set up his own workshop in the stable yard of the Hall. Issigonis was always very keen on his experimental work. Moulton was summoned to Longbridge to meet Leonard Lord – who gruffly surmised this toffish character was some kind of boffin who should best be kept at arm's length.

'Make some arrangement,' Sir Leonard instructed the BMC company secretary. They did. Moulton Developments was created with Moulton himself owning three-quarters of the intellectual property rights. Work would continue in Wiltshire – while BMC would have exclusive use of the technology – to be manufactured by Dunlop. Alex Moulton was happy with the arrangement; so would BMC be.

The first project of this little team was something called the XC9001, a completely new mid-market car of 1.5 litres but with many advanced features. It borrowed from the Alvis project, including a Moulton-developed, interconnected rubber suspension. It had rear-wheel drive and its styling had overtones of Bertoni's DS unveiled in Paris the year before.

One was built and that was that. Next was the XC9002, a Minor replacement proposal – with similar DS-like styling, this time with front-wheel drive from an engine mounted transversely with with an end-on gearbox. Like the experimental Minor of 1951–4 it required so-called constant-velocity joints in the front wheels to transmit power and steering forces as the car was pulled rather than pushed along, as with the rear-engined VW Beetle. Issigonis had no time for the Bug (it was successful because 'they built one car and thereafter concentrated on detail,' he would say later) and nor did Alex Moulton. The XC9002 was novel but not nearly as innovative as the next concept on the Issigonis sketchpad.

But in autumn 1956, pending the outcome of the Middle East crisis and some sort of quiescence on the labour front (there had been uncompensated lay-offs and a raucous protest strike at Longbridge that summer), the place for such cars, even of modestly advanced engineering, was in the balance. Farina would get their mid-range makeover commission and all those crisply styled Oxfords and Cambridges raised on existing floorpans would soon be coming on-stream. Even the intriguing yet-to-be-launched A40 was really thumpingly conventional. It was evolution in Brum, not revolution.

Meanwhile the petrol famine dominated. While publishing its small-cars-are-patriotic editorial, *Motor* printed an eight-page survey of the new wave of British microcars. It was a schedule of shame, blobby things printed in brown ink like leftover props from a low-budget sci-fi movie – the Fairthorpe Atom, the Petite, the Berkeley Bandit, the unfortunately named 'Tourette'.

Leonard Lord had an attack of the vapours. It was then he gave his famous pronouncement on 'bloody awful bubble cars'.

The Cowley design office was ordered to come up with an all-British bubble-beater with a two-cylinder engine and a retail tax-inclusive price of under £300. It was made 'a transverse rear-engined thing with the engine ahead of the axle so the weight distribution wasn't so bad' according to Charles Griffin, then chief experimental engineer; 'we showed it to [Leonard] Lord and it was then that he told Issigonis, "you'd better drop that bloody thing you're doing [the XC9001] and see what you can do to stop this thing they are building at Cowley".'

It was this, according to Issigonis himself, that 'there and then decided [him] on the Mini'. It was January 1957.

Petrol rationing in fact had only two months more to run.

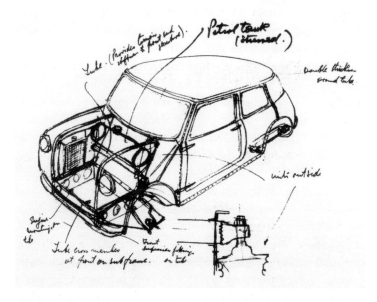

Mini back of an envelope: The best known doodle in British automotive history (made in early 1957) without which no published Mini account would be complete. Issigonis's sketches had to be interpreted by a team of production engineers and experimental testers to make the small car they called the 'Sputnik' into a reality.

Bubble cars were a 'craze'. They were hula-hoops on wheels. In fact their sales impact was tiny. A little more than 3,000 motor vehicles (other than motorbikes) in the sub-700cc class were UK-registered in 1957 – although the sub-one-litre class boomed. Morris Minor production peaked. But the genie was out of the bottle. Leonard Lord assented to developing a prototype baby car, saying something like 'you use any engine you like so long as we have it on our present production lines . . .' There was such an engine. It would still be in production, like the car it would power, over forty years later.

CHAPTER 8

The Monster We Love

We're married. This is a long-term commitment.
Theresa Galvin, 44, Manhattan MINI owner 2003

It wasn't just fuel crises and the cost of consumer credit that determined the speed of Britain's progress on the road to cartopia. It was the physical landscape of the country – with all those hopeless ring roads, unbypassed market towns and Victorian cities only recently furnished with lots of space for car parks courtesy of the Luftwaffe.

Where to put all these new cars? Even with the most stringent legislation in Europe, town-hall and ministry 'planners' seemed unable to do anything about the wave of metal engulfing the land. What was the solution? Knock it all down? There was an alternative. Make cars smaller. The UK Ministry of Transport discreetly began a study of very small cars to find a state-approved urban runabout. It would emerge as the 'Cars for Cities' report – of which more later.

But it would be tarmac first. The British Road Federation (founded 1932) had long been lobbying for a massive road-construction programme. A planeload of MPs had been flown to Nazi Germany to see the gleaming new *Autobahnen* in time to relax afterwards at the 1938 Munich Oktoberfest. They liked what they saw and had never forgotten. In the US the Eisenhower administration embarked on a massive programme of federally funded highway construction, the President invoking the Germanic prototypes that GIs had discovered during the conquest of the Reich.

All British political parties were pro-car and pro-road. The wartime-made plan for post-war London offended nobody by prescribing green belts, radial roads, satellite new towns and lashings of cars for deserving workers. It foresaw the capital of the not so distant future as a city of towers girt by cloverleaf motorway junctions.

It proposed three big ring roads circumventing the centre (a few historic chunks of which would become carless 'precincts'). 'There is a clean and lovely tidyness in a great new road', the great plan pronounced.

Mr Attlee's post-war government had toyed with an 800-mile national motorway network only to be halted by economic reality. The Trades Union Congress lobbied hard for road-building. Everybody wanted roads. They were just terribly slow in coming.

So slow that in 1955 the British Roads Federation launched a 'roads crusade' to get something moving. As planners drew lines on maps, there were mild objections from woolly-hatted 'ramblers' and the like but organised opposition to road-building was non-existent in Britain. The car economy was unstoppable.

There were some marginal voices of dissent. That same year a twenty-five-year-old topographer called Ian Nairn made his name with a special issue of the *Architectural Review* called 'Outrage' in which he coined the term 'subtopia' for the intra-urban space that had been claimed by motor cars with all their careless greed. Less iconoclastic voices had raised the same issue – where to put all these pesky cars. A very unusual policeman called Sir Alker Tripp (the pre-war Metropolitan Police Commissioner for traffic) had called for the complete segregation of pedestrians and motor traffic – and for something he called 'motorways'.

The most important voice, it would turn out, was that of a demobbed Royal Engineer called Colin Buchanan, who had worked at the Ministry of Town and Country Planning (est. 1947), seeking to reconcile traffic and environmental policies. At the time such an ambition was terribly cranky. He published a book in 1958 called *Mixed Blessing – the Motor in Britain*, setting out stark options on how to cope with what he called 'the monster we love' – the motor car. It was a terrific piece of phrase-making.

It caught the attention of Ernest Marples, Minister of Transport, a modernist, interventionist Conservative politician with commercial interests in road-building. Mr Marples was hugely controversial in his day. He appointed Dr Richard Beeching chairman of British Railways to implement a 'restructuring plan' (massive cuts).

Empowered to do so by the 1956 and 1960 Road Traffic Acts, the abrasive Mr Marples brought in yellow lines, parking meters and traffic wardens to vex the Jagworths. Further, he commissioned Professor Buchanan to study the whole question of the car and the city. It would result in one of the most famous discourses ever made on the social place of the motor car in the twentieth century – *Traffic in Towns*, published in 1963. The Rt. Hon. E. Marples ended up a hate figure both for Jagworths ('Marples Must Go!') and for branch-line nostalgists. He was also himself a Mini driver (of which more follows).

But in his early days as minister, Mr Marples seemed to be just what the road lobby had been waiting for. In December 1958, the first eight-mile stretch of what might be recognisable as motorway opened, the Preston bypass. Harold Macmillan cut the ribbon. There were votes in superhighways. The winning Tory election manifesto of that year had promised to match 'the rising volume of traffic, a yardstick of rising prosperity . . . by an intensive drive to build better and safer roads'.

It also promised to tackle traffic congestion in towns. Everyone could agree – more roads, more cars – jolly good thing. The working class trooping like L S Lowry stickmen into sooty factories would soon be staunchly independent motorists.

Then, oh happy day, on 2 November 1959, after two years of moving earth and pouring concrete, Mr Marples declared open seventy-two miles of M1 between Watford and Rugby. On that day, of the more than 13,000 private cars that hit the concrete-surfaced m-way, over a hundred broke down. One shed its entire engine. The old warriors weren't up to this kind of thing. The MOT roadworthiness test for vehicles more than ten years old (introduced in 1960) would soon cull the rest of them.

Seats four in comfort: That's what early publicity promised and the BMC baby car (sort of) delivered.

For a while it was Jagworth heaven. Getaway People charged up the fast lane. There was no speed limit. In the middle lane, middle-class Philip rushed home to Oxo-Katie in a crisply modernist Austin A40.

Advice was given to slow-lane dullards in public-information films: 'Do not picnic on the hard-shoulder.' Who were the masters now? Whoever could go fastest. The British class system on wheels progressed up and down at its varying rates, a linear strip seventy miles long – to mingle, should they choose, at classless Scratchwood service area amid rubber plants, overcooked vegetables and orange formica tabletops. It seemed motor-car heaven. All too soon it would be motor-car hell.

CHAPTER 9

Market Research Is Bunk

I have never liked the steering position of the Mini – it made me feel as if I had a soup plate on my knees at a picnic . . .

Lord Montagu of Beaulieu, *Town* magazine, 1962

Alec Issigonis had his commission to create a miniature car. But who was it for? In the Longbridge boardroom, market research was an unknown science. Motivational stuff from America was regarded as bunkum. When BMC at last produced a thin document on the topic in 1960 it was not for product planners but for dealers – advising them to allot a 'senior staff member and a clerk' to monitor who was buying what on their territory.

But there were certain givens in the economics of car production that could not be ignored. A strong domestic market was the necessary base on which to develop new models – that might then be exported. In 1952 the newly merged British Motor Corporation had manufactured 235,770 units. Now seven years on, it was producing double that. But although profits had risen, BMC's domestic market had dropped from 39 to 36 per cent. Ford was beginning to catch up fast with 30 per cent of the UK market, double its immediate post-war figure.

After seven merged years, Britain's biggest car manufacturer could congratulate itself on having more or less integrated its production. Its products were conventionally engineered but now (most of them) were trendily styled in their Farina makeover. The revamped Minor 1000 chugged on, too good to drop. At the time BMC was earning around £40 in profit on each Minor sold.

On the cusp of the new decade, Sir Leonard Lord and George Harriman could just see ever greater expansion. Government policy meanwhile was pushing new-build factories to sites in the 'depressed' regions. Overseas buy-ups and joint ventures in the old white Commonwealth and the booming new Europe would swell the tide of growth. More volume, more profit, more cars.

And now the scramble for dollars was not so desperate. A short-lived recession in the US had benefited the European importers who were stressing economy and practicality in their products. But by the time the 'sixties dawned American customers saw 'imports' as either fancy sports cars or the constantly uprated, updated Volkswagen.

In the US market the Dauphine had self-destructed; the export Minor and Hillman Minx glowed dully, Sprites, the big Healey, MGs, Sunbeam Alpines, Jags, Triumph TRs, a few Rollers maybe, that was about it for UK importers.

In 1958–9 the 'Compact Car' wave from Detroit would break: the Chevrolet Corvair, Ford Falcon, Plymouth Valiant, Studebaker Lark and AMC Rambler. A compact was defined as a vehicle with an overall length of less than 200 inches – big, big, big by European standards. But the Detroit fightback worked – for a while at least. Total import sales would be halved.

What could BMC do? America was now a hostile shore and at home the car-hungry years when you could sell anything were over. But there was an untapped market under their nose – the great British working class with their rising income and rising aspirations. Politicians, sociologists, novelists, dramatists and TV advertisers were scrabbling to make contact with this newly discovered tribe. What sort of car did they want? They wanted something cheap, surely.

Alec Issigonis had been banging on about his 'charwoman's car' since the Minor days. It wasn't because of his personal politics, which were distinctly conservative. It would be fair to call him a snob. It was because he was obsessed with the challenges of small-car design. The BMC chairman's 1956 injunction to develop the miniature seemed a heaven-sent opportunity to make it happen. But it would be much more than just a British bubble.

The designer began to think. Those famous doodles had begun to appear around him, annotated memos, sketches, flatplans and skeleton views, gathered up by an eight-strong platoon of draughtsmen and engineering assistants who must turn them into engineering blueprints. The development operation was as secret as it could be – conducted in a design cell isolated from the Kremlin and the rest of the Longbridge works. The pace was amazing.

As was the degree of new thinking. European automotive designers had already come up, it seemed, with every possible variation of getting power to the road – front engine, rear engine, air-cooled, water-cooled, two-stroke, four-stroke, front-wheel drive, rear-wheel drive. There was no paradigm other than that a private car should have four wheels, two of which were driven by an engine that used the internal-combustion principle.

In Sweden the Saab company had mounted a two-cylinder engine transversely in the Model 92 of 1947. The sideways-on arrangement had also been used for the West German Borgward's Goliath GP700 and 900 small car of the early 'fifties – known as the 'Plastic Bomber' by its fans. It was an oddity but it worked.

Designing a small car was much harder than designing a big one. The start point for the BMC miniature was the human body – how to fit four adults in a minimalist sheath of metal, glass and rubber in which the bits that make it go take up no more than a fifth of the given space. And the engine must be already in production. It would obey an existing design principle, that the engine should be at the front with the passenger cabin and some sort of luggage accommodation staged in line behind it.

The A-series measured three feet two inches from the radiator to the back of the gearbox. One way of shortening it was to chop off two cylinders. It was tried but was too lumpy-running and too feeble. It would be the full four-cylinder engine or nothing – with an amazing sleight of space-saving hand by tucking the gearbox in beneath the cylinder block. The radiator was mounted at the left side of the car so that the engine-mounted fan could be retained, but with reversed pitch so that it blew air into the natural low-pressure area under the front wing.

Everything must be configured to the ideal of space-saving. A veteran of the Lucas company recalled a brusque encounter with the great designer during the early development period, to discuss electrical components. The hapless executive blithely assumed the company's standard model C93 dynamo would do. 'Ludicrous! Far too large!' said Issigonis, sketching an outline of the proposed vehicle. 'There! That's what my car will look like – and you want me to have an electrical power source like this . . .' he said indignantly. As he spoke a sketch of Battersea Power Station, chimneys smoking, filled the engine compartment. He wanted a much smaller dynamo, especially designed and manufactured if necessary.

In fact the BMC baby car would end up with the 'ludicrous' unit – because as the executive recalled in a fascinating reminiscence forty-one years later:

> No one at Lucas thought the car would survive production for more than two years – because at the time it was such an oddball concept. What's more, there was no way our board would sanction product-development expenditure on a piddly little dynamo for what they often referred to as a 'piddly little car'. In their view it was doomed before it even went into production.

The famous four big innovations – the transverse engine, the gearbox in the sump, the tiny wheels positioned at 'each corner', plus front-wheel drive were not themselves entirely new. But bringing them together and putting the gearbox below the cylinder block to share the same lubrication and sump oil was a tremendous leap of faith.

As to a lesser extent was front-wheel drive, fashionable thus far in France, but not in Britain. The necessary front-wheel constant-velocity joints capable of accepting a wide angle of change through the steering process were adapted from submarine control gear made by an obscure company called Unipower. Dunlop made the required ten-inch-diameter wheels, smaller than any made before for a production car – the Minor's had been fourteen-inch.

The little wheels were crucial to getting the look of the car right – but they were at the frontier of innovation. Could they accommodate adequate brakes? How to keep water out of a tiny drum in a tiny wheel spinning away so close to the ground? But the small size meant minimum unsprung weight (a good thing), and the smallest possible intrusion into the cabin space (another good thing).

The suspension in theory must absorb the bumps and grinds of the road that the little wheels could not adequately soak up. It was initially planned to use an interconnected fluid system – similar to the one that Issigonis and Alex Moulton were working on in the mid-1950s at Alvis – but the short development time of the car meant that this could not be ready in time. Moulton's solution was to use compact rubber cones instead of conventional springs. The variable-rate properties provided by rubber as a springing medium had the further advantage that, in a small car, the weight difference between fully laden and driver-only was proportionally greater than it would be in a larger, heavier car. Furthermore they would scale down and this would shrink the overall size of the suspension, aiding the great quest for compactness. The ride might be stiffer and bumpier but this rigidity, together with the wheels being pushed out to the 'corners', would give the car its revelatory handling, to which front-wheel drive with its inherent dynamic stability and under-steer was the key.

Early testing by Dunlop on a water-sprayed test track would later show the prototype taking a corner successfully at 44 mph. An Aston Martin DB4 managed 2 mph faster. The rear-engine Renault Dauphine tipped over at around 28 mph.

What should the experimental car now codenamed XC9003 look like? The great designer at least recognised that the way a car looked played a part in its sales success or otherwise. But engineering came first. In one of the many annotated notebooks from the XC-series development period he wrote about styling thus: 'Simple shapes, if well balanced last longer . . . The basic envelopes are governed by engineering. If this is not right no amount of additional styling will put it right . . .'

And basic envelopes was how it began. One then lowly employee would recall how 'a guy with rather a large nose [Issigonis] came in one day with a sheet of plywood, laid it on the floor with a set of Morris Minor seats bolted to it. They were sticking bits of wood over the seats and making sure they could get in and out.'

Issigonis would later make it very plain just how far he was above the vulgarities of market trends. 'Style', he would declare, 'has to do with architecture – furniture and ladies' dresses. What we do is engineering . . .'

'Cars have become fashion goods,' he would later proclaim. 'A woman will say, "We will buy that car because I like the mirror in the sun visor." Or the car will be bought for some other totally irrational reason.' That was the trouble. People were irrational. 'Market Research is bunk,' he was fond of declaring. But in America they were already routinely using sophisticated sampling techniques to read the consumer mind (although they could still get it spectacularly wrong).

America was singled out as the guilty party. 'This preoccupation with trivial things comes from the other side of the Atlantic, I am afraid,' said the great designer. 'The French are not like this at all; that is why I admire their work. The Italians do it to a smaller extent. We are transatlantic, and the Germans too . . .'

The designer's prejudices were gender- as well as nationality-based. 'What could be worse than a suburban housewife with money,' he would later say of those empowered females who now seemed to be deciding what sort of car the family should have. 'They're so stupid – they buy Fords. Some are intelligent – they buy Minis.'

Although the hubristic Issigonis would repeat many times afterwards that he never asked the public what they thought because he did not think they could give him the right answers, this did not mean they were not important. He would just do the thinking for them.

So functionalism, not fashion, was the keynote, Issigonis insisted, just as BMC was about to unveil its Italian-styled range of middle-class pleasers. Was his miniature car going to be starkly utilitarian on purpose, or would it too be sent into society wearing a Turin-tailored suit? It almost happened that way.

One day an executive from the Lucas electrical-component company was discussing the tail lights with Issigonis when the MD, George Harriman, arrived to see the complete car for the first time. He walked round it for a bit and then said: 'It's very tiny, isn't it, but it's good. When we get the chromium plate on it and get the styling done it's going to look quite nice.' The designer replied: 'If you do anything to that car, I'm leaving. It's finished.'

And so the doodles progressed from concept to prototype. The car was designed as a monocoque shell – 'two boxes' – engine, passenger cabin and a vestigial tail – with welded seams unashamedly protruding from the bodywork. To simplify construction further, the car would have external door and boot hinges. The vehicle codenamed XC9003 (the drawing office code

ADO 15 would be given after the production decision had been made) was emerging as an essay in form following function, the underpinning principle of modernist design since the Austrian architect Adolf Loos proclaimed eight years into the twentieth century that ornament was 'criminal'.

The cool logic of the design may have been obvious to the great designer but how it might be rendered into something that could be mass produced profitably and practically was harder for the little Experimental Department team to grasp. Issigonis gruffly communicated with sketches rather than words – expecting these drawings to be magically transmuted into reality.

Peter Tothill, who worked on the project as a young engineer at Cowley, recalled the experience after over fifty years: 'Alec Issigonis was ambitious, autocratic and arrogant. He was a brilliant innovator [but] became bored with the details as the project reached its conclusion. His right-hand man was Jack Daniels . . . I had a lot of contact with him and held him in very high regard. He was totally loyal to "AI" as he called him (never Alec). Issigonis put huge demands on him which he took on board in a completely unflappable manner . . .'

Jack Daniels himself would recall the scale of the challenge. Speaking over three decades later he said:

> We made a prototype by hand. That meant we had to create a body from scratch, together with the suspension, steering and subframes etc, design the special gear box and final drive to fit under the engine block and then produce them. The top of the engine was already there, the Austin A-Type, we only had to make a new crank, flywheel and clutch for that. But all the parts were made within four months and within five we had them running.

He made it sound simple.

CHAPTER 10

Sputnik

> My mum had a green Mini van that had a vent on the roof
> you could open. Big daft magic-wand-type gearstick and
> she had them long rubber switch extenders on the switches
> on the dash, and if we all went out in it, I was in the back.
> Sat on the metal floor, no seat belts or cushions or anything.
> Must have been about four or five, which will put that
> around 1971 . . .   Mini memory, 2008

By February 1957 the first hand-built experimental car was
running. It was painted a muddy yellow, 'with some paint we
had lying around'. It was soon nicknamed the 'orange box'. A
second prototype followed very soon afterwards. A35 grilles
provided a simple disguise with an alligator hood closing on an
engine lying west–east with the carburettor facing the front.

Testing was moved to Cowley. At night they were thrashed
around a well-used test route through the Cotswolds under the
supervision of Cowley's resident chief experimental engineer
Charles Griffin. 'Bad' drivers were deliberately chosen to show
up handling problems. The designer stressed afterwards that he
was concerned to make something that could be driven safely
'by the worst driver in the world'. During the day, they were
driven at the disused airfield at Chalgrove around the rutted
perimeter taxiway. In 500 hours the cars covered 30,000 miles.
They proved amazingly fast. One of the drivers turned over and
injured his head. There was a panic that the device was too fast,
too flimsy, too dangerous. It was going to kill people. Leonard

Lord and Sidney Smith insisted something be done. An immediate solution was to use a short-throw crankshaft to reduce engine capacity from 948 to 850 cc. Development testing continued. It was time to show the boss what they had made.

Issigonis wrote in his notebook: '9 July 1957 first run by Sir Leonard in XC 9003 with 4-cyl engine – also Mr Harriman. Good general impression . . . approved for production'.

This account would be much embroidered. In later interviews Issigonis would tell of driving round Longbridge at breakneck speed with the BMC boss beside him, screeching to a halt outside the Kremlin, where Lord gave the gruff injunction 'make the bloody thing'. That remark became a core text of Mini mythology.

Plenty of design faults and construction weak points had shown up in development, just as they should. The prototypes kept destroying their synchromeshes. The engine block was turned east–west so that transfer gears could be introduced but now the distributor and wiring harness were facing forward.

The unitary body shell proved far from robust enough and front and rear sub-frames were designed to strengthen the structure at the expense of weight and cost. Water somehow kept coming into the interior – something Issigonis is said to have repeatedly ignored, even if the wet was seeping up 'his tweed trousers'. The two orange boxes were joined by more pre-production prototypes – there would be eleven in total. Someone scrawled 'Sputnik' in road-sprayed mud on one (on 4 October 1957, the Soviet Union successfully launched the world's first artificial satellite, *Sputnik I*, which meant 'fellow traveller', or companion). The name stuck. In the winter and spring of 1958–9 test cars were sent on deep penetration missions into France and Spain. The problem with water coming into the cabin was reported; it was still unclear how. The summer of 1959 proved exceptionally balmy. The problem seemed to go away.

The interior strove to utilise every inch of space. 'We have deliberately made the car very small because we have found new ways of making the inside very big,' Issigonis told Laurence Pomeroy.

The driver sat ahead of a minimalist fascia with a single speedometer graduated to 80 mph with a fuel gauge at the bottom and a big parcel shelf below. The thing was in the middle, as on the Morris Minor, with a simple set of switches below. With the front seats pushed forward the steering wheel was angled steeply upwards, 'like driving a bus'. The gear lever was long and wand-like, but required the driver to lean forward to operate it. There were no seat belts.

The hugely famous racing driver Stirling Moss was given one for testing; he promptly crashed it head-on, proving as far as Issigonis was concerned the safety factor of having the sideways engine as a big lump of energy-absorbing metal out there in front. Moss complained about the seats being uncomfortable – Issigonis told him this was to ensure that people did not go to sleep when driving.

The great designer had plenty more contentious things to say about the safety and comfort aspects of the machine he had conjured into being. 'I never wear seat belts' was one – 'it's so much easier to drive without having accidents'. Nor would he sanction car radios, a monstrous distraction when one should be concentrating on the hazards of the road.

He had equipped the miniature with ashtrays (a pipe-size one was made available as a dealer-supplied option) although forswore smoking himself while driving. On the unfamiliar stiffness of the rubber suspension he would say: 'a firm ride is preferable to a mere feeling of physical comfort [in a conventional car] which soon gives way to nervousness as the car sways about'.

The machine he was describing seemed to be an ergonomic torture chamber whose prime function was to goad its driver into perpetual wakefulness. Actually some people would come to see it that way.

The front windows were sliding, which echoed the Austin

Seven saloons of the 'twenties. As did the floor-mounted starter button, also used on the original baby car. And because the window glass had no winding mechanism, there was room for large storage pockets in the base of the doors, configured apparently to accommodate bottles of milk – or rather Issigonis's favoured Gordon's gin (twenty-seven bottles and one of dry vermouth, according to legend, the recipe for the perfect if very large dry Martini). These hollow doors miraculously produced more elbow space in a car 1.37m wide at the waistline – while the door locks were opened by utilitarian pull wires.

The very first experimental cars also lacked external boot lids, the original idea being to allow access from the rear seat or through an opening back window. On very early production cars the number plate was hinged so it flopped down to remain visible when the boot lid was open, held on little retaining wires. This curious arrangement was discontinued when it was discovered that exhaust gases could waft into the interior while the boot was open.

When put together the sum of technical innovations resulted in a car with minimum overall dimensions yet practical space for both passengers and luggage. It was a minor miracle, a Tardis (although that phrase was five years from being coined) on wheels. And yet it looked right.

It was not a freakish bubble or upscaled invalid carriage. The round headlamps and wide grille gave it an endearing, coltish expression. The slightly rounded haunches and unswaged (smooth) side panels gave it a bottom-pinchable sensuality. The Farinas, father and son, were allowed a glimpse on a factory visit. The Turin arbiters of style could not have been more complimentary – 'don't change a line'.

What to call it? The prototype Sputnik tag lasted a long time in the drawing office and the wider company. Unlike the A40 Farina, there would be Austin and Morris badged versions to keep the dealerships happy. There was a brief vogue for Austin

Newmarket – Austin Cambridge . . . new market, you get it. Then it was Mini-Minor, it just sort of happened. And it was Austin Se7en with that fancy alphanumeric twist.

What about the price? Standard cars would go on sale at just under £500, of which £150 was purchase tax. It was priced to get to grips with the venerable Ford 100E Popular, a pre-war relic and still the cheapest new car on the road. BMC knew a new mass-market car was coming from Dagenham (the 105E Anglia) which must be contended with on price. After a brief post-Suez fling with bubbles, Rootes had embarked on 'Project Apex', an all-new small car (which would eventually emerge in May 1963 as the Hillman Imp). That too would have to be contended with.

Three hundred and fifty pounds to make this technical wonder, £350 which must cover the cost of labour (the biggest component), materials, bought-in components, intra-factory transport, overhead, investment write-down, dealers' commission, delivery, marketing, warranty claims and – somewhere – profit. It was either a miracle of management accounting or a stupendous error. Leonard Lord and George Harriman assumed that volume, simply selling lots of them, would sort it. It was assumed, not without reason, that all those sturdy, working-class budget motorists would ditch the old banger or the motor-cycle sidecar and sign up on hire purchase for the morally improving miniature.

Now it had to be made in volume. A new assembly line was laid out in CAB 1 at Longbridge. A purpose-built assembly shop was raised forty miles away at Cowley. The floor and the doors were pressed (from September 1960) at a BMC plant at Llanelli in Wales and delivered by train to the Longbridge or Cowley factories. The rest of the body was made by the BMC subsidiary Fisher & Ludlow in Castle Bromwich; the engine and gearbox came from Morris Engines in Coventry and the suspension components came from the former Wolseley factory in

Birmingham. Cowley was also supplied with bodies by Nuffield Metal Products in Birmingham. Shuffling this lot around cost time and money.

So the Sputnik was 'over-engineered', as the expression goes, in a way that the Morris Minor had not been a decade before. And it would go on sale at a price that did not represent its true manufacturing cost. Strict financial discipline, the very key to effective mass production when fluctuation in manufacturing costs could rapidly accrue into enormous losses, was lacking from the corporate psyche of a business that had been founded and run by old-school engineers suspicious of outsiders. In the labyrinths of BMC, promotion was from within. Graduate trainees were an unknown species.

The Director of Sales, James Bramley, had been an associate of Herbert Austin himself and had been at Longbridge since 1932. His deputy had joined Riley in 1930. Austin's domestic sales manager had been with the company since 1925. They were traditionalists, deeply nervous of the new car, although they might not say so in public. Now they had to sell it. That would be done the old-fashioned way.

On 4 April 1959, the first pre-production unit came off the new line at Longbridge, body no. 101, engine no. 101, finished in white. It would be registered 621 AOK and badged as a Morris. According to a Longbridge veteran: 'When Harriman saw the first production car stood in our shop all polished and ready to go he said, "What a bloody mess. We'll never sell that. Spend another few quid and jazz it up a bit. Put some chrome plate on it or something".' On went bright wheel discs and a strip of chrome around the wheel arches.

A month later, cars started rolling off the second production line at Cowley. By June, 100 cars a day were being built to build up dealer stocks in preparation for the international launch now timed for late August – as the Se7en and Mini-Minor – two years and five months since the miniature had been approved.

Jack Daniels drove one to the British Grand Prix being held at Aintree but 'incredibly it was hardly noticed'.

The Austin Se7en was finished in Farina Grey, Speedwell Blue and Tartan Red, while the Morris Mini-Minor came in Old English White, Clipper Blue and Cherry Red. Paint colour aside, the cars were exactly the same apart from badging and grille differences (the Austin's was crinkly). It was that old badge engineering obsession. Both versions would be sold in standard and deluxe versions. The standard models had cloth upholstery and a rubber mat on the floor, the deluxe version had two-tone leather-cloth upholstery and carpet.

We're all going on a Mini holiday: Janet and John plus Mum and Dad set off on a Mini adventure in this wonderfully evocative image from around 1960. Note the legendary door pockets.

The marketing departments had been busy. Austin and Morris press releases and publicity material were drafted quite separately – and different ad agencies had been hired to make the birth announcements. What to go for? Economy? Technical innovation? That was never the marketing man's friend. Price? An internal briefing document for Austin salesmen was head-lined: 'A new revolution in personal transport' – a big statement. 'The announcement of the new Austin Seven 850 ushers in an exciting new phase of motoring for the masses,' it continued.

But were the masses ready for a revolution? Salesmen were advised to stress roominess, ease of parking, handling, perfor-mance, economy ('the cheapest form of transport available today') and safety, in that order.

The baby car seemed to be the answer to everything. Female buyers were supposedly enticed by its suitability for shopping: 'Women of the world, rejoice . . . in a man's world a car has been designed with women in mind', said the Austin selling copy.

The British motoring press were given an exclusive preview. It was held at the British Army's Fighting Vehicles Research and Development Establishment at Chobham south-west of London. It lasted two days, 18–19 August, proceedings advancing on a tide of Château Margaux, one day for the clubbable British hacks, the second for foreign. The great designer was on hand to goad proceedings along in a flurry of over-the-top pronouncements. It all went swimmingly.

Motoring correspondents returned to labour blearily over their typewriters and wait for the press embargo to come off on Wednesday 26 August 1959 – Mini Launch Day. On that day, slightly less privileged journalists were summoned to Longbridge to see a 'magic' show in which a huge prop top hat was pulled aside by two showgirls (otherwise employed at the Aston Hippodrome) to reveal the 'Incredible Austin Seven'.

A stream of people emerged from the spot-lit tiny car – three large male adults, the junior sales manager's wife Ruth and their baby son Kevin, followed by another young woman and two size-able dogs. They returned to unload a huge stack of luggage, golf clubs, a baby carriage, wicker baskets, picnic hampers, a briefcase, a football, a child's doll, car rugs, etc., etc. It was tacky but it was impressive. A similar magic stunt was staged at Cowley.

Whopping great newspaper ads appeared: 'The Morris Mini-Minor – wizardry on wheels' with a thirty-something mum and dad in the front seats (dad driving), with two girls and a boy on the back seat. 'You've never seen a small car like this before, front wheel drive, full independent suspension, up to 50 mpg, over 70 mph and that's only the beginning . . . Yet the Austin Se7en is less than £500 tax paid.'

The ads featured Janet-and-John families, clean-cut, forward-looking, and middle-class. Cinema ads showed the little car's practicality in the congested 'chaos' (it looks pretty empty) of central London.

Huge efforts had been made to get cars into dealerships across the United Kingdom and indeed the world. In wintry Belfast a twenty-six-year-old professional rally driver (for the rival Rootes), Paddy Hopkirk, saw a display in the window of Ferguson's, the BMC main dealer opposite City Hall – and thought, 'What's that funny little thing?'

Alex Moulton was in Coventry in launch week and remembered the inhabitants of motor city slack-jawed in amazement when a BMC baby appeared. But it wasn't approving. The first reaction was laughter. Then it was ridicule.

The most startling element was the new car's price. BMC proudly proclaimed it as 'a real breakthrough in automobile production . . . and yet it is one of the lowest priced cars in the world'. In that statement lay a profound paradox. It was one the Mini's makers would only wake up to years later.

The press reviews were in. And they were good. Laurence Pomeroy wrote of a car that possessed 'a standard of road-holding and steering much more akin to a racing car than the popular conception of a family saloon'. *Autocar* hailed it as 'an outstanding all original small car that bristles with originality, yet there is nothing remotely freakish about it'. *The Times* said 'it really can accommodate four adults comfortably including the driver wearing a hat'. Well, that was something.

The *Motor* could only pour praise 'on a compact car . . . which offers a remarkable combination of speed with economy, roominess with compactness and controllability with comfort'. Some of its readers disagreed – why bother with a 'glorified bubble car' furnished with 'scooter like wheels', capable of haring around at inappropriate speeds courtesy of a 'hugely complicated front-wheel-drive layout'? wrote an especially grumpy correspondent.

The London design establishment was distinctly snooty. Not that they cared too much about what went on in the west Midlands, but this was clearly important. *Architectural Review* gave what it called the 'BMC Miniature' its prestigious design-review slot in December 1959 and – although it praised the technical package as 'a functionalist dream of a motorised box on casters' – it thought the 'very frank styling' was marred by 'untidy and ill-considered' details and trim with rustic-looking seams and tail lamps that 'appeared to be stuck-on as an afterthought'.

Design magazine, guardian of good taste, had loved the square-cut, edgy (literally), Italian-styled A40 – but were not so keen on the BMC baby's outward appearance. Its September 1959 editorial did concede however: 'In spite of the substitution of the pudding look for the crisp look, I suggest that design conscious citizens will soon be transported with delight.'

The snooty *Economist* magazine thought the 'new design is neither inspiring nor inspired . . . we accept the appearance of a plum pudding, and so may the public if it is full of good things . . . The crispiness and modernity of Farina finds no reflection here.'

It thought the production target of 1,000 a week disappointing and the car resultingly overpriced at 66 pence per lb weight of the 1,275lb vehicle compared with the A35's 58 pence. How calculating.

Alec Issigonis was on the stand at the 1959 Earl's Court Motor Show two months later with a batch of his unfinished puddings when he found himself in conversation with a cabinet minister who asked him: 'How do you get the pipe [the propeller shaft] down to the back wheels?'

It was the Rt. Hon. Ernest Marples, newly appointed Minister of Transport and motorist's friend (for now). Other novelties on show included the Triumph Herald (which had been launched in April – the first British small car with all-round independent suspension), the Ford 105E Anglia, the Renault Floride, the Citroën Bijou (a 2CV with a plastic body) the NSU Prinz and the Soviet Moskvitch.

BMC issued instructions in a handy pocket-book guide for its show-going executives to be at the Hyde Park Hotel prompt at 12.30 for luncheon at 1.00. 'Ladies are not permitted,' it said sternly. Issigonis meanwhile instructed the cocktail barman at the Knightsbridge establishment how to make his favourite dry Martini (place a gill of dry vermouth in a glass, swill it round, empty it, pour in a measure of Gordon's gin and serve without olive).

The Mini-Minor and Austin Se7en (on separate stands at Earl's Court) gathered huge attention. There were three and a half (cut down the middle to show off the whizzy innards) on each. They were the tiny stars glowing amid the suddenly outdated-looking mainstream.

Issigonis meanwhile was sought out by the press and, as was now to be expected, gave a number of opinionated interviews. He was emerging as Britain's first 'celebrity' car designer. At least for now he kept his remarks about suburban housewives to himself.

On the road at last: One of the early ADO 15 prototypes under test, autumn 1958.

CHAPTER 11

Look at Us, We're Poor

But what I can't understand, is how the name 'Mini', synonymous with the same car for over forty years, just seems to be forgotten by the general public, and has been replaced with MINI after only a few years. It would appear that the legend of the classic Mini is fading into insignificance . . .

Mini lament, 2008

And so they waited. Was the new baby going to sell? Autumn turned to winter and that vital sales tool, word of mouth, went from cautious enthusiasm to I'm not so sure. The tiny cars had a funny smell. It got worse, mustiness turned to all-round mush as carpets dissolved in a squelching sludge. Frantic splash-tank testing revealed that floorpan seams had been designed in such a way that they would billow between the spot welds, inviting moisture from the road into the cabin rather than keeping it out. One journalist, so it is reported, turned up to a Longbridge press show with ironic goldfish swimming in the driver's door pocket. The 'water ingress' problem had shown up many times in pre-launch testing but Issigonis had ignored it. Management squabbled about who was to blame. It wasn't me, said the great designer.

The distributor and plug wiring (they were right behind the front grille) got drenched in a downpour. Owners resorted to putting plastic bags over them before rubber sheaths were produced as a factory retrofit. One hapless executive was sent to the arid Middle East with a boatload of sealing kits. About 8,000 cars already exported around the world had to be modified.

Other problems included oil leaking on to the clutch plate, and a mis-specified synchromesh that resulted in crunchy gear changes and fractured exhausts. 'There was another problem we discovered later,' recalled Alex Moulton. 'I remember being in the back of my Bentley when we overtook a Mini. I looked down and saw the driver's head moving up and down. His seat, strung on rubber webbing, was resonating. We had to fix that . . .'

The first owners were being used as guinea pigs and they knew it. Slowly the immediate faults were redressed (the ones like rusting rear sub-frames would take longer to show themselves) but ownership was clearly not for the faint-hearted.

The car had been sent into the world half-formed, a premature baby. It was too clever by half, a box of tricks, a transistorised Morris Minor with none of the straightforward practicality of its well-regarded predecessor. Just how self-flagellatingly modernist did you have to be to buy one?

The US journalist Vance Packard had published a famous exposé of the new black arts of US advertising in his 1957 book *The Hidden Persuaders*. He quoted motivational research from Detroit on how people felt about 'small cars' that had invited the responses: 'Jolted – cramped – tense – personally small and inferior'. Were the great British public so different? Nobody at BMC had asked them.

Business was slow. Suburbia was perplexed. The masses were indifferent. Motoring hacks poured praise on it but the sturdy crofters and enfranchised cleaning ladies of Issigonis fantasy didn't exist. Worldly-wise motor dealers were nervous. The car was cheap, no bad thing, but margins were wafer thin. Those nice salesmen grew ever more embarrassed as leaking floors and dud electrics clogged up the works with warranty claims. The juries in far-flung export markets had yet to pronounce. Issigonis and his backers had risked ridicule – and ridicule, it seemed, was what they were about to get.

There was a Mini wobble at Longbridge. But BMC management

kept its nerve. In late November, Chairman Sir (he was knighted in 1954) Leonard Lord introduced the 1959 annual report thus:

> The past year has seen Operation Changeover [the Farina models] begun. The new Austin A40 combines the best Italian styling with the advanced engineering of our own highly experienced designers . . . [but] by far the most important investment completed and put into service in the year was the £10 million devoted to establishing production facilities for a new small car of revolutionary design.
>
> Of the Austin Seven and Morris Mini-Minor, it can be said that no small car had ever had such a welcome as this one. I am confident that once its quite exceptional qualities are experienced and appreciated by the motoring public, it will go from strength to strength . . .

The Graduate: Early Morris Mini-Minor noses down The High, Oxford. The university city was a frequent photographic location for Cowley-made cars.

But the chairman's statement was an admission that the motoring public had yet to vote with their wallets. The miniature car had been developed on a combination of prejudices and assumptions – the chairman's against Teutonic bubble cars and the great designer's that he was on a mission to make a machine for Everyman.

Coming the other way, supposedly, was an enfranchised, educated, new mass market, hungry for the personal freedom exemplified by car ownership. The Conservative government saw them as its future electoral constituency and was only too pleased to spend public money on new roads (and let the railways wither). Was the BMC baby really the machine to set the people free?

Development at the edge of technology had been crashed through by a gifted but very small team. Alec Issigonis, its presiding 'genius', had expressed his hatred of committee meetings and lofty disdain for market opinion and (almost) everyone had gone along with the gag. Marketing was a question of some cheesy press stunts, a briefing for dealers and, very successfully as it turned out, making sure enough cars were in the dealership chain at launch time.

Then everyone held their breath. It was terribly ironic really. BMC's super low-price people's car was being spurned by the people.

BMC's advertisers were doing their best. As well as the posher prints, the wizardry-on-wheels campaign had been splashed all over the mass-market newspapers. The pitch to the aspirant was straightforward – enough of cycle clips and old bangers: 'BUY YOUR FIRST NEW CAR' the ads proclaimed – for £100 down, followed by monthly payments of £13 10s 2d per month for three years.

The *Daily Mirror* ran a competition (for women only) in conjunction with Ful-O-Pep dog food – to 'win the sensational Austin Se7en, the fabulous new baby car that everyone is talking about'. (That women-only thing would continue – a little later the *Mirror* in conjunction with the Danish Lard Council offered a fabulous Mini-Minor as a competition prize – 'ideal for shopping and taking the children to school'.)

It had all looked so terrific. The Mini was the cheapest car on the market, aimed at a rising wave of entry-level affluence. But on then-current US marketing theory, the British Motor Corporation had got everything disastrously wrong. A car bristling with newness was aimed at the most innovation-resistant slice of society. A glance under the bonnet was alarming. How I am supposed to mend that? What would happen if it crashed? Those wheels aren't up to anything. Is that what they call a family car? How can I fit my lot in that? And this was when 'obesity' was a word unuttered outside obscure medical literature.

One new owner returned the car to the dealer when he heard 'funny noises' coming from the front end (the wheels were scrabbling for traction on his gravel drive).

Maybe all those early adopters would pick it up and let their five-step approval process trickle down as the price fell. Yet it was cheap, cheap, cheap to begin with. Young people (well, some of them) could just about afford it. A Lambretta scooter cost about £250, while a basic BMC baby was £495. In 1959 the average male manual worker earned just over £13 a week.

Perhaps they were going for the wrong end of society. In October 1959 Issigonis took the thirty-three-year-old housewife and mother of two, Queen Elizabeth II, for a Mini ride round Windsor Great Park. Her Majesty seemed impressed. She had studied small-car maintenance as part of her service with the wartime ATS. But no order followed. She already had that nice Dauphine.

What the industrial classes wanted was something that reflected their rising status as aristocrats of labour. As a do-gooding survey of the state of the nation noted in 1961, 'Miners now take their families on continental holidays and drive to the pit in their own car.' What would be the end of it?

To be seen in BMC's miniature said 'look at us, we're poor'. Here was a bunch of patronising do-gooders sprinkling design on the workers like it was an aesthetic charity. The working class wanted chrome. They wanted status. They wanted America. There were cultural and political cheerleaders on left and right who were anxious to show them the way.

And right then Britain was booming – or so it seemed. In autumn 1958 all hire-purchase controls had been removed. The country was sailing towards the polls in October 1959 with the Tories campaigning under the slogan 'Life is better with the Conservatives'. New roads and the car-based economy underpinned the message. The Conservatives won a renewed term in office – with the fourth successive rise in the party's parliamentary majority. But the funny little car launched two months before was in all sorts of trouble. It just wasn't selling.

Issigonis retreated behind camp hauteur. When warned by his friend Laurence Pomeroy that buyers were more concerned with how a car looked on their front drive than with its fuel economy or how well it cornered, he replied: 'Yes, my dear Pom. I know there are tens of thousands of such people, but I will not design cars for them!'

Ford sniffed the air, sensing opportunity. It could have been the end of the Mini story but in fact it was the beginning.

CHAPTER 12

Getaway People

We have all driven or ridden in a Mini at one time or another. Like an unexpected whiff of long-forgotten perfume or the embarrassed acknowledgement of a song adored in adolescence, a chance encounter with a Mini rekindles lost love . . .

Review of the Mini-30, *Autocar and Motor*, July 1989

Provided you already own a Mini, a Rolls-Royce makes an ideal second car.   *Motor*, November 1959

The little car was out and into the world. The press reaction at home and across Europe had been ecstatic. *Vogue* magazine's October 1959 car issue was full of praise: 'I like its fox terrier jauntiness and the capable qualities that lie beneath the endearing perky charm,' wrote the BMC-sponsored Monte competitor Nancy Mitchell. 'Alec Issigonis has done a remarkable design job in coaxing the utmost comfort and practicality out of every inch of interior space', she wrote, 'the Mini Minor is a honey for parking.'

Le Figaro reported: 'The new car from BMC is much admired in France and particularly in Paris . . . It is appreciated by the young of all ages, when the buyer is middle-aged he is slender and well dressed with the look of a sportsman.'

In America the car was so small that they hardly noticed it was there at all. *Road and Track* magazine declared: 'The new

British miniature car is too little too late. On top of that it's just about the funniest looking roller-skate you can imagine.'

But the BMC baby had never been aimed at North America in the export-hungry manner of a decade before (although some hundreds of early Minis were destined to be shipped there to be marketed as the Austin 850 and Morris 850). It was sales in Britain that mattered, in the Commonwealth and – if they could get round the Common Market shutters – in Europe.

In 1959, the first year of production, just short of 20,000 cars were completed. The target market of enlightened workers remained totally indifferent. Out there in suburbia the talk was of wet feet and the uselessness of British industry. The ranks of 'decent, respectable, dim liberals' would rather have a nice Triumph Herald. It looked like a national humiliation. The only headlines BMC was getting that first Mini winter were about strikes – 'Baby Car Men Walk Out'. Variations on that headline would run and run for years.

In November 1959 the little car had won the Mobil economy run, returning a fabulous 61.7 mpg over 1,000 miles. But that was too worthy. What people wanted was frivolity.

The new baby was about to provide it. Early adopters were discovering something – its amazing handling. Motoring writers drooled over its acceleration and leech-like grip going round corners. It was 'chuckable', and just as eager to please going full out in a straight line. You could run rings round the Jagworths and beat most things off the lights or into a parking space. You could do things in BMC's baby and get away with it as in nothing else on the road.

Alex Moulton would later say that he and Issigonis built an extra safety margin into the car's handling because they knew it would be driven by students and young people once they reached the second-hand market. These were the days when car safety was a marginal matter, when people like Ralph Nader were regarded as dangerous seditionaries, when advertisers dared not mention 'safety features' because that implied that a car might crash in the first place.

These were also the days (in the US, certainly) of pedestrian-mangling chromework and 'meat cleaver' dashboards – while there was no consensus that seat belts improved anything. Issigonis thought they were an incentive to unsafe driving. He was echoing global auto-industry wisdom when Lord Snowdon showed him the seat belts he had had specially installed in his Mini and the great designer had replied, 'safety never sells, dear boy'.

But when the car was launched it wasn't young people who caused Mini outrage. It was grown-ups in love with its handling and acceleration. It made them feel rebellious. It was like riding a motorcycle while still wearing a suit. The Mini's antics chimed with a mood of angry young men, 'satire', the end of class deference and the Campaign for Nuclear Disarmament. The Establishment took fright.

Civil servants and senior policemen began to complain that the car's qualities were 'conducive to inconsiderate driving'. Stirling Moss became the first celebrity Mini martyr when he was prosecuted in September 1959 for dangerous driving, in an Austin Seven on a road in Shropshire, overtaking a Rover 90, to the 'horror of witnesses'. He told the court he was testing the minicar 'for a Sunday newspaper'. That was no mitigation apparently. (He got a twelve-month ban – on public highways anyway.)

The new baby could also play cute. Its very lack of styling gave it more style than any Turin *carrozzeria* could have tacked on to it. Neo-Freudian motivational marketeers would later discover an urge among Mini owners to 'mother it'. As a cultural commentator beguiled by its pre-pubescent appeal wrote soon after the car's launch: 'The Mini-Minor attracts devotion from the large middle-aged man who probably hasn't read *Lolita*.'

It was gawky and noisy like an adolescent. It was also 'round, cuddly and vulnerable', in one description – and as such it 'inspired the emotions of a parent for a child'. 'Like a child the little car might be wayward but would always be forgiven', as a clever Mini chronicler wrote on its twentieth birthday. Mini love was unconditional.

Whatever the trigger for Mini desire, as the car's makers were soon to discover, they had created not a transit system for deserving workers but a technological toy for the urban élite. The ultra-trendy menswear mag *About Town* gave its judgement 'Posh Practicality' – pairing the little car with 'an Italian-styled shirt-cum-pullover in plum and black' for its modish driver. Practical, yes, but posh? That was never the idea at Longbridge. Issigonis himself summed up the paradox many years later when he told this author: 'When they first saw it people said, "What's that thing?" The reception was bad. Then *to our horror* we discovered that rich and intelligent people bought it first.'

Alex Moulton had a slightly different memory of the time. 'It wasn't really an élite thing. It was just *so sensible* that its appeal was universal. Actually all sorts of people liked it. But Alec was of course delighted when smart people took it up.'

To possess one was to be 'with it'. It was those trendy early adopters beloved of US marketing theory. BMC had helped the process along when sales were sticking in autumn 1959 by lending test cars to a hundred journalists and opinion-forming 'personalities' so that they might talk the thing up. And they did.

At fashionable London dinner parties the message was getting across. It was just 'so nippy round town'. All sorts of people, young, not so young, trendy and 'square', were buying them. The architect Sir Basil Spence traded his pre-war Rolls for 'a Mini-Morris which he found much more serviceable'. Another fogeyish early adopter was rising political star Conservative MP John Profumo, CBE, the Minister of War, who acquired a red

Morris Mini-Minor. Both the car and its owner would have an eventful future.

Steam Mini: The BMC's people's car was launched just as the Government was resolving to drastically cut Britain's railway network – especially those snoozy branch lines. Everyone should be self-mobile in the new autopia.

In spring 1960 the never-had-it-so-good economy was over-heating. In April came a renewed credit squeeze and hire-purchase restrictions were back again. A mini breath of austerity swept the land. Then after a few months of Stop it was Go again. Then it was Stop. On one summer day in 1961, car showrooms were packed by buyers getting in quick before a much-heralded hike in purchase tax. As the economy roller-coastered, the little car fought for a second chance as the supply chain and the factory struggled to fix the leaking floors and less-than-water-proof electrics. It all looked dead dodgy. But its faults would be forgiven.

CHAPTER 13

City Car

When my mum was rushed off to hospital to have me she was driven by Dad in their white Mini, covered in paintings of dragons and fairies and castles done by my older half-sister Trina, and when I was taken home for the first time, it was again by Mini! I only discovered this tonight because she is writing a book about our family.

Mini memory, 2008

The Mini's faults would be forgiven. Because it had such intrinsic strengths. Its 'parkability' for one, in the days when motor vehicles could still legally occupy all sorts of urban crevices. That too was changing. After a report to Parliament on the growing perils of parking in London, the Road Traffic Act, 1956, had given local authorities powers to regulate on-street parking and levy charges via metering. The first parking meter in the UK was installed in June 1958 in Grosvenor Square, central London.

Miniature motoring became a tremendous perceived advantage for town dwellers (and that was most of the country). It wasn't just parking. It was getting anywhere at all. Forward-looking civic authorities began drawing lines on maps for vast new roads to plough through outmoded ranks of huddled terraces. Nobody who mattered objected.

Meanwhile even the most recently built urban infrastructure was clogging up. The cultural critic Reyner Banham noted in 1963: 'Harlow New Town has traffic problems – having been designed for those permanent working-class things like riding bicycles. Only the working class don't have bikes any more. They have Ford Pops,

107

Cortinas – and Minis. There is a fair chance that cars will be banned from Harlow before they're banned from London.'

He was wrong in that prediction but it was already clear that increasing regulation was on its way into the motorist's freedom to roam and plonk himself down at will. With wardens already swarming when you attempted to park, in 1962 the Macmillan government commissioned a panel of experts under the statistician R. J. Smeed, the deputy director of the British Transport and Road Research Laboratory, to investigate the idea of 'charging' even when you were trying to roll along.

The report concluded that it could work – that cities should be zoned – with a charge of 10 shillings per hour for driving in the centre of London – and that such costs should vary according to the location, time, and *type of vehicle*. Size did matter.

The whole thing was politically abhorrent of course. The Jagworths would rise in rebellion. The new Conservative government of Sir Alec Douglas-Home forswore it very publicly – but many of its conclusions and proposals would be consistent with those of congestion-charging schemes implemented in Britain some forty years later.

The most influential contribution to the question of burgeoning motoropolis came in early 1963 with the publication of that report that Ernest Marples had commissioned – *Traffic in Towns*. When it was published the question of what to do about the motor car was at the heart of national debate. It was a bestseller – and influenced politicians and planners around the world for decades to come.

Having ruled out 'hovercars' and personal flying bubbles arriving in the near future to change everything, the good Professor Colin Buchanan had ventured to predict what he thought would be the reality of the automotive future. 'The present number of vehicles per 1,000 head of population is 127', he reported (1960 figures); 'in the [much physically bigger] USA it is 409.' But 'to reduce the ratio of vehicles per mile of road to current US proportions, Britain would have to increase its present 193,000 miles to 1.6 million'.

He predicted 26 million private cars and 'saturation' by the year 2000 as the population hit 65 million and car use per head expanded at the same rate as it was already doing. He turned out to have been almost right – an equivalent figure for vehicles was reached in 2005, when there were 460 cars for every 1,000 people in the UK, compared with 750 in the US.

At the time, capital investment by private business and individuals in cars versus public expenditure on highways was grossly mismatched, his report demonstrated. The government promised to do something – they always did.

'Unless the greatest care is exercised, it will easily be within our ability to ruin this island by the end of the century', the professor concluded. 'We have taken a bull into a china shop and there are only two answers, shoot the bull, or more creditably, build a new china shop specially designed for bulls,' he wrote. The second option would prevail.

The *Sunday Telegraph* went to Birmingham to hear Alec Issigonis's comments: 'It is obvious that family cars may have to be banned from central London,' said the great designer, who was sure that his petrol-powered, tiny town-car concept could only prosper further as rational beings saw the light. Inter-city cruisers were a different matter, they were all right – although they would have to be consigned to gigantic suburban car parks and not allowed near city centres.

Alex Moulton would recall Issigonis dismissing criticism of the Mini's aerodynamics – 'do stop going on about wind resistance,' he told his collaborator, 'if people want to make long, high-speed journeys we can develop a detachable nose cone.' Moulton wasn't sure whether that was a joke or not. His own solution was to build a Cooper S with a five-speed gearbox and a hydragas suspension that gave a superlative ride – a motorway cruiser and city car all in one.

Motorway city: Austin Seven meets the new urban order in the shape of the Hammersmith Flyover in west London, almost completed in 1961. The advent of the BMC babies chimed with a growing national debate about 'Traffic in Towns' as growth in car numbers exploded. A 1966 government report called 'Cars for Cities' actually recommended the building of aerial roads exclusively for Mini-sized vehicles.

There was a growing chatter about alternative powerplants. Issigonis expressed himself as sceptical of electric cars (the batteries were going to be too heavy) but confident that 'pollution will be banished by the devices [catalytic converters] that are being tested in the US'. He pointed out how archaic the conventional internal-combustion engine had in fact become, unchanged in basic principle for over sixty years – and in fact woefully inefficient.

BMC marketing barged in opportunistically meanwhile with big ads declaring: 'Never mind the Buchanan report, get a Mini – mercurial, manoeuvrable – get through traffic smartish. Make the most of your road ration. Buy a bright new Mini!'

The professor was in fact much more pro-car than many might have assumed. In May 1965 he gave a disarmingly frank interview to *Small Car* in an article headlined 'Is Your Mini Really Necessary?' A car two persons wide and two persons long, for all intents and purposes a Mini was very handy for parking, he suggested. But by the time you factored in braking distance and driver-reaction times, when cars were actually moving, length was irrelevant. He thought it very unlikely that parking space would be rationed by overall size. 'My planning proposals are based on making even more use of motor cars possible . . . which means more speed limits, more policemen, more fines . . . conformity is the only hope,' he said.

He was 'thinking about buying a Mini for his wife' but he himself drove a Jaguar, he revealed. He admitted to feeling 'a sensual thrill every time he got behind the wheel'.

So Professor Sir Colin Buchanan turned out to be a Jag-loving Mini hater. He thought the little car was 'noisy and conducive to bad manners on the road'. Safety, silence and comfort rather than speed, cornering power or undue compactness should be the defining factors of automotive design, he insisted, 'until the final traffic jam made it time to discard the whole idea of individual motoring completely'. But the last car moving would be Mini-sized.

There was a fleeting moment when it looked as if government

policy would ensure that was the case – that a Mini or equivalent would become the *only car allowed* in urban centres. That working party set up by Mr Marples to study 'Cars for Cities' finally delivered its report in 1966. Although it couldn't be seen to favour a specific model over another, it adopted a vehicle ten feet long by four feet six inches wide (a Mini) as its paradigm.

The report examined the state of electric-propulsion technology illustrated by an electric Mini, a Traveller. But even with its load space crammed full of batteries it had a range of a mere 36.8 miles when driven non-stop at an average speed of 30 mph.

The report concluded that in an all-Mini city, road and parking space would be increased by a third. Meanwhile, to really get things moving, they recommended the early development of 'aesthetically acceptable special overhead structures' configured exclusively for small cars – in effect Mini-sized roads in the sky. Also on the agenda were exclusive Mini-sized parking arrangements for small cars where three would fit in the space of two ordinary ones.

From the mid 'sixties onwards, super-small 'town car' designs became very fashionable and were intensely pursued across Europe, as they had been already in Japan. It wasn't an oil-price spike driving it (although that was coming), it was a high-level conversation between industry, academics and independent designers concerned with just how future, car-based, urban societies were expected to function.

'In the boardroom of nearly every motor car company in Britain you will find a number of drawings of way-out motor cars [and] among them . . . someone's vision of a town car,' reported *Design* magazine in August 1966, 'small, compact and usually looking quite unlike any car that you can see on the road today'. Pint-sized cars on roads in the sky. The age of the miniway seemed about to dawn.

CHAPTER 14

Room at the Top

When I was seventeen all my friends had Minis. I really
wanted one. My parents thought it was dangerous so I was
given Grandad's old Hillman Avenger. Then I got a bit older
and got my own way. I bought a 1991 Mini Cooper. It was
fantastic . . .   Mini memory, 2008

All this early 'sixties chatter about road rationing and state-
sponsored city cars was terrific for Mini sales. But there was still
that problem of perception that the little car was a carriage for
social invalids. Then, in a stroke of early-adopter magic, the BMC
baby would find itself at the very pinnacle of the fashionable
Establishment. It happened like this.

Issigonis had a good friend called Jeremy Fry, a member of
the Fry chocolate dynasty. Born in 1924, old-Gordonstounian Fry
was a social entrepreneur and gifted inventor-engineer. He
founded a company, Rotork, to progress his technological ideas
that would later employ the young James Dyson (of vacuum-
cleaner fame) straight out of the Royal College of Art. He lived
at Widcombe Manor, a 'miniature palace' outside Bath. Fry was
intensely social. His friends included the film director Tony
Richardson, Cecil Beaton, Alec Issigonis, and the young photographer, Tony Armstrong-Jones.

Fry would regularly take a skiing chalet at Davos for the season.
In 1958 his guests included Issigonis and the already fêted
photographer Mr Armstrong-Jones – the nephew of stage
designer Oliver Messel – who had set up a fabulously fashionable studio in the Pimlico Road. They became enduring friends.

The Morris Minor-driving photographer was by now a reluctant celebrity. His romance with Princess Margaret, the Queen's younger sister, was fabulous tabloid fodder – especially after the agony of the princess's doomed romance with the divorced Battle of Britain hero Peter Townsend. The group captain, exiled to be air attaché in Brussels, had acquired a caddishly foreign Renault Frégate, which had been 'often seen parked outside Buckingham Palace' according to prod-nose newspaper correspondents.

Mr Armstrong-Jones was not divorced and (after a dalliance with a Fiat 500 Topolino) drove a very British Morris Minor. He married the Queen's sister on 6 May 1960 at Westminster Abbey. Alec Issigonis was a guest. He was delighted to be seated next to Noël Coward. Jeremy Fry was supposed to be best man but dropped out at the last minute (a 'creepy hack' had sniffed out that he had once been involved in a youthful homosexual scandal).

BMC misjudged the mood by presenting the royal newlyweds with a vulgarly American Austin Metropolitan as a wedding gift, black with a green interior (the couple's choice apparently). Its fate is unknown. What Tony Armstrong-Jones (created Lord Snowdon in October 1961) much preferred was his Austin Mini.

There were several cars in the royal garage, two Rolls-Royces, a VW Type 2 Kombi and the Austin. Lord Snowdon had the sliding windows replaced with wind-ups, reportedly to keep the princess's hair from blowing about on their way to engagements. Other sources ascribe it as means of better getting rid of cigarette smoke.

The couple visited Longbridge where, according to *BMC News*, the princess 'chatted animatedly' with polishers Mrs Doris Beddard, Mrs Dorothy Payne and Mrs Margaret Millinder as they buffed up a batch of Austin Se7ens. The royal imprimatur was beyond marketing price. How democratic, how modern and practical it all seemed. The newspapers loved it when Princesses Alexandra and Marina were caught in a traffic jam in a Mini-Minor and the world could see what was on their parcel shelf. A 'raincoat' and 'sweets', apparently.

Early adopters: Princess Margaret and her husband Antony Armstrong-Jones (soon to be Lord Snowdon) were big fans of the BMC baby – and the newlyweds often appeared round town in an impeccable Morris Mini Cooper S. But when the Princess was on the move, a Rolls from the Royal mews was never far behind.

London in 1962 was not you might call generally swinging. Carnaby Street was a dingy collection of rag-trade cutting rooms. But further west in Chelsea, where Mary Quant's shop, Bazaar, had served to clothe the beautiful and daring young women of the capital since opening in 1955, trendiness on wheels ruled. As Miss Quant remembered: 'King's Road on Saturday was a parade of vintage Hispano-Suizas and Bentleys – E types, Mini Coopers and miniskirts.'

The new mood was spreading – although fashion was still dictated by the wealthy and well connected. But what more and more of such people wanted was the cultural and sexual freedom the working class were tangibly beginning to enjoy.

The Queen magazine, a venerable title alarmingly reinvented in 1958 as something ultra-fashionable, discovered this febrile mix of old money and class mobility long before the mainstream press.

Alongside gushing accounts of débutante's balls, models were photographed in gritty industrial landscapes. Advertisers piled in – including Morris, who got their cheeky wizardry-on-wheels advert into the glossy pages in the month of the Mini-Minor's launch.

'*The Queen*'s typical reader', it was said, 'had long hair, was named Caroline, had left school at age sixteen, was not an intellectual, but she was the sort of person that one ended up in bed with.' You would get her there in a Mini.

The magazine's motoring correspondent was the Scottish racing driver Ron Flockhart (killed in an air crash in Australia in April 1962), who at first ignored the BMC baby. It was all Renault Dauphines and Sunbeam Alpines until suddenly in spring 1960 the super-glossy owned up to what it called the 'Baby Car Craze', a survey of those fashionable, urban taste makers who were suddenly in love with those funny little cars designed for the working class. *The Queen* clearly thought such people were going too far. How long would it last? Then three months later it was: 'The Baby Car Has It! Amid the traffic chaos, the small car is here to stay.' So the arbiters of fashion proclaimed. And leading the pack were BMC's brilliant tiny tots. King's Road Caroline would do it in a Mini-Minor.

As would slightly less posh types. A 1963 piece by the very observant journalist Nicholas Tomalin in *Town* magazine identified the 'scampi-belt', the new downsized, middle-class suburbia that had blossomed in the Macmillan era where it was 'all Beatles records, Goon voices and Minis'. The little car was ideal for young married homemakers to seek opportunities for outdoor sexual intercourse in the rapidly disappearing countryside. There was a picture of two of them, with a nice white Mini, emerging from a bush somewhere in the Chilterns to enjoy a post-coital cigarette.

Modernism was meeting miniaturisation whether you liked it or not. As the Mini was being launched, the working class were being uprooted wholesale from their bathless, carless slums to be packed into gleaming tower blocks with their utopian 'streets in the sky'. But where could you show off your newly acquired car? Style pundits scoffed as they decked their system-built hutches with lace curtains and china ornaments. The working class didn't do 'modern'.

BMC had kept their nerve. The original target market might have been a bust but who cared. The sales chart began to climb. In 1960, 166,677 would be built, some 23,000 more than the good old Morris Minor. Foreign 'small car' competitors were becoming irrelevant. The Renault Dauphine faded fast – although Welbeck Motors of Vauxhall, south London would send a fleet of them on to the roads of London in September 1961 as rivals to traditional taxis. They called them 'minicabs'.

It was time to stretch the brand – and the basic vehicle itself. The chassis was lengthened to make estate versions (launched in autumn 1960) sold as the Morris 'Mini Traveller' and the Austin 'Se7en Countryman' with half-timbered woody rear bodies. *The Queen* magazine hailed them as perfect for fashionable 'just marrieds'.

Then in 1961 came the Mini van. Built on the longer chassis but without side windows it was classed as a commercial vehicle and was thus exempt from purchase tax. The same applied to the little pick-up, a motorised wheelbarrow supposedly for farmers, launched the same year. The Mini Van would take on a life of its own, not just as a tradesman's runabout but as a student favourite – with a foam-rubber mattress in the back.

In January 1962 that fancy Se7en titling was dropped for the Austin badged versions. It would be the Austin Mini henceforth (Morris Mini-Minor would continue for a few years yet). It was really 'Mini' now – minicab, mini-budget, mini-this, mini-that. The baby car was growing up and its name was now part of the English language.

CHAPTER 15

Bit More Steam

Fifty years on and the original Mini is still terribly important to me. I've got one in the barn. I keep it in a special air-conditioned bubble. Here was this cheap family car that in Cooper form beat anything the rest of the world put up against it. It was a David-and-Goliath thing. The Mini was the British underdog triumphing again and again and people loved it for that. I was just lucky enough to be there.

Paddy Hopkirk, November 2008

Only a few weeks after the new baby's launch, a handful of enthusiasts had begun turning up in them at weekend racetracks. They were amateurs who brought their quick-handling machines along just for the fun of it. Professional drivers began to do the same a little later. Most people's initial response was laughter.

As a sport, production saloon car racing was in its infancy. But those first competition drivers very soon developed a repertoire of wheel-twitching, accelerator-tickling techniques to get round a track with grit-spraying dexterity that was adored by spectators. As an eloquent historian of the Mini described it:

In 1959 racing cars were racing cars and the start of the saloon car race was the signal for the initiated racegoer to make for the beer tent. But the sight of Minis arriving at Silverstone's Woodcote Corner all at once leaning on each other's door handles was enough to empty the tent for the rest of the season and transform the attitude of spectators to saloons.

Mini triumph: After the Monte Carlo Rally victory of 1964 a Cooper in either of Austin or Morris versions became the most desirable sporting car in the world. Especially the Cooper 'S'.

Cars regularly came to grief with the strain of it all, engine mountings broke up, exhausts sheared off, centres simply ripped out of their wheels. It happened so often that Minis were banned from the racetrack. The management at Longbridge seemed indifferent until it was pointed out that the same might start happening to hapless district nurses on their rounds. Specially strengthened wheels, stamped as such for the attention of RAC invigilators, got them going again.

The adventurous Miss Christabel Carlisle was given a BMC baby for her twenty-first birthday in 1960, 'a little red Mini, sweet, shiny and beautiful', as she wrote. She began to go on raffish early-morning 'treasure hunt' rallies in it – then was lured by the competition track. She published a how-to-do-it guide in 1963 called simply enough *Mini Racing*.

'When first produced at a race meeting it was greeted with uproarious laughter from everyone,' she wrote of her own Mini début. 'This was reduced to quiet chuckles when the crowd noticed how fast the car went round corners and changed again to gaping amazement when it began to pass larger cars in the straight and round bends and at every conceivable point where it could squeeze by.'

After much lobbying by enthusiasts, BMC had set up a competition department based at Abingdon (home of MG) in 1954, conscious that motorsport success promoted car sales at home and abroad – on the well-proven US model of 'win on Sunday, sell on Monday'. The new outfit, steered by the pre-war racing driver Marcus Chambers, tinkered around with what the corporation had in its line-up until the big Healey 3000 seemed to open the doors to rallying glory. When the 'fwd Sputnik' (as it was still referred to internally) appeared in summer 1959 it was ignored. Those tiny wheels, that vacuum-cleaner ground clearance. It seemed ridiculous to think of it bounding through Alpine snow-drifts or along dirt tracks. Nor was its originator that interested. 'When the Mini was designed and in production I never gave [competition] one single thought,' Issigonis would later tell a BBC interviewer. 'We were preoccupied in the design in getting good road-holding and stability for safety reasons and to give the driver more pleasure, but it never occurred to me that this thing would turn out to be such a fantastic rally car.'

Thus, at first, it was outsiders who rose to the challenge of making it go faster. Tuning shops began to pop up, run by hopeful mechanics offering trick carburettors and magical camshafts, widened track and lowered stance. A proportion were fly-by-nights turning out 'undrivable little screamers' that might top a ton flat-out but had no pull lower down. Others were much more professional – offering Mini 850 owners something that might be considered Cooper-like performance. Among the movers and tweakers in those early years were Arden Racing and Sports Cars Ltd of Solihull, V W Derrington of Kingston, Surrey, Yimkin Engineering Ltd based in a mews behind Sloane Street in west London, Speedwell Performance Conversions Ltd (with mus-tachioed racing driver Graham Hill as a director) in north London and Broadspeed Engineering Ltd of Birmingham, founded by Ralph Broad, an eager Mini early adopter who scored big success on the racetrack using Minis (he would grumpily switch to Ford in 1965). There was Nerus of St Leonards, Sussex, Taurus Performance Tuning of west London and Oselli Engineering of Eynsham, Oxford. Others would follow through the 'sixties as the Mini modification boom just kept on going. Tech Del Ltd of Chiswick began offering their famous 'Minilite' magnesium wheels in 1967 without which no go-fast Mini was complete.

But one Mini modifier would shine way above the rest. Just south of Salisbury, Wiltshire, in the village of Downton, a Mini wizard was building a business that would become legendary. Daniel Richmond, proprietor of the Downton Engineering Works, was a gifted engineer with society connections who tended venerable Bentley and Rolls-Royces for a posh West Country clientele. He had encountered a BMC A-series engine in a Morris Minor owned by a grand customer's wife and had seen its potential for tuning. His partner Bunty (they never married) was the niece of Somerset Maugham. She did the book-keeping. Also around 1957 Downton employed two Hungarian refugees from the Budapest uprising, called George Toth and Jan Odor. Toth became the head of the firm's cylinder head shop and Odor became an exhaust specialist.

According to a well-informed history, the Downton garage was next to the Bull public house, which was rather apt, as both Daniel and Bunty Richmond, the latter being the business brains in the outfit, were notorious for their alcohol consumption. It was even said that engine parts were bathed in gin (for super cleanliness apparently). Bunty favoured dry Martinis while Daniel preferred Krug champagne. He also chainsmoked Gauloises cigarettes.

In 1964 the tempestuous Bunty objected to Daniel giving Jan Odor a bonus. He walked out to found his own tuning firm, 'Janspeed', which undercut Downton's prices and which would eventually take the Mini tuning crown without any of the 'works' backing that Downton enjoyed from BMC.

Daniel Richmond was the classic early adopter of the tiny car and began straightaway to play with its A-series engine. Tricked up as it was to be mounted transversely, it was still the basic unit he was used to. In January 1960 he offered his customers a conversion job complete for £39 – a reworked cylinder head with modified inlet manifold and twin carburettors.

In May 1960 his own tuned 850cc Austin Se7en appeared in racing guise, driven by a professional driver called Jimmy Blumer on the track at Spa, Belgium, causing a Mini sensation; which it repeated on August Bank holiday at Brands Hatch, where it outpaced the beefy 2.5-litre works Ford Zephyr in the ten-lap saloon-car race to general delight. Word began to spread.

The Abingdon operation meanwhile was waking up to the potential of the new babies, especially in international rallying, where big publicity rewards might be garnered. In September 1959 a car modified with nothing more than a sump guard and a map light was entered in the Norwegian Viking Rally, acting as support car to Pat Moss's A40. It finished fifty-first with 'broken wheels, leaking boot and floors'.

Six works cars and six private entries went in for the January 1960 Monte, of which four finished, one being placed twenty-third overall. It was terrific at cornering and all of that – but it just wasn't powerful enough to be a serious contender.

A works-entered Se7en came tenth in the May 1960 Dutch Tulip Rally. In the 1961 Monte, none of the three works cars entered reached the finish line. The buzzing little car was draining to drive for extended periods. The handling was terrific, everybody knew that, the problem was lack of power.

An acclaimed racing-car designer also took notice of the infant prodigy's potential – John Cooper, thirty-six years old in the year of the baby's birth – whose mid-engined Cooper Climax machines had won the newly introduced Formula 1 Constructors' Championship in 1959 and again the following year. The Cooper company, based in Surbiton, Surrey, was also pursuing the new Formula Junior, the nursery slope for aspiring GP drivers, with front-engine cars with an engine capacity less than 1.1 litres. Negotiations for the supply of BMC A-series to power them were in hand – with Cooper's old friend Alec Issigonis as the intermediary.

Cooper was also working at the time on producing a go-fast version of the fashionable Renault Dauphine, using a Coventry Climax engine. But the French specialist Amédée Gordini had already tuned the standard-engined version to within a cubic centimetre of its life and a Renault Dauphine Gordini won the 1958 Monte Carlo Rally. Cooper dropped the Renault project once he'd driven an early-production Austin Seven, YOK 250, lent to him by BMC's publicity department; he had been enthralled by its handling.

—and now
QUALITY FIRST **MORRIS**
MINI-COOPER
For the fast lane

Life in the Fast Lane: When the Austin and Morris Mini Coopers were launched, BMC boss George Harriman doubted whether they would sell as many as a thousand. Alec Issigonis was also deeply sceptical. Such doubts were overcome and the result was a sensation.

He took the Austin to Monza for the Italian Grand Prix in September 1959. For years afterwards, John Cooper liked to tell the story of how Aurelio Lampredi, the chief designer for Fiat (formerly of Ferrari), swooned over the machine, pronouncing it to be 'the car of the future' (Enzo Ferrari eventually bought three Minis, including a Downton-tuned car that he used to take fast-paced but soothing drives into the hills around the Maranello factory).

John Cooper went to Longbridge for a convivial meeting with Issigonis and Harriman, the MD. He had a proposal. A production car was very quickly handed over for 'modifications', including a boost to cylinder capacity. Morris Engines in Coventry did the job of making a long-stroke version of the 848cc engine to take capacity to 994 cc. The Lockheed brake company was already engaged on a speculative disc brake of just seven inches, to fit the BMC baby's ten-inch wheels and give the required stopping power. It was the power to go that was about to make the big difference.

A prototype was completed at Cooper's south-west London works from an existing production Mini-Minor. Alex Moulton remembered proceeding in his patrician Bentley along an early stretch of motorway in the direction of Birmingham 'when I suddenly noticed a Mini in the rear-view mirror, doing eighty-plus. It just stayed with me all the way, I couldn't understand it.' It was John Cooper on his way to Longbridge to show off what he had made.

Alec Issigonis was not so sure. What had been done to his car-for-everyone? It was something for the district nurse to potter around in. Cooper reportedly said to him, 'we ought to build some of these for the boys, you know . . . bit more steam'.

George Harriman was keen enough. A deal was struck. The 85mph-capable car (now codenamed ADO50) would be put into production. A royalty of £2 would be paid to Mr Cooper on every one manufactured. Over a thousand would have to be built and sold on the open market if the car was to be entered in competitions as a 'production' machine according to the rules of so-called homologation. 'Do you think we'll sell that many?' asked Harriman. He was prepared to take the risk. With the 997cc tuned A-series engine putting out 55 bhp at 6,000 rpm, a 62 per cent boost in power, remote gear change, front disc brakes and better instrumentation they would be sold as the 'Austin Se7en Cooper' and the 'Morris Mini Cooper'. Would enough people really want to buy them? There were grave doubts at Longbridge.

In 1960 the Cooper Car Co. dominated Grand Prix racing, a bigger name at the time even than Ferrari – but even so (or perhaps as a result) the badging was ultra-discreet. The body shell was unchanged – although the paint jobs featured roofs of contrasting colour, something shared with the 'Super' version of the standard car launched a little earlier.

This was not badge engineering. It was much cleverer, grafting a pulse-quickening name from motor racing on to a not-yet-formed 'brand' that was quickly sloughing off its utilitarian roots (in spite of its originator's objections, and he would soon be basking in the all-round glory). The press launch, on 17 July 1961, featured ten hand-built cars – all there were in the world. The glittering guest list included twenty-seven Grand Prix drivers. The whole affair oozed automotive glamour – even if it would be another two months before 400 cars had actually been built and put on sale. At £679 including tax, the Cooper was £153 more than the standard baby.

There was scramble to get hold of them. Urban early adopters now had something expensive and exclusive to show off about. Lord Snowdon was described by a breathless profiler of the time 'whizzing about London after dark in his Mini Cooper, venturing to the bohemian districts of Clapham and Hammersmith'. The production line (for both versions) was at Longbridge. Ten thousand were manufactured in the first year, a fabulous figure.

It was go-fast heaven. Cooper's own stable of drivers, Jack Brabham, Bruce McLaren and Roy Salvadori, were hopping in and out of them all the time.

The reanimated BMC Competition Department would run the rallying programme, using the car, while the Cooper Car Company would semi-officially concentrate on track events with a ready supply of factory money. A big chunk of BMC competition cash was already going to Donald Healey to fly the sports-car flag in the USA.

An American actor meanwhile was flying the Mini flag in England. An offbeat western, *The Magnificent Seven* (a title picked up by Austin Mini marketing), had been a big international hit in 1960. One of its stars was thirty-year-old Terrence Steven McQueen, a big motorcycling fan and self-confessed 'car nut'. Steve McQueen had been racing semi-professionally on US tracks since the late 'fifties.

127

In late summer 1961, the actor was in England to make a film called *The War Lover* – co-starring as 'Buzz Rickson – a daredevil World War II bomber pilot with a death wish'. The Columbia studio heads warned him that, if he tried to race cars in England and was injured, he would be sued for the film's production costs. He ignored the warning, choosing instead to seek out Stirling Moss – who introduced him to the joys of the very first batch of Mini Coopers. As it was reported by a biographer: 'McQueen stayed out of cars during the weekdays on the set [the principal location for the shooting of *The War Lover* was in Cambridgeshire] but each weekend he'd wangle a ride at club events. He was fifth at Oulton Park, an also-ran at Aintree but took a solid third overall at Brands Hatch [behind Sir John Whitmore, the 'racing baronet', and Christabel Carlisle, also in Minis]. His newfound friend, Stirling Moss, helped Steve learn the fastest way round various circuits by signalling with his finger for second, third gear and so on.

Girl on Top: The beautiful film actress Charlotte Rampling found stardom aged twenty in 1966 in the Swinging London flick 'Georgy Girl', and felt inclined for some reason to climb onto the roof of a Mk I Mini a little while afterwards.

It was at Brands Hatch that Steve got into trouble. "I was running in the wet with this Mini Cooper when a brake locked on me. This threw my car sideways as I was coming out of a fast turn, and I knew I couldn't hold the road. Not on a wet track".

The actor hit the embankment hard and bloodied his lip (close-up photography was scheduled for the next day) but as McQueen himself recalled it: 'the director saved the day by letting me do all my scenes in an oxygen mask in the cockpit, so everything was cool'.

'Racetrack success at home was fine but rallying success was fabulous international publicity. The first years of rallying the 850cc cars had been brave experiments but devoid of trophies. Then in 1961 a new success-hungry competition manager took over at Abingdon. He was called Stuart Turner, a twenty-seven-year-old accountant and keen amateur rallying navigator, co-driver to Pat Moss when they achieved the first ever competition win for the little car in the October 1959 'Mini Miglia National Rally' in a Morris Mini Minor 850.

The mild-mannered wordsmith would prove ruthless in pursuit of sporting victories. In the 997cc homologated (meaning enough had been built for it to be considered an 'ordinary' car on sale to the public) ADO50, the BMC Competition Department now had the means to achieve it. In May 1962 Pat Moss won the Dutch Tulip Rally to score the car's first outright international win. The veteran Rhodesian-born driver John Love won the British Racing and Sports Car Club national saloon-car championship in September the same year. In January 1963 Rauno Aaltonen and the Belfast-born driver Paddy Hopkirk finished third and fourth in the Monte, driving Coopers. They were getting closer and closer to a big outright win.

With excellent sales figures, John Cooper was already proposing a more potent development of the car. At Downton Engineering in sleepy Wiltshire meanwhile, Daniel Richmond was playing with a version with an engine enlarged to 1088 cc, capable of well over

100 mph. Drooling journalists tried it out. Issigonis, now appointed technical director of BMC, got behind the wheel and drove it 'like a kid'. He was amazed that his 'Mini could have that amount of acceleration'. In December 1961 the *Autocar* published a glowing road test of what it called the 'Mini-Ton-Bomb'.

The 0–60mph time was reduced to 9.6 seconds and top speed was a blistering 103 mph. *Autocar* commented: 'A direct result of this is a marked gain in torque but the chief object of the conversion as a whole has been to provide outstanding tractability and top gear acceleration over a wide engine speed range, rather than the ultimate in top speed.' That was a Downton signature – and why Daniel Richmond enjoyed BMC backing. His conversions were the best. Production of the further-uprated machine was approved. It was a turning moment in Mini history.

Richmond, whose tuning business was never an official part of BMC, was brought into the fold, working with Issigonis and the Cooper operation as a consultant on what was now being loosely referred to as the 'special'. Under the deal the Downton concern would take an annual fee for an exclusive contract (although they could take on individual commissions). And BMC would provide factory cars to be breathed on at the request of illustrious customers who had approached the corporation direct. Downton meanwhile was obliged not to publicise the relationship (although the cognoscenti knew). The Cooper name must shine alone – and once again 1,000 cars must be built to meet the homologation rules. Harriman apparently wanted to call it the 'Special', but John Cooper objected. It would emerge as the beguilingly simple 'S'.

In March 1963 the Mini Cooper S made its public début with its Downton-developed cylinder head and engine capacity boosted to 1071 cc putting out 70 bhp at peak power. The 95mph-capable car was stopped by 7.5-inch disc brakes. Paddy Hopkirk recalled:

I remember I was at Oulton Park racetrack, where I met Stuart Turner. He said, 'Come over here, I want you to take a look at this car.' It was the 1100cc Mini Cooper S. I got in just to give it a quick drive somewhere off the track. It had disc brakes and a very torquey engine. It was a revelation. 'My goodness,' I told him. 'This is to die for . . .'

The Abingdon competition operation under Stuart Turner's direction now had a truly world-beating saloon car in their hands. But it was on the Continent that sports success seemed to feed directly into sales – before the wider British public really took notice. In Europe the little car was already chic; now it would become heroic. In the Tour de France run in September 1963, the Ulster-born rally driver Paddy Hopkirk and co-driver Henry Liddon in a Morris Mini Cooper S led most of the way. The event was partially televised. The tiny car consistently outpaced and outdrove the big US Ford Galaxies with their monstrous engines, something that seemed especially to please the French.

According to Hopkirk: 'The French went mad about it . . . and the dealers all turned up saying we want Mini Coopers. I think it was the first time BMC realised the potential of the publicity value. I mean it was more chic to pick up your girlfriend in Paris in a Mini Cooper than in a Bentley.'

And it was true. By 1965 France was the biggest market in the world for the Cooper, in spite of a Common Market tariff barrier of nearly 20 per cent. On the other side of the world, the Japanese had been showing more and more interest ever since the first Austin Seven had arrived in March 1960. The Cooper absolutely wowed them. The Mini Cooper was on its way to being the trendiest thing in the universe.

CHAPTER 16

Conspicuous Thrift

As far as I am concerned, the one thing that has never occurred has been the recognition of Issigonis's achievements . . . that is one of the reasons that we would like to produce vehicles bearing his name. Many enthusiasts would argue that his design was actually lost permanently . . . when the new Mini, the Mark III, arrived in 1970 [and] many of his original space-saving ideas were thrown out of the window . . .

We want our new Mini to resemble the Mini that Issigonis designed back in 1959 . . . taking out what BL put in . . . wind-up windows, thick reclining seats and jazzy colours and all that sort of thing. We go back to originality and recreate it.

Deposition to use the trademark 'Issigonis' to market retro-rebuilt Minis, successfully opposed by Rover Group, 2000

The Cooper mystique was terrific, of course. No marketing plan could have anticipated the fabulous accident that transformed the shopping-car-for-housewives into a stellar object of masculine desire. The fashionable élite had taken up the original car and was embracing the Cooper even more eagerly. On US consumer-psychology theory, the BMC baby had been through the early-adopter phase and was now into trickle-down. Actually it was working out pretty much like that.

In its main home market the car was selling itself. The half-million production mark was passed in December 1962.

Premature release had been a huge gamble – but it seemed to be paying off. Rival Hillman, with their rear-engined small car, the Imp, were still a year away from launch.

The Austin Mini Countryman and Morris Mini Traveller, Van and Pick-up did what they did happily enough. Sales were encouraging. There was no MG version; why bother when the Cooper grabbed the sporting laurels? But BMC could not resist its old badge-engineering obsession when, in early 1961, the Dick Burzi-styled Riley Elf and Wolseley Hornet were announced, in an attempt to make the Mini safe for the Home Counties by adding an extended bustle boot, vestigial tail fins, wind-up windows, 'traditional' radiator grilles and 997cc engines.

The Elf was marginally more expensive, priced at £694 to the Hornet's £672, with three instrument dials set in a walnut fascia and a chrome gearbox handle. The styling was done by the competent enough Dick Burzi but nevertheless they looked faintly ridiculous. Quite whom they were aimed at was never really clear. Issigonis loathed them, especially the wind-up windows.

But still there was no real marketing policy. BMC's appointed admen grabbed at every sporting success, news event and passing trend as they happened. The Janet-and-John family of the launch vanished in a puff. Now it was all 'bachelor girls' and jazz musicians. There were zany rag-week stunts as students packed as many in a Mini as possible. It would be called a 'Mini cram'. BMC marketing was always keen to help this youthful jape along.

And why not? So much of British society and the wider world was changing at breathtaking speed. BMC's annual report for 1962 alluded to the febrile, Cuba-missile-crisis-period mood. Signed off by George Harriman, it used the metaphors of then-imminent-seeming nuclear war: 'It is unfortunate that our nation is passing through this miasma with industrial conflict gravely undermining Britain's world economic prestige when it needs to be strong for economic negotiations now taking place in

Europe . . . Every industrial explosion at home adds to the fallout.'

The established social order was imploding from within anyway.

A new generation had emerged through the 'fifties of what would later be called 'upwardly mobile' young people, products of the 1944 Butler Education Act. They thought themselves rational and socially aware. They read *Which?* magazine and tut-tutted over general British shoddiness. They read the new Sunday glossy mags that pushed homewares and trendy furnishing as approved by the Design Council. They read the theories of J K Galbraith on the perils of affluence and applauded Ralph Nader and Vance Packard in their exposure of the US-led conspiracy to poison the world with dud stuff. They liked to think of themselves as classless and forward-looking. They were the sort of people who bought Minis.

They lived both in the new scampi belt and the gentrifying parts of inner-urban Britain. And this was the thing – brought up as children in wartime austerity they eschewed both socialist asceticism and jukebox excess. Mrs Thrift would covet a 'plain, plain Mary Quant dress pared right down to formal simplicity'. Mr Thrift fancied a Mini (a Cooper actually).

Of course they loved to consume – but things that were stylish and minimalist. Such things could be expensive. This generation would dominate high-end British consumer taste until the advent of Margaret Thatcher. Less was more and Minis were even more of less.

In 1963 the trend-spotting *Town* magazine in a piece by Nicholas Tomalin called them the 'Conspicuous Thrifters' – who wore 'denim and leather' – to whom a Ford Consul was absolute anathema – and whose 'ideal of dress and manner was a romanticised, teenage building-site worker'. CTs liked foreign cars – Volvos, Karmann Ghias, Dauphines – but of course loved Minis best. They also loved Moulton bicycles (Alex

Moulton launched his defining, rubber-sprung small-wheel bike in 1962).

You could be stinking rich, royal even, and still be a CT. The Duke of Kent was one, his 'lank knees doubled through the roof of his Mini-Minor as he goes to work in sheepskin at the War Office' – as were the Snowdons. 'Lord Snowdon works for a living . . . he has a dozen cars . . . but prefers the Mini.'

Sir Hugh Casson, the royal family's favourite architect-interior designer, adored his Mini, describing it as his 'private bubble'. Later, when he was President of the Royal Academy of Arts, his yellow Mini became a familiar sight buzzing in and out of the courtyard at Burlington House.

Once upon a time a rich young man would get a flashy sports car – but now that seemed 'a foolhardy extravagance' in the age of CT. 'The Mini Cooper is its rebuttal, neat, casual, democratic yet of course everyone knows it is neither ordinary nor cheap, but a quart of power poured into a pint pot,' pronounced *Town*.

Conspicuous Thrifter: Lord Snowdon, aristocrat of early Mini-adopters, shows his egalitarian credentials in this 1962 cartoon by the perceptive Wally Fawkes ('Trog').

The CTs were the kind of people who warmed to the campaigning rhetoric of opposition Labour Party leader Harold Wilson, with his promise of a technological revolution. 'It is the working classes of all of us who still guiltlessly enjoy the excesses of conspicuous waste,' said *Town*. 'It is the Jag parked outside the council flat that defines the workers.' And it was true.

Actually it wasn't Jags the workers wanted but Fords – especially the Consul Cortina launched in September 1962, cleverly conceived and marketed by Ford UK's product planner Terence Beckett as a glamorous family car pitched above the Mini. In the new age of package-holiday travel it was named after an Italian ski resort. It said, 'look at us, we're not poor'. The launch ads featured men in white tuxedos and women in mink stoles. Mini and mink didn't really work.

In September 1962 a new magazine was launched called *Small Car and Mini Owner*, in tune, so its backers hoped, with the new CT mood. The title said it all really. Its publisher was the unusual clergyman Marcus Morris, founder of the *Eagle* comic. It was fabulously innovative in its graphic design and editorial style, a long way from the sycophantic reviews and ponderous road tests of the *Motor* and *Autocar*. It was sexy, fashionable and drenched in Mini-ness.

'Here is a new kind of motoring magazine produced for the conditions of today aimed at the small car owner because most drivers are small car owners . . .' its launch editorial announced brightly. 'Crowded roads started the scaling down and manufacturers finished it by making small cars so good that we don't need big ones any more.'

Well, that's how it seemed at the time. Eventually it would ditch *Small* to become the deeply fabulous *CAR* magazine. But that's another story.

Small Car and Mini Owner rejoicingly logged the politicians and entertainers, the rich and the famous who were proving

Mini celebrity early adopters. They included President Kekkonen of Finland, Miss Shirley Bassey, Sooty man Harry Corbett, the Duke of Kent, Dame Margot Fonteyn, Giovanni Agnelli (boss of Fiat), Norman Wisdom and Princess Grace of Monaco, who took delivery of a very pretty Austin Mini Cooper with whitewall tyres. Film director Roy Boulting had one with green and black vertical stripes. He would commission another for his wife, the actress Hayley Mills. The theatrical farceur Ray Cooney had a Morris Mini Traveller. Lord Hartwell, proprietor of the *Daily Telegraph*, acquired one (with chauffeur).

An early edition of the mag featured 'Paula Noble, a twenty-four-year-old London model who spends 21 guineas every few months having her Mini resprayed to match her clothes. She began with Rolls-Royce silver grey, now it's shocking pink . . .'

You could feel the buzz already. Conspicuous thrift was getting a bit dull. What those cool, neat, casual, democratic, Mini drivers wanted to really do – was swing.

Mini adventuress: Christine Keeler was another early fan of the BMC baby. Her choice in cars and men seemed to symbolise the end of the old order when the 'Profumo Affair' hit the headlines in 1963.

CHAPTER 17

Mini Scandal

> When I argue with a car salesman that I must postpone the purchase of a new car because I fear a depression – it is up to him to sell me not only the new car, but even before that, to sell me a positive philosophy of life.
>
> Ernst Dichter, *The Strategy of Desire*, 1959

Certain sections of Mini-owning society were pretty swinging already. Those small-car rationalists of the early 'sixties were also the sort of people who sniggered knowingly at the revelations of the 'Profumo affair' – which dominated domestic British politics in the spring and summer of 1963. Some of them would not have been at all surprised to learn that some of the principals in the unfolding drama of scandal in high places were also Mini adepts. The little car was sex on wheels, after all.

In March of that fated year, Mini-Minor-driving John Profumo, Secretary of State for War in Harold Macmillan's Conservative government, denied to Parliament that there was any truth in the rumours swirling in the press. Well-informed, Mini-loving *The Queen* magazine had been dropping gossipy hints since two summers before. The minister admitted an acquaintance with one of the young women allegedly involved, but insisted there was no 'impropriety' involved. Then in June he confessed to having had a sexual relationship with topless showgirl and fellow Mini owner Christine Keeler.

There is a delicious press picture from that lurid-headline-bathed spring and summer of 1963 of Miss Keeler getting into her Mini in a London street as a frowning clergyman strides by. One assumes it was the driver rather than the car that invited his disapproval.

The twenty-one-year-old club hostess became even more of a modernist icon when she was snapped in May by the theatrical photographer Lewis Morley, naked, straddling an Arne Jacobsen Model 3107 bent-plywood chair (actually a knock-off imitation of the 1955 design classic). It was a promotion for a film (which was never made) but when one of the prints was stolen and published in the *Sunday Mirror* it caused a national sensation. This was thoroughly modern design – and sexy with it. Just like a Mini.

Her by-now-ended sexual liaison with Mr Profumo had been adventurous. Within a week of meeting in summer 1961 at a midnight skinny-dipping session in a country-house swimming pool, the first 'screw of convenience' as she would describe it was enacted. A further encounter took place, she would later reveal, in the War Minister's red Mini-Minor.

Her friend, Marilyn Davies, meanwhile had already taken Mini honours in a less gymnastic way in 1960. It happened like this. Marilyn, who would become famous as Mandy Rice-Davies, had grown up in Solihull near Birmingham, although her parents were originally Welsh – her mother, a miner's daughter, her father, an ex-policeman working for Dunlop tyres. At the age of fifteen she began to work at a posh Birmingham department store. An admirer spotted her in the fine-china department. He had a friend who was an executive for the Austin Motor Co. who was looking for a Miss Austin to grace the stand at the forth-coming Earl's Court Motor Show. She was offered twelve guineas a day plus expenses, a fabulous sum of money. She was just sixteen.

The show was opened on 19 October by the Trade Minister, Reginald Maudling. The Se7en was once again the main attrac-tion on the spotlit stand, especially the brand-new estate version. 'I stayed at a hotel in Earls Court,' she recalled not long afterwards, 'but every night brought an invitation to dinner from the crowd of admirers jostling around . . . I basked in the flattery of handsome, well-dressed men like a seal on a rock.'

Or was it the baby Austin that was the centre of attention? There was a stream of VIP visitors trooping through to take a look, politicians, movie stars, royalty. *BMC News* splashed a front-page picture of Princess Margaret and Mr Anthony Armstrong-Jones being greeted by Alec Issigonis. As Miss Rice-Davies herself recalled: 'the Mini was the most photographed, most publicised car ever. My work, if you could call it that, consisted of looking cute. I was taken to receptions and met the Mini's designer . . . he was very famous at the time.'

Girl in a Countryman: Sixteen-year-old Birmingham shop-girl Marilyn Davies came to London in October 1960 as 'Miss Austin' to decorate the stand at the Earl's Court Motor Show and help launch the brand new estate version of the baby car, as this grainy newspaper photo shows. After all that automotive glamour there was no going back to Brum. She changed her name to Mandy Rice-Davies and found a rather different calling.

She was a star. There was picture of her in the London *Evening News*, dark-haired, in the 'new Austin Seven Countryman with model Marilyn Davies gracing the interior'. 'I thought it was wonderful,' she recalled after almost fifty years, 'it was white with shiny varnished wood. It was glamorous and it was young.' There was no going back to humdrum Brum after all that. The teenager 'was introduced by a girl on a neighbouring stand' to London's nightlife. She went home for one day, packed her bags and sold her sewing machine to buy a one-way ticket back to the bright lights.

She got a job as a dancer at Murray's Club in Beak Street, Soho. There she met Christine Keeler, who introduced her to her friend, the society osteopath Stephen Ward. He would prove the conduit for the former Miss Austin to meet a section of society which was interested in more than miniature motor cars.

Mini downfall: Looking glum, War Minister John Profumo is caught by photographers on the eve of his resignation outside his Regent's Park home in June 1963. Even his Mini-Minor (an alleged trysting place with Miss Keeler) seems to want to stay out of the picture.

Another cabinet member linked at the time by innuendo (and nothing else) to the sexual shenanigans in London was Ernest Marples, the Transport Minister. In spring 1963 he was looking for a new car suitable for his position. On 29 April he wrote to Sir William Glanville, director of the Road Research Laboratory, to ask his advice, as a letter preserved in the National Archives reveals.

'As Minister of Transport I must set an example and be seen to be reasonably up to date,' he wrote. 'I have almost decided to get a Mini Cooper.

'I plan to have the new Antilok anti-skid system fitted and of course seat belts [not a legal obligation under UK construction-and-use legislation until 1967].

'Is there anything else you think I should have fitted to my car . . .?'

The minister was reassured. He would indeed be seen to be 'up to date' – after an encounter with John Cooper at the 1963 Racing Car Show in London that resulted in an order for a 1071cc-engined Austin Cooper S, specially modified at Longbridge to the minister's requirements, including a full-length opening tailgate for his 'golf clubs'. And, so it was reported at the time, that easy-access boot was used for forays to his own French vineyard in the Beaujolais to 'collect crates of wine'.

CHAPTER 18

Mini Converts

All girls who own Minis are old and wrinkly . . .

[Reply] There are a few girls around Tunbridge Wells that drive Minis and one that drives a Beetle and they're certainly not old and wrinkly! Very nice looking girls . . .

Hot girls in Minis, Mini forum 2008

I had an E-Type which got stolen. Then I had a Mini later on in the 'sixties, a Cooper S in racing green. I loved it. I'd drive it round Kensington and get lots of admiring glances, but I never knew whether they were for me or the car . . .

Mini memory, Mandy Rice-Davies, 2008

The Minister of Transport came late to the great Mini adapt-and-improve boom. The work of Daniel Richmond and John Cooper represented the top end of an extraordinary explosion of automotive DIY that began almost as soon as the car was launched. *Motor Sport* had noted just weeks after the launch that owners 'even now are modifying and tuning them for high speed'. Maybe it was the car's utilitarian, half-finished nature. It needed to be made whole, pampered even. The premature baby soon became a spoilt child.

Every manner of Mini variation crowded into the pages of *Small Car and Mini Owner*. In January 1963 the magazine featured the 'Minnow GT', built in Hackbridge, Surrey, by MPG

& H Engineering, constructed clumsily on a Mini Van chassis with a weird kind of estate-car back fitted with a 'Fish carburettor', an American device bought in by Mr Bob Henderson, the vehicle's deviser, who drove his Minnow, he said, at high speed regularly from the south London suburbs to his ruined castle in Scotland.

The magazine's advertising waxed on the burgeoning range of accessories that otherwise sensible buyers abandoned their powers of reason to eagerly acquire. How about 'the Panorama Airscoop' by the Panorama Radio Co. of Putney, a kind of tiny spoiler that promised to keep 'a fast moving air stream down across the rear window'. Or why not complement your Mini with the Allcar leopardskin door armrest that clipped on to the utilitarian door bin. You might choose to 'double the boot capacity of your Mini with the LMB Mini boot'. If that was a bit tame you could give your Mini the 'rally look' with the Desomo Continental spare-wheel carrier. The Styla company promised to 'make your Mini different' with sundry chrome strips, mud flaps, wing mirrors and gaudy wheel spinners.

You could buy a 'Murmaride' sound-deadening kit or sheets of something called 'shamkane', stick-on plastic wickerwork to emulate the Edwardian coach-built look that was suddenly so fashionable.

There were rear-wheel spats from Cosmic, or more practically a remote gear change to replace that flailing wand, which was hard to reach for a driver wearing a seatbelt. The same was true for the toggle switches, which could be brought within reach with flexible 'Extendaswitches'. Seat extensions and steering brackets promised to push back the front seat for more legroom and drop the wheel a couple of inches for a more reclined driver's body position. All of that was a mercy for fans of the car who were taller than six feet.

If that was the case you could even sleep on the roof in the extraordinary Mini-sized 'car tent' that sat in a roof rack: 'just stop the car, open the tent and climb in, no need to worry about animals or creepy crawlies . . .' All you had to worry about was falling out.

But like entry-level Mini owners bolting on all those bizarre goodies, the temptation for Mini-tinkering went right up the income scale. Princess Margaret's Mini was shadowed by a chauffeur-driven Rolls from the royal mews on her forays round London. What if limousine comforts could be packaged into the baby car itself?

Another Mini girl on top: As a solution to interior space constraints, how about the Car Tent of 1960? Of all the myriad accessories that bloomed on the baby car's success, this was one of the strangest.

In March 1964 *Small Car*'s women's editor, Kay Christiansen, interviewed the radio comedian-turned-film-actor, Peter Sellers, about his Mini. She encountered him at Elstree Studios, making the second movie in the Pink Panther franchise, *A Shot in the Dark*.

He had 'bought and sold 85 cars in fifteen years', Mr Sellers confessed – no less than £130,000-worth, he thought. He had bought a Mini Cooper on the general fashionable buzz about the car, registration no. 6189 PK, and, as one did, he took it via the Rolls-Royce dealer H R Owen to Messrs Hooper, coachbuilders, with instructions to improve it with 'anything you can think of . . .'

The result was the '£2,600 Mini', featuring Bentley headlamps, electric windows, 'the very best quality HMV transistor radio with two speakers, two-speed wipers, a mahogany instrument board, servo brakes, bucket seats in terracotta hide, beige carpet, safety belts, and an anti-dim driving mirror'. The car was finished in 'roman purple and shamkane'. One might say it teetered on the brink of vulgarity. In June 1963 it appeared in Downing Street, where Sellers had been invited to a private luncheon with Harold Macmillan.

Skinny Mini: Miss Lesley Hornby, 'Twiggy', the quintessential 'sixties personality, was born in Neasden, north London, exactly ten years before the BMC baby car was launched. She was caught by a photographer aged nineteen in November 1968, having just passed her driving test – in a luxuriously equipped Mini with wind-up windows, radio and lots of exciting dashboard dials and switches.

'I'm mad about it – although I've got an E-Type and a Lincoln Continental anyone can have those but no one at the moment has a car like my Mini,' said the actor.

A chauffeur drove him to the studio. His passengers were almost always his children Michael and Sarah; although ten-year-old Michael preferred the E-Type. He had clocked only 3,000 miles in six months, his interviewer pointed out. 'I don't have the time,' he confessed.

'I never drink when driving, not even one, I don't think one should smoke and I never have the radio on unless I'm on a wide open carriage way – and because I'm on actors' insurance there's no rallying.'

The story of the 'luxe' Mini was only just beginning. Harold Radford (Coachbuilder) Ltd of Hammersmith, west London, who had produced woody-bodied Rollers and Bentleys for sporting gentlemen of the early 'fifties, caught the trend in 1963, offering three versions of what they called the 'Mini de ville': the £1,080 'Grande Luxe'; the 'Bel Air', with slightly reduced spec; and the 'de luxe' which had all sorts of interior comforts but retained the standard car's outward features.

A high-specification car was shown at Earl's Court in October 1963, causing a general stir with sun roof, stereo radio, electric windows and lamb's-wool carpets. In spite of lots of sound-deadening, the gear-change rattle of the cooking Mini was apparently still very audible.

HH Sheikh Khalifa bin Salman Al Khalifa of Bahrain ordered one – a Morris Mini Cooper S with all the Radford tweaks – plus a second one with a (so it was stressed, non-alcoholic) cocktail cabinet.

In October 1965 the 'Mini de Ville GT' appeared with loads of important-looking switches and instruments. It was also offered with a one-piece rear tailgate. Peter Sellers ordered one for his second wife, Swedish-born actress Britt Ekland. For the Mini limo's launch, Sellers drove it through a gigantic prop 'cake' at the Radford showrooms, surrounded by popping flash-bulbs as Britt beamed from above.

The Fab Four were earlyish adopters. Their original manager Brian Epstein shrewdly set up a car dealership called 'BryDor' that was used to get cars at trade prices as a pay-off for the mop-top publicity. That included a string of Minis. John Lennon had a black 1965 (the year he passed his driving test) Austin Mini Cooper S, reg. LGF 696D, in which he moodily flitted round the place (actually, like Princess Margaret, he seemed to have preferred his Rolls).

Paul McCartney had a 1965 Radford Mini Cooper S, registered GGJ 382C. Ringo Starr owned a Radford Mini, LL0 836D, first registered on 5 May 1966. George Harrison had a Radford Austin Cooper S, registered LGF 695D and finished in metallic black until in early 1967 it went all psychedelic. As did its owner. In this guise it featured in the TV musical movie *Magical Mystery Tour* filmed that September, driving round and round a disused RAF airfield at West Malling, Kent, apparently chasing the rest of the mystery trippers in their six-wheel Bedford VAL coach.

Posh Minis began to pop up all over the place in films and newsreels. Marianne Faithfull arrived at the law courts on 1 August 1967 in her duo-tone Radford Mini de Ville for Mick Jagger's appeal against his drug sentence. Four weeks later John Lennon was filmed arriving at the Apple Studios in west London in his Radford Mini de Ville hatchback after hearing of the death of Brian Epstein.

The BBC drama department caught the mood when they gave Adam Llewellyn De Vere Adamant, Edwardian gentleman adventurer, frozen in a block of ice since 1902 only to be defrosted sixty-four years later in swinging London, a Radford Mini de Ville to convey him into action.

The Mini Cooper would also burst on to the small screen as the star of the show. In fact it did it twice.

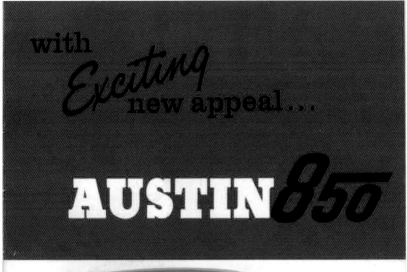

with *Exciting* new appeal....

AUSTIN *850*

Mini appeal: From almost the very beginning the BMC babies were aimed at the US market as the Austin or Morris '850' (the expression 'Mini' did not figure) – but were so small that hardly anyone noticed. *Car and Driver* magazine called a test car a 'roller skate'

© Simon Elgood

(*Left*) **Nippy round town:** The Mini's cheeky ability to squeeze through traffic and into impossible parking spaces was a big part of its initial appeal – stoked here by Morris advertising circa 1960

(*Below*) **Early adopters:** Morris versions of the BMC baby were being called 'Minis' right from the start. Austin abandoned the cute Se7en branding after a couple of years – by which time Today's Car really was a Mini and firmly aimed at hip city dwellers rather than the 'working class' car-buyers of Issigonis's imagination

© TopFoto

(Right) **National treasure:** By the mid 'sixties Alec Issigonis was Britain's foremost celebrity car designer – in fact the nation's only one. On the occasion of his 1969 knighthood he was pictured with an eclectic array of enduring design and craft icons from around the world, including a (very English) Chippendale chair, a (German) Meissen figurine and a (Swedish) AGA stove

(Below) **Mini Monte:** The Coopers' rally success of the mid 'sixties poured glamour over the whole Mini range. Here Timo Mäkinen and Paul Easter head through the January snows in a Mini Cooper S towards victory in the 1965 event. But as Paddy Hopkirk reminisced, it was still a modified 'shopping car' and its glory days were about to be eclipsed

(Right) **Portrait of the author as a young man:** Me with my dad's Mini – circa 1975. We've all got a pic like this somewhere

(Below) **Mini idyll:** For generations of British children, the Mini was not some swinging lifestyle accessory, but Mum and Dad's car that took you to school or to the seaside and in the memories of millions, it still is

© Kazushige Tanase

Small in Japan: The Mini had been a hit in car-culture obsessed Japan since the 'sixties, something that pleased Sir Alec Issigonis greatly. The reborn Cooper of 1990 was like a miraculous second coming (sold as a 'Rover') – and Japan was its biggest market until the end

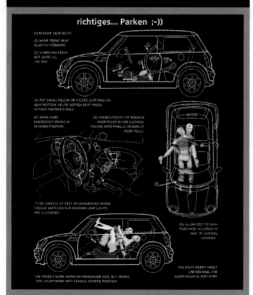

(*Above*) **Mini endgame:** Right to the last, the classic Mini could be regarded as a practical car for chic urbanites. Its glamour may have been fading but its boho-bourgeois charms never palled

(*Left*) **You can do it in a MINI:** The internet offers abundant advice on MINI-related sexual athletics including this spoof BMW information sheet from the German website MINI2IG

(Above) **Dynasty:** BMW strove to ensure that the classic Longbridge-made Mini was supplanted in the showrooms by the Oxford-made MINI without too long a break – so that the heir apparent should be seen as just that. Launch publicity stressed the idea of a seamless succession but die-hard Mini-purists were hugely suspicious

(Left) **Mini Winehouse:** Fresh-faced, twenty-one-year-old singer Amy Winehouse heads for a press call in Brit-award branded MINI, January 2004, shortly after the release of her first album *Frank*. The car and the singer have changed quite a bit since

(Left) **MINI forever:** Production of the MINI Mk II at Plant Oxford (better known to BMC nostalgists as Cowley) peaked in 2008 – before the economic crisis began to rumble through the global car industry

(Below) **We shall remember them:** Alive or just resting, Minis are everywhere – including halfway up a Spanish mountain in this 2008 image. The cat in the foreground may have nine lives; the Mini-MINI has thus far had two

Sunday Night at the London Palladium

Do you know 'Moke'? The 'Moke' car had have long-standing history civilization, which is been first manufactured by the UK. Longbridge plant for 1964–1968. We developed new 'Moke' jeep again, the new 'Moke' car keep its aboriginal manner, we not only remain the original style, but also improve it to meet current requirements of modern traffic such as original especial rubber shock absorber, gear box, chassis . . . and use electron control injection engine to meet exhaust emission standard . . .

China Chongqing Big Science & Technology Co.,
sales brochure, 2007

The success of the Cooper 1071S in international competitions and on weekend racetracks had bathed the ordinary Mini in borrowed glamour. Sunday fantasists in Antartex car coats and Dent's stringback driving gloves could toss a copy of *Motor Sport* on the rear seat of a humble 850cc car and let rip.

The rallying successes continued. Rauno Aaltonen won the 1963 Alpine Rally in a Cooper S. Paddy Hopkirk came third in the Tour de France and fourth in the RAC Rally of that year.

Hopkirk revealed one big reason for the continuing success:

One of the great things about the Mini was it was a small car in a big family – the British Motor Corporation

– which could really get things done if they wanted. Alec Issigonis could order a design change just like that – he could sit down with George Harriman, have a gin and tonic and come up with a whole new car if necessary, that's more or less how the Cooper started. When Stuart Turner came along he might say we need to get that part changed; Alec would make sure it was done tomorrow.

Now the Cooper S would be aimed at the highest-profile international motorsport event of all, the Monte Carlo Rally. For 1964 BMC entered six Minis – and twenty-four more were entered by private teams, not all of them British. But three red-painted Minis with their white roofs would shine like stars, the Morris Mini Cooper S (33 EJB) driven by Paddy Hopkirk, LBL 6D with Rauno Aaltonen at the wheel, and AJB 44B driven by Timo Mäkinen.

The Monte was a big event with a huge popular following. Hundreds of entrants in a fabulous variety of cars – some professionally prepared, others with not much more than a map-reading light – would set off from points all around Europe, from Glasgow to the Urals, to converge on Reims in northern France. Then would come fiercely competitive stages, a tortuous mountain transit and a final day on the Monaco Grand Prix circuit to decide the winner. It wasn't over until it was over.

Hopkirk and co-driver Henry Liddon's point of departure was Minsk in Byelorussia, in January 1964 gripped in deepest midwinter freeze. As Hopkirk would tell the story many years later:

I think most of the ordinary Russians were simply bewildered; we were in the hotel one afternoon, listening to a band playing Viennese waltzes and, when they went off for their tea break, one of the Dutch rally drivers produced his guitar and we all took to the floor when he struck up Chubby Checker's 'Let's Twist Again'. From all round the room, doors opened an inch or two and you could see all these bewildered waiters looking at us as though we were stark, raving mad.

This was at the height of the Cold War and, knowing such luxuries were in short supply in the Soviet Union, I'd taken a generous supply of ladies' nylon stockings, which I swapped with the hotel chef for a huge tin of Beluga caviar.

Once in France, it was a 'giant killing' epic as the Coopers duelled with big Mercs and 4.7-litre-engined Ford Falcon Futura Sprints all the way to the Mediterranean, front-wheel drive besting the brute force of the American cars.

'There were no electronics, just sheets of paper with calculations on them brought back here to headquarters after each stage,' according to Hopkirk. 'I didn't even know I'd won the rally until I got a phone call at four in the morning the Sunday after [the rally finished on Saturday 25 January] from [a newspaper] reporter. He said, "You've won." I thought he was joking. I had another beer, and went back to sleep.'

He had subsisted for the past five days, he revealed, more or less entirely on dexedrine. In retrospect the victory seemed all the more extraordinary having been achieved with what he described as 'a modified shopping car'.

Issigonis was in Monaco to see them do it. They celebrated at the Hotel de Paris, with among other things the caviar from Minsk. *Vogue* correspondent and Monte veteran Nancy Mitchell wrote to congratulate the great designer on a 'splendid' win. 'Such a small car and British too,' she gushed.

Hopkirk got congratulatory telegrams from the Beatles and the Prime Minister, Sir Alec Douglas-Home. Britain really could make it.

In a rolling *coup de théâtre*, the winning car was flown from Nice by British United Air Ferries Carvair (a modified C-54 freighter) to Southend airport – and on 26 January drove into the wintry West End of London and through the stage door of the London Palladium variety theatre (the hardest bit of the drive according to Hopkirk).

After a brief rehearsal, in a high-camp wedding of light entertainment and sporting jingoism, EJB 33 and its crew shared the stage on live TV with the compère, Bruce Forsyth, Kathy Kirby and another Cooper, Tommy. As the bizarre spectacle came to a climax and befeathered Tiller girls revolved around the car and its crew, the orchestra struck up 'Rule Britannia'. More than twenty million viewers watched it all in glorious black and white. Four months earlier the same famous theatre had been mobbed by screaming teenage girls when the Beatles had played the *Sunday Night* show. Britain was changing.

When Paddy met Brucie: Paddy Hopkirk shows off the fabulous 1964 Monte-winning Cooper, flown in straight from Nice, to the showgirls on the revolving stage at the London Palladium in the hugely popular 'Sunday Night At' show hosted by Bruce Forsyth. Britain really could make it.

Two months after the Monte triumph, more Cooper S variants appeared. The 970S was designed to compete in the one-litre competition category and just under a thousand were made in a year. The other variant was the much more significant Mini Cooper 1275S. With capacity boosted by a longer stroke it was capable of 97 mph and accelerating from 0–60 mph in eleven seconds. Here really was a giant-killer on ten-inch wheels.

The fastest Mini yet was naturally pitched back into the renewed rallying fray. Timo Mäkinen and co-driver Paul Easter in a 1275S took the January 1965 Monte in dreadful weather with a first-place margin measured in minutes. The car went on to take win after win that year, culminating in Rauno Aaltonen being crowned European rally champion.

The British Motor Corporation, in spite of continuous rumbles on the labour front, was looking glossy and successful. It was even trendy. The Mini had turned the company from a large-scale maker of middle-England pleasers into the manufacturer of the world's most advanced affordable car. Still, the press stayed on-side as rivals came along and proved wanting. *Small Car and Mini Owner* may have been partisan but it expressed the general mood when it proclaimed in October 1963:

> Looking back we can now all see the underlying wisdom in Issigonis's long shot at the basic transportation problem in Britain. We can see how he tackled the rock-bottom rules of tiny car production and beat them one by one to produce a four-seater car 23 per cent shorter than the average of its European rivals. Putting road holding before everything, making this tiny saloon the equal of many big sports cars . . .
>
> Getting round corners, the Mini will still lick the pants off any other mass-scale vehicle [the rear-engined Imp got a general thumbs-down]. In our experience all you need do is sit there and steer . . .

'The Mini is almost as much out on its own as it was four years ago,' said the mag. 'Rivals have come and gone [the newly launched Hillman Imp bore no comparison in their view] and the Mini remains the better buy all round. The Cooper has no British rival and the Cooper is unique in the world at the price. Take it or leave it!'

And people took it. Foreign baby-car opposition on the home market was fading: Fiat 500s and 850s for those who really wanted to be different, a trickle of DKWs, BMW 700s, DAFs and NSUs (all those acronyms), perhaps attracting eclectic customers by their very obscurity as much as by their innovative engineering. The Beetle, the funny-foreign-car paradigm, was a steady seller. The froth of bubbles had otherwise blown away. In 1965 the tiny Daihatsu Compagno Berlina became the first Japanese car to be officially imported into Britain. It had an 800cc four-cylinder engine and a radio as standard.

Autocar liked the build quality but thought the little Daihatsu was 'outdated and of inferior design'. British buyers ignored it completely. *Small Car* covered that year's Tokyo motor show under the gloriously un-PC headline 'Nip Nip Array' and conceded, just maybe, the new wave of Nissan Cedrics, Toyota Coronas, and Subaru 450s, 'one of the many people's cars that are the bread and butter of the Japanese market', might find a few takers at home. Meanwhile Mini was best, thank you very much.

Something for the weekend: Early Minis (this is an Austin Cooper S) featured a special boot with fold-down number plate for extra luggage.

CHAPTER 20

'Sixties Sexpot

Profile of a Face: Michael Lumley (aged 24). Profession: Fashion designer. Lives: Chelsea. Educated: Charterhouse and Sorbonne. Restaurants: Alvaro's, the Popote. Pubs: The Queen's Elm, Fulham Road. Suits: Vincent. Shirts: John Michael, Mr Fish. Shoes: Annello & Davide. Smokes: Gauloises. Drinks: Vodka and tonic. Drives: Mini Countryman. *Swinging London, a guide to where the action is*, Karl F. Dallas, 1967

The Mini was what made England swing. You knew England was swinging because that is what American observers of the national condition were now reporting. They might have once found the first import Morris and Austin 850s to arrive on their own shores 'ridiculous roller-skates', but five years later, on the dollybird-crowded streets of good old London Town, they looked just perfect.

Observing the passing parade on the King's Road in 1965 one US journalist described it as: 'The visible froth of a deeper turbulence that boiled up in Britain around – if we must date it – 1958 – though some would set it as late as 1960. In that period [exactly when the Mini was fledged] youth captured the ancient island and took command in a country where youth had always been kept properly in its place.'

Maybe so. Mostly however this seemed to be about sex, sex, sex and a 'deluge of pretty girls' who seemed eager to provide it. The American essayist Tom Wolfe wrote a word picture of the city featuring sixteen-year-old 'Sue . . . her London yellow straight hair hanging down to her shoulder blades' picked up by a bloke with a car at a 'brainless deb's cocktail party'. The big question hovers in the air. Is he going to invite her up to his flat? But first he must get her there – and he does it in a Mini.

The couple are 'driving along Maida Avenue W.2. – and he cocks the wheel of the Mini Cooper [of course] and sends it into a four-wheeled drift. London is full of such fierce Mini-aces', wrote Wolfe, 'and they skid, drift and bump as the decayed stucco of Little Venice goes by in the dark . . . and Sue sinks back into the Mini-seat and closes her new eyelashes . . .' He does invite her up to his flat.

And she naturally enough is wearing a miniskirt. That definingly 'sixties item of female apparel was either invented by Mary Quant circa 1962 or by Frenchman André Courrèges a little later, according to which fashion historians you believe, some of whom also ascribe the coming of the miniskirt to the already accomplished triumph of tights. She knew where the inspiration for the word miniskirt had come from – her Mini. As she said: 'The Mini was fast, simple, nifty, easy to park and manoeuvre. Girls loved it. It was easy to drive, young-looking, it did not look like your dad's car, nor your husband's. With the tank full of petrol and evening shoes in the door pocket it was cute, loveable, young and sexy, and yours.'

Actually having sex in a Mini was pretty difficult. Cabinet ministers might manage it, but there were always stories floating around (school playgrounds anyway) of firemen being called to cut conjoined couples out of Minis with hacksaws. Over four decades later, with the launch of the beefier, upscaled Mini, handy guides appeared on how to have sex within its still-constricted interior envelope. 'Take care to be presentable before you open the door,' remarked one forum poster, 'as your Mini will turn on the interior light.'

The Mini Cooper's bird-pulling power was legendary. They were coveted by men – City types, officers from fashionable regiments, 'Hooray Henrys' who hung out in west London mews pubs before taking the Cooper for a thrash down the A3 to the parents' place outside Guildford. Chris, Tony and 'hello chaps' Dominic, the getaway drivers in *The Italian Job*, were perfectly cast – public-school chinless wonders who willingly turn to a bit of high-class larceny as long as they can drive their fabulous cars screamingly fast. Coopers were always slightly caddish. The Conservative MP villain in Len Deighton's modish 1963 thriller *Horse under Water* had a Cooper S (and a Bentley Continental).

And for a while this is it how it really was. There was a strange period in the middle of the decade when a handful of Mini tuners achieved godlike status. The roster of personal customers at Downton Engineering looked like a page out of 'Jennifer's Diary'. Downton meanwhile were producing up to 100 tuning kits a week for BMC and were employing over eighty people.

Coopers and especially Cooper Ss were for the real grown-ups. Younger, poorer aspirants had to make do with those wheel spacers and magical cylinder-head kits you found in magazines like *Car Conversions*. But were girls impressed by that? Not really.

It was the much-commented-upon 'classlessness' of the ordinary car that made it the trysting place of the time. And girls bought them too, independent modern misses and proto-Sloane Rangers with 'dirty hair and fierce fathers in the country'.

When the Prince of Wales was given an Aston Martin DB6 Volante by his mother as a coming-of-age present in 1969, his one-day-second-wife, Camilla Shand, was nipping between Fulham and Berkshire polo matches in a British Leyland Mini.

There was another Mini derivative of the 'sixties that would swing pretty remorselessly, a strange machine that burst on the 'scene' from unlikely origins. Or maybe not so unlikely when it might be remembered by some that a very modish set of wheels at the time was an army-surplus Austin Champ, the jeep-like vehicle that BMC had produced for the War Office from 1952 onwards. But the Army now preferred Land Rovers and Champs were being flogged off cheap. In mid-'sixties London, de-mobbed Champs prowled the King's Road nightly – their military drabness relieved often enough by splashes of purple and orange.

Alec Issigonis had designed lightweight military vehicles before for Nuffield. In early 1959, with the baby car tooling up for production, he returned to the theme with a warlike derivative using the engine and running gear in a new punt-like body of soapbox simplicity designed, like his wartime Gosling, as an air-droppable runabout for burly paratroopers. It was dubbed the 'Moke'.

The first pared-down prototype had a lawnmower-like front end of startling ugliness. In July 1959, of all strange things RAF Bomber Command issued Trial Directive 87492 to test its suitability in defence of the realm. It was thrashed round RAF Wittering for three months and found to be an 'entirely satisfactory squadron transport in fair weather'.

'The vehicle is a bodiless BMC Minicar having the associated transverse-mounted engine, front wheel drive, four wheel brakes and independent suspension . . . it is thought it might be suitable for carriage by a Vickers Valiant,' said the report. Tests stowing it in the bomb bay of a V-bomber in a special pannier showed the scheme's feasibility. But what was the strange combination of nuclear bomber and Mini actually for? For a sneaky overland penetration of the Soviet Union? For a high-speed robbery getaway? Sadly it was never put into service.

Mokes with revised bodies were tested by the British Army in the summer of 1960 but rejected for their low ground clearance. The wheels were too small (although the thing could be picked up by its crew by four big grab handles and carried over obstacles). The Royal Navy acquired some to be stowed on aircraft carriers and used as on-shore runabouts on port visits. For a while dashing naval officers whizzed around London in them. HM Armed Forces meanwhile acquired quantities of Mini vans and pick-ups, plus some Mk II 850s for very junior officers (known as 'Staff Car, Grade 5 Morris Mini').

A 4 x 4 Moke with two 1098cc engines and two transmissions giving 87 bhp of power at each end (the 'Twini') was built in 1963. The outlandish machine was tested by the US Army but failed to find a government order.

After its passing largely unfit by HM armed services, BMC put the Moke on general public sale in January 1964 as either an Austin or Morris Mini Moke in a single colour option: spruce green. The price of £405 undercut every other four-wheeled device on sale because it was not actually a car. Supplied with just a driver's seat it was classified as a commercial vehicle, on which no purchase tax was payable. It was just about capable of 65 mph, took almost twenty-two seconds to reached 60 mph, and was utterly comfortless.

There was some vague idea that sturdy smallholders would buy the things but, like the technology-minded charwomen of 1959 marketing fantasy, they did not exist. Farmers generally couldn't be bothered, and trendier country sportsmen looking for something at home both on the King's Road and the grouse moor found it all just too wet and too cold. A nice cosy Land Rover would do much better.

But like its more civilised cousin, the Moke rapidly became a swinging accessory. Lord Snowdon and Princess Margaret opened the Amsterdam Trade Fair of 1965 in one. Cheesy come-to-Britain ads featured Mokes tootling round Buckingham Palace, packed with bowler-hatted gents and dollybirds. Just like London really was.

The Moke flared all too briefly before it all shivered to a halt. It was not so much the British climate that ended the fun but the moment in 1967 when the taxman reclassified it as a car rather than a commercial vehicle, raising the price by £78. UK sales stopped dead and in October 1968 manufacture at Longbridge ended after 14,518 had been built (all but 1,467 of them were in fact exported). The Moke tooling was shipped to sunny Australia, where Mokes had been assembled by BMC since 1966.

Going for Moke: Work on a utility version of the BMC baby was actually completed before the 1959 launch – but after all sorts of strange tests and wheezes like carrying it in a V-Bomber, the military rejected it. Relaunched as a swinging fun car (seen here with some decorative German ladies), it was too leaky for Britain and production moved to sunnier climes in Australia and Portugal. In 2006 the Moke was revived yet again – in China.

In 1972 it was renamed the Leyland Moke. In 1974 came a pick-up version. The Australian Army bought 500 of them and, by the time production stopped in 1981, another 26,142 had been built. And nor was that the end. Nine thousand two hundred and seventy-seven more were made in Portugal as beach cars and fun-car rentals for Algarve sun seekers. In 2007 the Big Science & Technology Co. of Chongqing, China, put a replica on sale with a choice of three-cylinder 800cc engine, 1050cc and 1275cc four-cylinder engines or an electric motor – registering the name 'Moke' in Australia where the trademark had lapsed. A little later, after some legal hanky-panky, it was branded as the 'Big Machine'.

Of all the myriad Mini variations, the Moke would have a fictional life on screen that went far beyond its minimal impact in the real world. 'Ordinary' Minis were on TV screens routinely in action series: *The Baron*, *The Saint*, *Man in a Suitcase*, *The Persuaders*, etc. etc. as part of the streetscape or in thrilling chase sequences. But movie art directors of the period seemed to love Mokes especially. Perhaps because they figured in the Swinging London movies *Catch Us If You Can* and the artier *Blow-Up*. Mokes featured in the cryptic TV series *The Prisoner*, with stripy canvas tops as 'taxis' in 'the Village'.

'Mother' was conveyed around in a Moke in the late Emma Peel-era *Avengers*. Bond villains loved them, ideal for scooting around their underground headquarters (*Moonraker*, *The Spy Who Loved Me*, *You Only Live Twice*). In *Live and Let Die* (1973), Roger Moore's Bond actually drives one on a Caribbean island – the only time 007 ventures near any sort of Mini.

The film *Carry on Camping* (1969) featured a Moke packed with what look like miserably cold hippies in Afghan coats. You might say that was the point everything stopped swinging.

Macca Mini: Beatle Paul McCartney acquired a fancy Morris Mini-Cooper S with Radford tweaks (note front quarter-light) late in 1965 in which to fashionably flit about north London. It would end up in a Florida museum. John had one (after he'd passed his driving test in early 1965), so did George (which went all psychedelic in 1967). Ringo had two – a Radford mini-limo and as he said at the time 'an ordinary Mini for just popping about'.

CHAPTER 21

Third Time Unlucky

When I was very small I had a major hip operation. My mum told me that I used to be strapped with a long piece of bungee rubber into a special cot in the front seat of her Mini Traveller. No, it isn't a bad memory at all. It was a lovely car. It was Harvest Gold.   Mini memory, 2008

The Mini feel-good factor sloshed over the corporation's other products of the time – including the bigger family car (code-named ADO16 when it was in development) that had been launched in August 1962 as the Morris 1100. It had Issigonis engineering principles throughout – including front-wheel drive and a transverse engine – plus 'hydrolastic' interconnected fluid suspension. This time Farina styling had been applied over the Issigonis engineering with a certain sensitivity. The public loved its whizzy technology in a reassuring package. The 1100 quickly established itself as Britain's best-selling car (to be toppled in 1967 by the Mark II Cortina).

In summer 1964 the Mini was also offered with the hydro-lastic suspension system. Once again it was all very innovative but not quite fully formed. It was expensive to make. The system lost pressure easily and did not make the ride significantly softer. Paddy Hopkirk, however, was quoted as saying that, in rallying, hydrolastic suspension was worth ten seconds a mile.

In January 1966, BMC went for their Mini Monte hat trick, this time in the 1275S. The four works Coopers entered were favourites, of course, and received enormous press and public attention. From the start they lived up to their promise, leaving the competition far behind. But it was the beginning of the most tortuous Mini drama of the decade.

As the BBC reported:

> The Monte Carlo Rally has ended in uproar over the disqualification of the British cars expected to fill the first four places.
>
> The first four to cross the finishing line were Timo Mäkinen, driving a British Motor Corporation Mini Cooper, followed by Roger Clark (Ford Lotus Cortina), and Rauno Aaltonen and Paddy Hopkirk, both also driving BMC Minis.
>
> But they were all ruled out of the prizes – with six other British cars – for alleged infringements of complex regulations about the way their headlights dipped . . . The official winner was announced as Pauli Toivonen, a Finn who lives in Paris, driving a Citroën [DS 21].

The Fédération Internationale de l'Automobile in Paris had claimed that the headlights fitted on the British cars were not standard production and the four additional driving lights mounted on the radiator grille contravened the homologation rules. They demanded an exhaustive technical inspection before the apparent 1–2–3 win could be announced. French newspapers were extremely hostile, declaring the 'cheats must be exposed'. According to the BMC competition manager Stuart Turner:

> We got thrown out. I passionately believe it was because the cars were so quick that people thought that we had swapped cars. The organisers looked at the times and simply did not believe them. People

blamed it on the French just trying to fake it for a French car to win. I think it was the French trying to chuck out the English, who they thought had been cheating.

I think if they had not thrown us out on the lighting they would have thrown us out on the colour of Paddy's socks . . .

It was a ghastly mess that would drag on for months. The immediate aftermath was another burst of super-patriotism. Once again the cars were flown back to Britain, all three of them this time, driving on to the stage of the Palladium to go round and round on full lock in darkness with their 'illegal' lights blazing. Your host, Jimmy Tarbuck, announced: 'ladies and gentleman, the real winners of the Monte Carlo Rally'. The audience went wild.

Hey, hey . . . etc: Monkee Mike Nesmith seems transfixed by the novelty of the Mini's transverse engine layout as he inspects his just delivered Radford-modified 1275cc Mini Cooper S in July 1967.

CHAPTER 22

Mini Troubles

There is a very pretty lady I see some mornings in her red Mini driving into Leicester from Sharnford. Got a bit of a librarian look about her but she's really cute.

Hot Girls in Minis, Mini forum, 2008

It was right over the top. Two Finns and an Ulsterman being diddled out of victory by the beastly French, who were pushing the claims of another Finn (who was profoundly embarrassed by the whole thing), with a Liverpudlian comedian stoking the nation's emotions. This was high politics as 'foreigners' and the Common Market excited ever more volatile feelings (a renewed British bid to join was about to be launched) and the nation's economic woes and old-fashioned class war intensified.

BMC's Longbridge citadel, once the nation's engine of prosperity, had become the symbol of all that was wrong. In spite of non-stop-seeming strikes, the factory's highest production figure ever was in 1964–5, when 345,245 vehicles were turned out. But growing foreign competition, a reputation for poor quality and prehistoric industrial relations were alienating the nation's affections for its still-biggest carmaker (Ford were coming up fast). BMC's home-market share was in sudden decline. In 1966 the embattled corporation merged with Jaguar Cars and Pressed Steel to create 'British Motor Holdings'.

Like the people's car being bought by the rich and fashionable, another Mini paradox was bubbling to the surface. The greater the car's sales success, the bigger the financial grief. It went back to the start, to that decision to sell the baby car at a toytown price. Volume was fine. Profitability was another matter. Terence Beckett, the gifted Ford manager of the period, would tell an interviewer: 'I can remember in one month in 1960, the Mini achieved a 19 per cent market penetration. That was just one model.'

The base Mini's selling price had undercut the Ford 105E Anglia's by £93. How? Ford of Britain naturally enough acquired an early production car and its own engineers took it apart to work out its manufacturing cost. They calculated their rivals were losing £30 on every baby car it made. 'You can track the decline of BMC from that single product. It took up a huge amount of resources, it sterilised cash flow and it was a pretty disastrous venture,' according to Mr (later Sir) Terence Beckett.

It seemed impossible to turn round. Every car sold in the UK contributed to the company's fiscal malaise, even if export sales remained marginally profitable.

A production engineer recalling the 1966–7 period told Alec Issigonis's biographer: '[By then] they'd come to realise the massive cost penalty being incurred by the Mini . . . The trouble was [it] was over-engineered, there was so much cost built into the car with, for example, a penalty of £20 to £25 on the subframes and suspension.' Small was more expensive. Even the tiny wheels (because they required more rubber in the tyres) were more costly than larger ones.

The Mini's inability to earn its own living was reflected in the nation as a whole. On 20 July 1966, three months after winning the general election, the Prime Minister, Harold Wilson, announced the tightening of hire-purchase restrictions and public-spending cuts – measures to alleviate the continuing weakness of sterling – plus a 'voluntary' price and wage freeze. The country seemed on the ropes. Ten days later, at Wembley, the England football team won the World Cup.

It really was a tempestuous year. The British Motor Corporation robbed by the French of Monte Carlo rallying glory. Then, in a kind of redemption, it was England four, West Germany two. Novelists and movie scriptwriters took note. Post-imperial Britain was being weighed not on its old-style military or economic power but on its sporting prowess and cultural trendiness. And in a pre-globalised world, a country's car industry remained as powerful a statement of national pride as its football team.

The Mini shone through with the best of them. In 1968 BMC

Mobile phone: How about this for the acme of modernity? – a Mini carphone launched with the help of a mini-skirted blonde at the Paris Auto Salon, 1966. Those door latch pulls and capacious pockets would stay a feature until 1969.

was by far the largest and most profitable car manufacturer in the UK. Mini Cooper Ss had finished the Monte Carlo Rally first four years in a row, fitted with engines built by the BMC Competition Department at Abingdon, using components supplied by Downton Engineering Ltd. It looked as if it would never end.

Swinging London was already beginning to metronome to a less frenzied beat; but the little car now approaching its tenth birthday had one more truly fab trick to play.

Tunnel vision: The climactic escape by gold-bearing Minis through the Turin sewers in the 1969 movie *The Italian Job* was in fact filmed at Stoke Aldermoor, Coventry, as this production still demonstrates.

CHAPTER 23

Turin Car

Although the Mini has changed, and changed significantly, it remains the small car that raises the spirits. Like many entering their late 40s, the Mini has something of a chequered history, combining glory years with lean times. Yet it continues to be made, and continues to be held in high esteem by the British public and across the world. It is a brand that is forgiven its shortcomings, and its absence from the market in the early 2000s seems only to have made the heart grow fonder . . .

BMW internal market-research document, 2004

He was ever so slightly late but the TV scriptwriter Troy Kennedy Martin picked up on the national mood with a pitch for a crime-caper movie. All those mid-'sixties populist rumbles – rallying Minis robbed of victory, football frenzy, celebrity criminals, balance-of-payments crises, funny foreigners, the Common Market, I'm Backing Britain – came together in the film *The Italian Job*. It was made in the summer–autumn of 1968 and released the following year.

Rallying Minis had stayed in the news. In 1967 BMC had taken its revenge for the French takeaway of the year before in the Monte Carlo Rally. Rauno Aaltonen and Henry Liddon drove to victory in the rally of their lives and the Mini and its drivers once again received a hero's welcome back in Britain. What flight of a scriptwriter's imagination might send Mini Coopers back over the Alps?

The production, put together by the British producer Michael Deeley, had begun with a story idea from Mr Kennedy Martin's brother and fellow scriptwriter, Ian, about a daring robbery set in London. A confected traffic jam was a key plot device. It was reworked with patriotic brio to take place in Turin, Italy, a convoy of Chinese gold being taken to a bank, suitably enough in payment for a Fiat car-production line to be set up in the People's Republic.

Paramount Studios took it on. Michael Caine was in the frame to play the lovable lead villain Charlie Croker (whose on-screen, just released from a two-stretch, persona lived as if London had never stopped swinging); and a British director called Tony Collinson, to make it. His godfather was the venerable actor and playwright Noël Coward, who would play Mr Bridger, the posh criminal mastermind whose imprisonment at Her Majesty's pleasure did not impede the staging of an outrageously daring bullion robbery so far from home.

Issigonis liked the film and was especially pleased by the role played by his friend Noël Coward. He hired a Birmingham cinema (British Leyland paid the ten guineas fee) for a private viewing.

But the real stars were the cars. They would have to be Mini Coopers of course, with the diminutive stars of the London Palladium still going round and round in the national consciousness. You would have thought that the manufacturers would have loved the publicity. Especially because in January 1968 the Mini Cooper's Monte Carlo winning streak had ended as more resilient rally cars gained the ascendancy. Those tiny wheels just could not get enough power to the road, however brilliant the handling. There would be no more Monte wins.

But as the film was being put together, the real automotive drama was taking place at Longbridge. After the Jaguar merger to create BMH, the mighty descendants of Austin and Morris and all their badge-engineered offspring had, under intense government pressure, in January 1968 been shunted into the

Leyland Motor Corp. (owners of the Triumph marque) to form the British Leyland Motor Corporation under its new chairman, former wartime REME lieutenant-colonel Donald Stokes. By creating a single British auto manufacturer with the capacity to produce 1.25 million motor vehicles per year at a time of seemingly in-exhaustible world demand, the merger seemed entirely sensible; though its badge of a letter L apparently disappearing down a plughole was dubbed by some the 'Flying Arsehole'.

Just as Austin had submerged the Morris men, now the corporate Leyland management legacy would dominate Longbridge. Ex-Triumph man George Turnbull was drafted in to run the Austin-Morris volume business with the intention of improving profitability. Daniel Richmond's contract was terminated. Alec Issigonis was marginalised and replaced by a new chief engin-eer, Harry Webster from Triumph.

Those first few merged months were spent 'rushing round, turning off all the expenditure taps', so Mr Webster would later comment. 'Money was rushing out of Longbridge, and we had nothing to show for it – it was quite terrifying.'

So when Mr Deeley & co. approached BLMC, looking for some Mini sponsorship, the answer was frosty. Michael Deeley remembered: 'My association with [BLMC] was sadly very limited. There was a very nice man who was head of PR who was blind. He had been blinded dismantling a bomb on Brighton pier at the end of the war. Very sweet and nice but he didn't seem to have much clout.'

Michael Caine was tougher: 'That's why the company no longer exists and that's the problem with British industry: No foresight. We hated British Leyland,' he told an interviewer.

According to Paddy Hopkirk, recalling the film's pre-production stage: 'The competition department was approached to do the stunt driving. I was up for it. But the actors' union Equity wouldn't allow it.'

So the stunts were performed by the Frenchman Rémy

Julienne's *équipe* as the action progressed through the piazzas and ornate arcades, over the roofs and into the sewers (actually the Birmingham–Coventry Tithebarn Main Sewer, which was under construction at the time) of the north Italian city.

The Italians could not have been more co-operative. When pre-production scouting began in Turin, local firm Fiat offered as many cars as were needed. That did not fit the plot line. Eventually BLMC sold the production company six Austin Mini Cooper 1275Ss at trade price, and an extra twenty-five Minis were bought from Switzerland. But fans of the film have never been quite sure how many of these were Coopers or regular Minis tricked up for filming.

The three-Mini jump was filmed at the Fiat factory at Lingotto, in the Turin suburbs, with its circular banked test track on the roof. M. Julienne calculated that each car would need to be moving at 50 mph to do the jump. Fiat employees turned out as extras and all said goodbye to him because they thought he was going to be killed.

Fiat were immensely accommodating while the British car company was miserably Scrooge-ish, but some sources claim that BLMC did help a bit by building a car with a 1798cc engine with sufficient torque to climb all those marble steps. There is an abundance of mythology surrounding the film and everything about it. According to a fan site, Ken Morris, one of the last of the production crew members to leave after filming in Turin, stated that there were six surviving Minis and thirty sets of mag wheels in the lock-up garage that they were using. He said that he locked up and headed for the UK and, as far as he was aware, the film's producers never returned to collect them.

A 2003 interview by the now-ennobled Sir Michael Caine revealed an alternative to the famously frustrating cliff-hanger ending with the coach see-sawing on the edge of a precipice.

'The next thing that happens is you turn the engine on,' he said. 'You sit still until the petrol runs out, which changes the equilibrium. We jump out and the gold goes over and at the bottom the Mafia are waiting for it. We try to get it back and that is the next movie.' But according to Sir Michael, the sequel was never made because 'the original movie flopped in the US'. It was released a year after the Mini was withdrawn from sale in America. Hardly anyone noticed either mini-occurrence.

As British cinema audiences warmed to the Mini's transalpine antics, in fact the car was heading for trouble. Its lack of profitability was steering its parents towards the rocks. It was greedy for attention, costing as much to put together in production-worker wages as a much bigger car. The ten-year-old baby was looking like a spoilt brat.

CHAPTER 24

Not So SuperMini

In 2000 I bought one of the last production Minis, a Classic Mini Seven. The Rover dealer seemed quite pleased to sell it. It was very different to older Minis, in fact it was like a bigger car, I wouldn't say the handling was the same. I looked under the bonnet and didn't have a clue. It was just like other 'modern' cars.

I must say it did disappoint me. The suspension was smoother but it wasn't nearly as much fun to drive. No bumps or thumps and I didn't feel quite so much in control as with my older Mini.   Mini memory, 2008

The Mini was far too good to scrap. Thus far, rather than be subject to any substantial revisions, the Mini had been allowed to chug on with only minor mechanical and cosmetic bodywork changes. At the end of 1967 the Mk II Mini had been introduced, with a larger rear window and mildly reworked front end, new badging, larger tail lamps and interior tweaks. The name Mini-Minor was formally dropped. In October 1969 a further redesign concentrated on the doors, introducing wind-up windows (to Issigonis's outrage) and concealed hinges.

In spite of being thus 'refined' (purists as well as the great designer were cross), the Mini was still a product of its crypto-experimental origins. A lot was still wrong with the overall design and could be made better. But this was the point – its creator was more than ready to develop an outright replacement. In 1967 he had been made Fellow of the Royal Society, the only car designer to be so honoured. It went to his head ever so slightly.

For BMC's management up to the Leyland merger, the question of what to do with the mid-range cars was more acute, although there had been plenty of design exercises for a son-of-Mini. In 1968 Issigonis and a small team began work on what would be codenamed the 9X, potentially as great a leap as ADO15 had been. It would emerge as a totally new car owing nothing to its predecessor. It was a very serious exercise, a chance for a renewed Britain Can Make It epic of struggle and survival. It would end in stillborn tragedy. It broke its creator's heart.

Mini future that wasn't: The innovation-packed 9X was created by Issigonis in 1968 as a potential outright replacement for the original car (a prototype is pictured here in his Edgbaston, Birmingham, garden). The future looked assured but the new men at British Leyland thought otherwise.

This little-known 'sixties UK moonshot was conceived around a specially developed, space-saving engine, lighter than the equivalent A-series plus transmission by 125 lb. The 80-inch wheelbase of the 1959 original was reduced to 76 inches. Unofficially it was being called the Mini-Mini by the five-man design team. The hatchback body (courtesy of a Pininfarina commission, their last for BMC, to soften the Issigonis lines) was forward-looking but still true to its Mini origin. The suspension reverted to steel springs all round – McPherson struts at the front and a beam axle at the rear. No fancy rubber or hydraulic fluids this time. In fact the great designer was going for the utmost simplicity. Importantly the whole thing was planned for the most economic production-engineering. Market sampling remained primitive but it looked at least as if the 9X, if it sold in Mini (i.e. big) volumes, would turn a profit. Alex Moulton's later judgement was that 'it would not have survived'. There it is in the archive photographs: the 9X's stance with a big tyre-to-top-of-wheel-arch-gap has nothing like the Mini's lithe packaging.

Issigonis, as he got older and crankier towards the end of his life, would turn on Moulton, saying in effect that the rubber suspension had been a mistake. 'I regret I ever did it, it was a novelty at the time,' he would say. That rapidly rusting sub-frame always remained a weak point and it was as a direct result of employing the seemingly so efficient rubber-cone system.

The 9X was also roomier inside, in spite of being shorter than the existing Mini. Corporate infighting killed it. Two prototypes were made. One was saved by Issigonis personally and survives in the BMIH trust collection.

It was just too advanced. Stokes stated the kind of cars that he thought were required would be not overly cheap but 'small, comfortable, fairly sophisticated, and capable of doing a lot of miles to a gallon of petrol'. The 9X would need unaffordable levels of investment to get into production and the original Mini was selling very nicely, thank you very much. But the stillbirth of the 9X ensured the Mini was as yet without a successor.

In its tenth year, Mini weekly production was running at nearly 7,000 units and it was the fifth best-selling car in the UK with 8.1 per cent of the market. The unsentimental Donald Stokes declared at the time: 'The success of the Mini is a great tribute to its original concept, and its continuing popularity all over the world shows the public's faith in this reliable, high-quality little vehicle. I see no reason why the Mini, albeit in other forms, should not continue for another 10 years.'

On 19 June 1969 Mini number 2 million came off the Longbridge production line. The *Daily Mirror* acquired it as a competition prize for 'women readers' (again) – to be won by Skoda-owning Mrs Ernestine Swift, fifty-six, of Harehill, Leeds. Issigonis gave the newspaper an interview: 'I am the last of the Bugattis,' he proclaimed, 'someone who designed the whole car . . .' The reporter described the domestic set-up *chez* Issigonis: 'where his 84-year-old mother, in the drawing room of the £15,000 house in the Birmingham suburbs, sits upright holding court like German film-star royalty; dressed in black, she still chides her son on the colour of his shirts . . .' Hulda Issigonis would die in 1972.

On 27 August 1969 Alec Issigonis was knighted. For his renewed Mini encounter with HM Queen Elizabeth II (they had become quite friendly in the meantime) he arrived at Buckingham Palace in an Austin Cooper.

BL meanwhile was going through something of a cultural revolution. The Ford stylist Roy Haynes (moulder of the Mk II Cortina) had already been recruited as product planner and proposed reducing BMC's model range down to five basic platforms with an end to all that fusty badge engineering. The exotically named, US-born Filmer M. Paradise, whom BMC had brought in as head of Europe from Ford a few months before the merger, became sales & marketing director of the Austin-Morris division.

His most portentous move was to initiate a cull of ye olde dealer network. One latter-day critic of the move noted: 'Unfortunately [he] aimed the hatchet at many family-run dealerships with a loyal customer base, sending them straight into the arms of foreign competition, notably Datsun [Nissan], taking faithful car buyers with them.' Old loyalties were going out the window. The Mini looked next for the chop.

In Donald Stokes's view, the front-wheel-drive BMC cars were not making a profit and the last car launched independently (the 1800) had failed spectacularly. The Issigonis legacy was a millstone. 'Issygonyet?' became the jibe among the thrusting new men. The about-to-be-launched ADO14, the 1485cc-engined Austin Maxi, the last of the Issigonis cars, looked to be another loser. The gearbox was a disaster and it was clearly under-powered. And yet it must be put into the showrooms – to public indifference and scathing press reviews that echoed the premature release of the BMC miniature a decade earlier. It seemed more than a good idea to revive a sense of Austin and Morris separateness, by making Austin the 'avant-garde' brand while Morris would be the rear-wheel-drive, tradition-ally engineered car to tackle the ever rising company-car market so resolutely courted by Ford. The result would be the Marina.

Marginal activities would be shut down. A strange BMC hang-over, the Fisher-Bendix washing-machine company, was sold. The range of paint colours was slashed from 140 to 18 across the board. The dealer networks and export franchises would be ruth-lessly pruned. The once all-conquering Competition Department was axed. Stuart Turner had already hotfooted it to the oil company Castrol and thence to Ford (to push the Escort as the rally star of the 'seventies). Donald Stokes eyed the Cooper contract warily, as he did that for continued production of the Austin-Healey.

Messrs Cooper and Healey would soon be hearing from the company's solicitors. Fancy outside relationships were doomed. Daniel Richmond had his contract terminated.

In 1971 Sir Alec Issigonis officially retired aged sixty-five. His leaving gift was a giant Meccano set. He would continue to work as a consultant, first with an office at Longbridge, later at his bungalow in leafy Edgbaston. He was allowed to potter around Longbridge like a mad professor playing with loopy-sounding schemes for steam-powered Minis and Minis with gearless transmissions that could go backwards as fast as they could go forward. L J K Setright of *CAR* magazine went to see him in 1971: 'BLMC has put Issigonis in the right place, a private little design suite with a few assistants who draw and brew tea while he doodles and brews the future,' he wrote. 'Retirement' began with a trip to Moscow to consult on a Soviet people's car (the only ex-WWII combatant apart from America that had failed to produce one). He was treated like a design god. Vodka flowed but in the end the pesky Russians went for Fiat.

New men were also in charge at the Midlands Kremlin. The immediate Mini task was to produce something to replace the Hornet and Elf at the top end of the range but with lower production costs overall. The result was the strange automotive diversion overseen by Roy Haynes that would be so derided by Mini purists. It was called the Mini 'Clubman'.

It was supposed to look upmarket. A chunky-looking longer nose was blended to the existing box, giving easier engine access and maybe an extra safety factor, but aerodynamically it was inferior. It aped the Ford-inspired vulgarities of the day: dinky-looking ten-inch Rostyle wheels and a Cortina-esque steering wheel and radiator grille plus stick-on go-faster stripes. The inside was tarted up with instruments plonked in a box of undistinguished design directly in front of the driver.

But the Clubman, hated by old-guardists for what had been done to the design essence of the car, did not supplant the original shape outright. Production continued, with 'Mini' now a marque on its own. Austin and Morris versions were dropped as if they had never been, and the 'Mini Clubman estate' arrived to replace the Traveller and Countryman. Production at Cowley ended (to make way for the doomed Maxi). It was all Longbridge now as far as the Mini was concerned.

In October 1969 the Mini 1275GT (a distinct model from the Mini Clubman, although sharing the same front-end body treatment) replaced the 998cc Mini Cooper. The Cooper connection was doomed. Many years later the now-Lord Stokes would comment: 'We lost about £20 per Mini. Then people wonder why I scrapped the Cooper. We were giving more money to Mr Cooper than we were making in profit.' Donald Stokes was dubbed the Cooper-killer. His enemies had already been calling him an 'over-promoted bus salesman'.

Innocenti in Italy, however, would continue to make their own version of the Mini Cooper for a little while yet. So would Authi in Pamplona, Spain, between 1973 and 1975. The Authi-built model is probably the rarest of all Coopers.

King's Road Caroline and her admirers had moved on to something flasher. The Cooper had gone well out of fashion. For now.

The last Cooper 1275S came off the Longbridge production line in June 1971, leaving the 1275GT as the only 'sporting' Mini in production. The much-maligned 1275GT could be brought up to S performance levels with a BL Special Tuning kit consisting of a polished cylinder head, additional 1.5-inch SU carburettor, and a twin carburettor inlet manifold and air cleaners.

At the time a 1275GT cost £898 new, and a 1275S (in May 1971) cost £1058. *Motor* magazine judged the 1275GTS (as it was dubbed) to be as competitive as the old Cooper 1275S; they just didn't think it felt the same. *Autocar* said of the machine:

> The cross-country performance of the Downton-converted car is quite amazing, and the ability of the car to regain its high cruising speed after any sort of hold-up gives remarkable journey times . . . There were no signs of any temperament from the converted car, and this conversion should appeal to anyone looking

for the handiness of a Mini and the performance of
a much larger-engined car.

Downton engineering was about to vanish into legend. The increasingly alcoholic Daniel Richmond died aged forty-six in 1974. A year later, his partner Bunty committed suicide. The Mini as a fashionable sports car seemed suddenly absurd. The first great tuning epoch, when sporting gents would discuss desired modifications as if they were visiting their tailors or wine merchants, was over. Mini modifiers were now back beneath the railway arches and in the Swarfega-stained pages of *Car and Car Conversions*.

Mini sales overall had dipped in 1969 but picked up again to make 1971 the best year ever for overall Mini sales at 318,000. But the corporation's UK market share was ever slipping. After the subsidence of the so-called 'Barber Boom' of 1973, when the Conservative government reflated the economy in an effort to reduce unemployment, it slipped from 40 to 33 per cent. Then came the oil crisis of October 1973, and worldwide demand for cars slumped.

BLMC management fretted over what to do with the mid-car mess: 1800, Maxi, and in 1971 the Minor replacement (after twenty-three years of production), the Morris Marina, of which Sir Alec said witheringly, 'that's not a car, anyone could make that'. It was supposed to be aimed at middle-range executives as much as family men. Neither group were convinced.

The Clubman estate had been supposed to give some extra carrying power at the small end of things but was coming up against the new generation of European 'superminis', something larger than a Mini yet smaller than a typical family car of the time. There were lots of them coming into the market from manufacturers who had looked at the original Mini concept and thought they might do better. The Mini was too small, they concluded. Buyers wanted a larger car fitted with a 'hatchback'.

The basic Issigonis front-wheel-drive transverse-engine layout had been slavishly copied but no other manufacturer had gone for the gearbox-in-the-sump trick. The Fiat-backed Autobianchi Primula of 1965 and the 1969 Fiat 128 had used a transverse engine driving the front wheels, employing an end-on transmission using a separate oil reservoir.

This would become the universally adopted system henceforth for small, front-wheel-drive cars (with the exception of some Peugeots). The supreme example was the Fiat 127, which emerged in 1971 as the first true 'supermini'. It had exemplary space utilisation. A three-door hatchback was launched after a year and proved hugely popular. Between 1971 and 1983, Fiat 127 production totalled 3,730,000, a million more than the Mini achieved in its first twelve years.

The ultra-basic Renault 4 of 1961 had featured front-wheel drive but with the longitudinal engine and transmission placed behind the front axle and the gearbox/differential in front, a layout repeated in the Renault 5 launched in January 1972. Between then and 1985, 5,471,709 'Five's would be turned out, more than the entire four-decade Mini production run.

The 1973 Middle East war and the oil-price hike that followed, like the Suez shenanigans that had been the Sputnik's midwife, boosted small-car development everywhere. Having analysed the BMC cost model soon after the Mini's launch and concluded that 'Mini cars made Mini profits', Ford for now chose to stay out of the small-car business. But a decade later, with new challenges from Japan and Europe, the automotive giant would launch their Bobcat programme, which would result in the 'Fiesta' of 1975. The front-wheel-drive Audi 50 of 1974 (which itself took over the NSU Prinz) would be rebadged as the Volkswagen 'Polo'. By the mid-'seventies, the supermini scene was getting super-crowded.

CHAPTER 25

Mini Heartbreak

The BMW MINI? I like it as a car but they should have called it something else. It's not a Mini.

I hate BMW forum, 2008

The much-derided Mini 1275GT actually outsold the Coopers, the original ones anyway. Miss Sue Cuff, the 1975 Miss Great Britain and then BL's most favoured publicity poppet, was routinely featured atop a 1275GT in publicity photographs of the period. But by now such cheesy echoes of Swinging London were about to be consumed in the vengeful bonfires of 'seventies feminism. Although black-stockinged, high-heeled, 'empowered' female sexuality would be used to sell motor cars in all sorts of enticing new ways in the decade to come, the Mini's cute little trick seemed effectively shot. The 1275GT especially looked like the oldest swinger in town.

There would be a late flowering of the unloved car. Driven by Richard Longman it took overall first in the British Saloon Car Championships of 1978 and 1979. But it would gain a kind of tragic infamy (like the Porsche Speedster in which James Dean self-immolated) for being the vehicle in which a pop icon of the 'seventies would be killed. And he wasn't even driving. It remains a difficult story to put together amid the obsessive clutter of fan worship (for the singer not the car) but it goes like this:

The Mini was just three years old when in September 1962 the ultra-fashionable *Town* magazine ran a piece about something called 'faces', teenage trendsetters in London, featuring fourteen-year-old Marc Feld from Stamford Hill, who possessed forty suits. He claimed he'd been riding a motor scooter for two years and was a Conservative – 'because they were for the rich'.

He and his pals didn't need to drive; they'd scrounge 'pickups' from older, less trendy acolytes, who would convey them from club to club for the privilege of being seen with the young arbiters of fashion. They flitted around the night-time capital, naturally enough, in Minis.

Fifteen years later the one-time king of the mods had become Marc Bolan, founder of T.Rex, pop icon, children's TV presenter and father. He still had not passed a driving test.

So it was his girlfriend Gloria Jones, mother of two-year-old Rolan, who was behind the wheel of her purple Mini 1275GT, registered FOX 661L, in the early hours of the morning of 16 September 1977. They were heading homewards to Richmond in the south-west of the capital after a night spent at the Speakeasy off the Edgware Road ('a music-business hangout' where the couple had first met) and Morton's, a louche nightclub in the West End of London.

It was a Mini tragedy of the highest order. Travelling fast on Queen's Ride at the southern edge of Barnes Common, the Mini left the road as it crossed the hump-backed bridge spanning the railway, went through a fence and smashed sideways into a sycamore tree. Marc's side took the impact: he was thrown into the back and killed instantly. The Ohio-born singer Gloria Jones was unconscious but alive and in hospital for several days afterwards. She did not learn of Marc Bolan's death until the day of his funeral at Golders Green Cemetery. The cause-of-death certificate read: 'Shock and haemorrhage due to multiple injuries consistent with Road Traffic Accident. Passenger in a private motor car which collided with a tree. Accidental.' Some fans vented their anguish on Miss Jones, who went back to America with her son. The crash site rapidly became an improvised shrine.

Long nose Minis: Mini 1275GT (foreground) with Clubman chums.

In 1999, TAG (the T.Rex Action Group) was formed to create a memorial shrine and preserve 'the tree'. The landowner, Railtrack, granted TAG a lease in perpetuity on the site. In September 2002 Rolan Bolan unveiled a bronze bust of his father, while in an epic display of bad taste, *Viz* comic offered its readers a spoof memorial tableau of the tragedy.

Conspiracy theories circulated for years afterwards. Police Constable David Hardman from Barnes police station was 'on the scene of the accident within minutes of it happening', and much later stated his personal belief that the Mini 1275GT was not being driven at excessive speed. The driver was not drunk, or on drugs. Ex-PC Hardman had 'reason to understand that a wheel had been removed to have a puncture repaired a few days before the crash. There is a possibility that the wheel had not been retightened enough, came loose, and affected the steering'. Marc's possessions were 'looted' by ghoulish fans, so it was reported, as Gloria lay in a coma. The fatal 1275GT was eventually scrapped.

There remain diehard fans who are absolutely obsessed with the Mini from the black lagoon. Ironically the original long-nosed Clubman had been engineered that way in deference to tightening safety legislation – which was always to be going to be the Mini's nemesis, or so it seemed.

The car had originally been designed on the principle of 'active safety': it should not get into trouble in the first place, or be pretty good at getting out of trouble. Issigonis was typically head-in-the-clouds about it: 'I make my cars with such good brakes, such good steering, that if people get into a crash it's their own fault,' he declared. 'I don't design my cars to have accidents.'

This all sounded a bit clunky as times were changing. There were stricter speed and alcohol limits now. Magistrates found drunken pranks in overcrowded Minis ever less amusing. In 1965 Issigonis's friend Laurence Pomeroy could get something like this into print (in *Small Car and Mini Owner*). 'There must be no overall speed limit in this country – the sort of thing that has turned America from a land of rugged individualists into a police state. They seem amazed that Britons can go from London to the Midlands at 150 mph' (and until 1965 they could, on the no-speed-limit M1).

In America the campaign by that pesky lawyer Ralph Nader had resulted in the 1966 Traffic Safety Act. Two years later the Mini was withdrawn from the North American market because it couldn't meet the new namby-pamby automobile construction regulations that had followed. There were plenty of lost sales in Britain as mums thought twice about putting kids in such a fragile-looking thing.

In 1974 a prototype Mini experimental safety vehicle was built with a crumple-zone nose, strengthened door sills, extra internal padding and recessed door handles. It looked weird. In January 2007 *Which?* magazine listed the Mini City in its list of 'ten worst cars for safety since 1983'.

Don't say it too loud, but there were some for whom the Mini was nothing without that frisson of vulnerability and risk. It was a high-powered motorcycle with some sheet metal wrapped round it. As a young Mini blogger wrote (way after the original had gone out of production): 'The Mini becomes the best car on the road because it's a potential death trap. Really. You constantly have a feeling that you're slightly out of control and that something is going to break at any second. You may think this is a bad thing, but it really keeps you into the driving.'

That was not far off how Issigonis had planned it.

CHAPTER 26

Mid-Life Crisis

I had a Mini Cooper, black with black leather seats and music machine. To own it and drive it with a tank full of petrol was true emancipation. I kept Caron D'Ache crayons and drawing paper in the door side pockets and a bottle of wine.

Mini memory, Mary Quant, 2008

The British-built Cooper was no more. The Clubman was dreadful. The Mini seemed to have divested itself of every vestige of glamour or even self-respect as a prelude to checking into the retirement home.

A decade and a half from its birth, the 'sixties sexpot now rusted gently on suburban front drives as a student shagmobile or a grungy runabout for a harassed mum. The slim young modernists who had bought those early Minis had grown too fat to fit inside.

Middle East war, miners' strikes, feminism, Harold Wilson's comeback after Edward Heath's Conservative intermission – the political times were as febrile as ever. The oil-price spike of 1973 was a tremendous boost to 'economy' cars but pretty quickly things returned to usual; as had long been predicted, the politics of production had indeed long been supplanted by the politics of consumption. There were too many cars. Pollution was the big issue: safety, noise, exhaust emissions, urban dislocation. People began talking about the 'environment' and politicians and planners had to take notice.

Promising to build ever more roads was no longer a sure recipe for electoral success. The building of urban motorways became fiercely contested by a new breed of protesters unknown before. Countryside-gobbling bypasses would soon excite the same level of excitement. But after the October 1973 oil-price shock, the three-day week and slump that followed, many ambitious projects for 'motorway boxes' and 'corridors of opportunity' fell into half-built limbo. The freebooting motorist was corralled by ever stiffer restrictions. Clunk click, every trip. Have you been drinking, sir? The Jagworths were not having it quite so good.

And the car industry was slowly 'globalising' (although the term was as yet something for academic economists). 'Foreign' cars were no longer any kind of novelty. British automotive culture had to adjust, especially to the advent of a new motoring power – Japan – and did so with a kind of early-adopter passion that had animated the first Mini buyers. Datsun Cherry owners honked and waved at each other as once had early Mini-nauts.

Common Market entry was now removing protective tariffs on European competitors in the UK market. Attractive, innovative machines like the VW Golf of 1974 became favourites of the baby-boomers who had grown up to be the new generation of early adopters. Trendiness was no longer Mini-shaped. The Golf GTI, introduced three years after the basic Giorgetto Giugiaro-styled car's launch (although it wasn't the first of the breed), kickstarted the 'hot hatchback' fashion explosion. Sales of Japanese cars motored on unstoppably. British manufacturers meanwhile were relying more and more on 'company cars' and fleet sales to sell anything at all. Their offerings were going back in technological time: banal, booted, boring. But no 'executive' would be seen dead in a Mini, or any other fancy overdesigned thing from BLMC. They liked cars with big boots to lock away their samples and little clothes-hangers inside with room for their executive jackets as they made those dynamic motorway forays. Alec Issigonis didn't help when he declared that 'large boots' were 'sales gimmicks' and that drivers needed to be 'uncomfortable to stay alert'.

Going up in the world: In the third decade of production, Minis as a whole got higher specifications to meet global competition in the small-car market. The Mini Mayfair (1982–1992) was offered with a radio as standard, front disc brakes and 12-inch wheels (from 1984) and a 1275 cc engine (from 1992). Issigonis (who regarded a car radio as a vulgar 'household appliance') pleaded for the 'Mayfair' name to revert to the de Luxe of the early years. The result was a letter terminating his design consultancy. Austin Rover meanwhile pitched the Mayfair at thrusting, Thatcher-era yuppies with a certain degree of success.

'The modern car is much too sophisticated for my liking because I still enjoy driving without being surrounded by an environment of domestic and household appliances,' he loftily declared.

But Mini economics made it worthwhile going on with the baby car's production, even when British Leyland was descending into seemingly terminal industrial crisis. It still delivered volume and 'economies of scale' both on the production line and in terms of the dealer network. It still enticed first-time buyers into what was optimistically called the 'British Leyland family'. New accounting procedures were beginning to show up just how much the car was losing. In European export markets its profit performance was dismal. Maybe some astute management moves could turn it all round. Some hope.

Meanwhile production at Longbridge was regularly brought to halt by walkouts under the leadership of the works convener, Derek Robinson, dubbed 'Red Robbo' by the tabloid press, who had embraced him as their favourite pantomime villain. The fault lines that would determine the politics of the decade to come were already rumbling seismically at the place they made the Mini.

And it seemed such a sensible car. But for some people the Mini's very Britishness was becoming a reason not to buy it.

With BLMC lurching from crisis to crisis, the Ryder Report of 1975 recommended putting the sprawling mess into 65 per cent public ownership plus granting £500 million in loans to enable the group to recover. Crucially it must produce a new Mini by 1980.

It was not enough. Within a few months BLMC had to be bailed out completely, bought by the taxpayer for 10p a share. Making the Mini was now a state-owned enterprise. Leyland Cars, as it was now known, remained the largest car manufacturer in the UK, employing some 128,000 people at thirty-six locations with a production capacity of 1 million vehicles per year – for all the good it did them. Stokes was 'kicked upstairs to be president of BL, where he remained an impotent figure for four years watching the group decline even further into chaos', according to an obituarist (he died in summer 2008).

There was a year of frenzied managerial infighting. In 1976 it looked as if the Mini would at last be pensioned off for ever and replaced by an odd-looking thing called project ADO 74 that put the Mini's engineering principles into a bigger, sleeker-looking body. Why be ultra-small any more? But there was no investment money to do it.

In 1977 another much-heralded industrial saviour, pint-sized South African troubleshooter Sir Michael Edwardes, was appointed chief executive to sort out the mess and face down the unions. Leyland Cars was split up into Austin Morris (the volume-car business) and Jaguar Rover Triumph.

That year a certain Mrs Lindsay Campbell was appointed head of Mini sales, brought in from chocolate/soft-drinks combine Cadbury Schweppes; she would tell a writer soon after her appointment that for the eighteen years that had gone before there had been *no real policy about how to sell the car.*

She at last had set out to use some of those market-research techniques derided at the beginning to see who might still be interested. Buyers were 'youthful' or, more importantly, they perceived themselves to be. A significant proportion were late-middle-aged, identified as 'colonel's wife' or 'blimp'. The Mini appealed to those who had never bought a new or even second-hand car before, and a lot of buyers were women – more than half of the total by 1978 (to put that in perspective, in the mid-'seventies, 69 per cent of adult men held a British driving licence, and 29 per cent of women). Male workers, skilled or semi-skilled, bought hardly any. It was a car for the impoverished young, the late-middle-aged and the housewife. It was a car for life's slow lane.

TV scriptwriter Carla Lane caught the mood in 1978, giving Ria Parkinson, the frustrated dentist's wife and incompetent homemaker played by Wendy Craig in the sitcom *Butterflies*, a red Mini in which to tootle round Cheltenham. A decade before, a Mini would have represented liberation. Now, for a woman on the cusp of middle age, it said the very opposite.

The Edwardes regime passed on the ADO 74. The money to develop it had run out anyway. The Mini was reprieved to chug along as bravely as it could until a proper replacement could be developed that would have to take on all those superminis that had appeared meanwhile.

But there was enough confidence in the dear old thing to give it an advertising boost. It was all those women buyers: they had to be addressed. The masculine Cooper was now a distant memory. Could men be tempted to drive a girlie's car? It was a dilemma that would trouble Mini marketers for ever.

Mini ads still responded to changing times. When the Sex Discrimination Bill became law in 1976, ads featured a grinning young couple with a bright red Mini under the saucy headline 'Sex Has Never Been a Problem for Us'. The cutesy copy squirmed under the new strictures of politically correct feminism: 'perhaps we shouldn't say this but women like the Mini because they're nippy, exciting cars to drive . . . the gentler sex go crazy about a Mini's ability to stay stylish and fashionable.' The implication was that Mr and Mrs Mini had just had sex in their super-sexy little car. That was one way of getting over the motorised shopping-trolley image.

'Sixties celebrities like Lulu, Twiggy and Spike Milligan were hauled in to take the fun factor forward. 'Small' was out and 'fun' was in – 'Joy Ride' – 'Happiness is Mini-shaped' – while Spike Milligan made an appeal to patriotism – 'Drive the Flag'. It was so retro already, but in fact the Mini's age-of-austerity origins had become an increasing embarrassment. By 1978 *CAR* magazine, heir to *Mini Owner*, had fallen right out of love. The old girl was 'a rough little beast, bouncy and rackety . . . cursed with a thoroughly nasty engine and transmission', so the mag declared that April.

'Why will people today pay so much for a spartan outdated

product?' *CAR* asked quite reasonably. 'Are they impervious to the awful ride and Noddy seats? Probably they buy it because it's what they know, a familiar companion for 19 years, once the pride and joy of our motor industry with its worldwide reputation in competition and wide and enthusiastic following in Europe.'

Well, it was a different matter now. It was 'decrepit and completely outdated'. If the show was going to continue at all, *Autocar* magazine called for a whole raft of improvements, including a hatchback and a front-mounted radiator with electric cooling fan. It had long been pulled out of the United States and Canada. The car was progressively withdrawn from once-healthy South African, Australian and New Zealand markets. In October 1983 the last classic Mini rolled off the assembly line at the Elsies River plant near Cape Town. Continental Europe stayed loyal. As did Japan, even though the Mini was fractionally too wide and its engine too big to qualify as a kei car.

Miniless America was having one of its spasms of automotive downsizing with the post-Iranian revolution second oil-price shock of 1979–80. But it was the Germans and above all the Japanese who cleaned up with ever rising US sales (they would never stop) of fuel-efficient, technically clever and reliable vehicles with which BL and its successors had no intention or chance of competing. But for a few Jags and the abysmal TR7 sports, the Mini's makers had abandoned the American market altogether. But memories among car designers were long. A graffito appeared at the then-embattled General Motors design HQ in 1980, declaring 'Issigonis was Right!' so Alex Moulton reported. It needed no more explanation than that.

Meanwhile at home the Mini's makers had reverted to that by-now established marketing trick, the limited or special edition, usually a sign that an old favourite was heading for the knacker's yard: the Mini Limited Edition 1000 in green and white with a gold body strip appeared in 1976; the Mini City, in 1979–82 (a quite sensible pitch for the urban car market) with an 848cc – later, 948cc – engine; the Mini Mayfair, launched in 1982 with radio and tinted glass as standard; the Sprite of 1983; and the Mini 25 of 1984, based upon the Mayfair model to celebrate a quarter of a century of Mini production. Plenty more tricked-up specials were coming.

The supermini project (codenamed LC8) would emerge in 1980 as the Austin Mini Metro (the 'Austin' and 'Mini' tags were soon dropped) launched as 'a British car to beat the world', depicted in TV ads as just the thing to 'send the foreigners [the harmless enough Fiat 127, Renault 5, Volkswagen Polo and Datsun Cherry] back where they belong'. Margaret Thatcher gritted her teeth and went to Longbridge to drive one of the first off the production line. Nineteen-year-old Lady Diana Spencer was chased round London by paparazzi in her red Metro L. Mini Clubman saloon production ended in August 1980 to make way for the Metro although the estate lingered on, renamed the 1000HL, until 1982.

But it was not the end for the original. Mini production volumes fell as buyers looked to the Metro as the new, small BL car, but as Longbridge had been stripped out in a massive modernisation programme in preparation for Metro production, the Mini had also benefited.

It rolled off the same production line as its bigger brother and benefited from the economies of scale afforded by the new plant. The Metro's launch also marked the point when the Mini at last actually started making real money for the company.

Nor had Sir Alec stopped doodling, dreaming and indeed making. Since the demise of the 9X he had pursued a strange obsession to produce a 'gearless Mini', achieved by using a bigger engine modified to produce lots of torque at low speed, propelling a lightweight body. Lord Snowdon was given it to test. The fact it would have trouble getting away on a hill start did not seem to trouble the great designer. There was another diversion, 'hydrostatic transmission', using oil under pressure to turn hydraulic motors at each wheel. It was applied to an experimental lawn mower but oil leaks killed most of the grass on the great designer's Edgbaston lawn. The steam-powered Mini was more successful but in the end it too proved a glorious dead end that expired in a hiss because the boiler and engine technology were not efficient enough in turning fuel into power.

Mini chiefs came and went. Longbridge had become a symbol of manufacturing incompetence and trade-union intransigence on which de-industrialising zealots would pounce. After Margaret Thatcher came to power in spring 1979, the new Prime Minister would demand to see the corporation's accounts. She described them as 'elliptical'. But after much anguish, the new government did sign off millions of taxpayers' money to get the Metro into production.

Things could not go on the way they were. In 1982 Harold Musgrove, an old Leyland insider, was appointed head of Austin-Rover Group Ltd (as BL Cars Ltd had been renamed). 'Bullet headed, teeth gritting, hyper-determined', as he was described, Mini-hating Mr Musgrove was thwarted in an early attempt to kill off the Mini by the fact it was now just about paying its way.

New mid-size cars, such as the Maestro and Montego, came on-stream. Amid continuing class-war rumbles over the Trade Union Act (which became law in September 1984, requiring secret ballots for strike action), the little car chugged on virtually forgotten. The last, big, old-style car-industry clash was the Austin Rover pay dispute of November 1984, at the time of the (much more protracted) miners' strike. The Longbridge strike collapsed after two weeks.

There was a Mini hurrah in 1986 when the five-millionth Mini was driven off the Longbridge production line by the television presenter Noel Edmonds. Not too many people noticed.

Market research discovered that most people thought the little car had long gone out of production anyway, but there was a core of Mini *cognoscenti* who not only knew their little friend was still alive but hoped it would remain so for a lot longer. The unsentimental Musgrove regime intended to dash their hopes by ending production in 1986–7 when the Mini's ancient A-series engine would no longer pass increasingly strict emissions tests demanded for cars sold in Europe. A date with the axeman was set.

Then reprieve arrived in the shape of Graham Day, another new boss, brought in from British Shipbuilders by the new owners, British Aerospace. Those market-research findings were interesting. Pleas for clemency came in bagloads from Mini lovers. The car was 'a nice little earner', so Canadian-born Mr (later Sir) Graham Day declared.

Instead of scrapping it, he told product planners to give the model a new lease of life with cleaner engines and some mild body revamping. It was made clear that as long as there was demand for the Mini, and as long as the necessary engineering changes could keep the car legally in the marketplace, then it would continue to be manufactured and sold. It was seen by some as a miracle that an engine rooted in the early 'fifties could be made to meet end-of-century standards.

Ironically the Mini's basic envelope was inviolate, as any serious tampering, even to make it safer, could not be done without invoking rules that would reclassify it as a new model and subject it to statutory crash-testing that it could not conceivably pass. It was the presiding Mini paradox. It was so old it must stay forever young.

Mr Day also discovered that the car was still an export star. In France they were beloved of women drivers, in Paris especially, where they judged 'the Metro to be too big'. 'One of the joys of France is to watch the ladies get out of a Mini because when you see a Mini park, you know what is going to get out is going to be really spectacular,' an executive confided to *Mini World* magazine.

In Britain the sales demographic was similar. It was very much a woman's car (and right then selling to the 'women's market' was very fashionable among carmakers). It was all at once a fashion accessory, a handbag on wheels, and 'a pet Labrador to be patted on the head', a survey concluded. That would do. A stay of execution was granted until at least 1991.

For the first time in a decade, Mini press advertisements appeared. The result was general public surprise that it still existed at all. A snowbound 'Minis Have Feelings Too' Xmas TV campaign ran at the end of 1986. Sales began to creep up. The Mini 30 special-anniversary edition was launched, with Twiggy (again) fronting a campaign proclaiming 'you never forget your first Mini'.

For People in the Know: Although traditional Commonwealth markets had been abandoned, Mini exports to Europe remained significant through the 'eighties. Germans especially seemed to like an urban-chic object of desire that was Made in England. As did the Japanese who would represent the biggest Mini-market of all until the very end of production.

Were these new-wave Mini lovers elderly nostalgists seeking lost youth or a new bunch of postmodern, retro-ironists rebelling against the bloated excesses of the latter Thatcher years? They were both.

Sir Alec was growing increasingly frail. He suffered from Ménière's disease, which affected his hearing and balance. Still he kept a wary eye on what was being done with his creation and still he couldn't resist disparaging remarks about lesser car designs (which was more or less all of them). He wrote to Graham Day: 'To change the Mini shape would be fatal as it is known worldwide, to do so would make it just another car. A reversion to the original model names of Mini and Mini de Luxe instead of Mini City and Mini Mayfair would be preferable.' The outcome was a letter received via his solicitor, terminating his consultancy.

He confided his thoughts to handwritten notes: 'Japan loves the Mini, so does Europe . . . BL just hates it. It's politics, they can't sell their Metro. They're giving it away with packets of tea . . .'

He had to give up drinking and smoking. He'd long been too frail to drive himself. Now he had to give up his chauffeur. A move from the Edgbaston bungalow with its attached workshop-garage to a second-floor flat became expedient. There would be no more going out. He talked about being put on the scrap heap. He became ever more cranky and jealous, forbidding any mention of the name Dante Giacosa (designer of Fiat's mid-century babies) and feuding ungraciously with Alex Moulton, whose advanced suspension work he now disparaged as a mistake.

The fate of 9X grieved him the most. He became convinced his work had been stolen by 'spies'. John Sheppard stayed loyal, as did Tony Dawson. But the ailing great designer remained immensely proud of his achievements. When Mini production reached 5 million, he said:

Don't expect me to be modest about the Mini. I'm very proud of the fact that it has run for so many years without a major mechanical change and still looks the car we designed. Five million people have bought my Mini and it just goes to show that they have a lot of common sense. If a car can't inspire you then it's not a good car . . .

Still those special editions poured out of Longbridge. The Mini Ritz in 1985, the Mini Chelsea and Mini Piccadilly, the Mini Park Lane and Mini Advantage (originally to be called 'Wimbledon') with a tennis theme. Thankfully there was never a Mini 'Carnaby'.

Designer genes: During the Mini's prolonged mid-life crisis, the UK market groaned under a plethora of 'Limited Edition' marketing stunts – but more innovative were those linked to fashionistas with the right credentials to boost a 'sixties icon when it needed a little extra help. What could be more appropriate than the poptastic Quant LE (known as the 'Mini Designer') of 1988 – with true Mini-fan from the start, Miss Mary Quant herself, doing the promotion?

Nor was there a Mini 'Issigonis'. But in 1988 there was a Mary Quant 'Designer' special edition that rummaged through the dressing-up box of a quarter of a century earlier. The steering wheel and bonnet badge featured Quant's daisy logo.

But like your dad doing a dance at a 'sixties disco theme party, these confections trembled on the brink of acute embarrassment. Truer to type than dragging up its swinging credentials was the Mini's association with Mr Bean, the TV character portrayed by comedy actor Rowan Atkinson, several of whose unfunny adventures of the early 'nineties featured a 1977 lime-green BL Mini Mark IV (although a number of different vehicles from various Mini epochs would appear in the series). From episode one, Mr Bean's Mini was often seen in hilarious conflict with a light-blue Reliant Regal Supervan III. The British Leyland car presumably symbolised the general dysfunctionality of its tweed-jacketed owner. At the time it wasn't a bad piece of casting.

But car-loving Mr Atkinson redeemed himself in the eyes of Mini purists when he reviewed the state of Mini play in *CAR* magazine in 1991 – by first attacking all those tacky-seeming special editions: 'Sprite, Ritz . . . Jet Black, Flaming Stupid . . . absurd marketingspeak, application of make up to what was perceived to be a tired old face'.

And deep down Mr Bean's creator was a Mini lover. 'In fact the Mini has timeless elegant features,' he said. 'The original Mini shape is so good that anyone who considers these nostalgia add-ons an improvement must be plain barmy.'

On 2 October 1988, Sir Alec Issigonis died in his sleep, aged eighty-one. The funeral was at the Anglican church of St George's, Edgbaston. The address, drafted by Sir Peter Ustinov, suggested that the Mini reflected Issigonis's 'own twinkling personality – his eyes, of a surprisingly intense deep blue, were recalled in the wide-eyed innocence of the Mini's headlights, childish but hugely sophisticated. The Mini was not only a triumph of engineering but an enduring personality, as was Sir Alec with his exquisitely caustic tongue and infectious humour.' Paddy Hopkirk was there; he was sad that, 'not being married, [Issigonis] had no children' at the service to mourn him.

Tributes were worldwide. An American eulogist noted:

Sir Alec was the most influential car designer of his time. His genius and practical engineering flair led to some of Britain's most successful vehicles, including the Morris Minor, the 1100 and 1800 and the Maxi.

But he will be best remembered for the Mini, which brought classless motoring to millions . . . It was just the car for the swinging '60s, a favorite with aristocrats, film stars and the bell-bottomed and mini-skirted young people who could, at last, afford a car.

Despite embellishments and refinements, its outward appearance has never greatly changed. The price has multiplied almost tenfold, but sales remain strong.

Auto-designer peers paid their tributes, like this one:

The Mini-Minor has provided the basis for the design of virtually all modern small cars. Honda was the first to follow the lead of front-wheel drive, transverse engine and 'two-box' body. Later, Volkswagen adopted the same formula for the successor to the Beetle – the Rabbit [US Golf] – and the stage was set for almost all manufacturers of small cars, as well as many of larger cars.

Thus the Mini-Minor is arguably the most influential design since Emile Levassor established the classic configuration of an engine at the front, driving the rear wheels through a geared transmission, for the 1891 Panhard. This layout determined the mainstream of automobile design to the time of Sir Alec Issigonis's masterstroke.

A memorial service at Birmingham Cathedral was held four weeks later. There were three cars outside, the first Morris Minor, the first Mini, and a new Mini taken off the line that particular week. It was number 5,100,001. Lord Snowdon gave the address, hailing a 'true engineer, designer and perfectionist'.

The thirtieth-birthday celebrations of 27 August 1989, focused on a giant international jamboree at Silverstone, were exuberant in the extreme: an astonishing 120,000 people and 25,000 Minis were there. The Japanese turned up in force. The Germans chartered a whole North Sea ferry.

A midsummer campaign of TV ads had ramped up the nostalgic mood. The evergreen 'sixties model Twiggy had been hired to star in a mini-saga in which she emerges from a smart restaurant and, when approaching her chauffeur-driven Bentley, catches sight of a 1968-registered Mini in the street. Sigh! There is a flashback to her superskinny old self standing by the very same car; there's a mash-up of *The Italian Job*, the Beatles, Mick Jagger and Peter Sellers before the heroine relaxes in the sumptuous back seat of her Bentley, looking wistful. Cynics interpreted the ad's message as 'thank God I don't have to get into that old thing any more'.

The knives were really out this time: 'We are gazing wistfully at an antique, a car that . . . never should have continued in production, virtually unchanged for three decades,' proclaimed the *Sunday Times*. There was more:

> There is scant cause to celebrate one of the greatest missed opportunities in automotive history, or praise a car that is slow, noisy, less safe than it ought to be and dying on its feet, save for a shrinking number of customers.
>
> The Mini's catalogue of failure leaves us with a car

thirty years out of date in style, merit and profitability. It was badly made and wrongly priced at the start, never earned enough money to keep its lead, and remains a monument to a management that never realised how distinguished it was.

Oh dear. Rescue, however, was close at hand.

CHAPTER 27

Cooper Reborn

I was given a Mini for my seventeenth birthday by my
parents – Surprise! It was a Mini Mayfair. It was G-reg so I
called it Gemima. There were four girls in the sixth form
at my [quite posh] school who had Minis. I suppose we were
rather pleased with ourselves – but who wouldn't be . . .?

Mini memory, 2008

Sprawling BL had been a long time unravelling. For Margaret
Thatcher and her more doctrinaire ministers the nationalised
concern had represented 'everything that was wrong with
Britain' incarnate. The volume-car Austin Rover Group Ltd (which
Mrs Thatcher wanted sold to Ford but they wouldn't have it)
had been formed out of the corporate mess in 1981 alongside
Land Rover Group. Triumph and Morris joined Riley and Wolseley
as ghosts in the Longbridge machine. MG limped on. Jaguar was
stripped out to stand alone to be eventually bought by Ford. The
once-mighty Austin name was dropped without ceremony in
1986–7. After that it would be plain 'Rover'.

Mini continued as a brand (no one talked of marques any more)
with minimal advertising. In 1988 the remaining Rover Group
(as BL had been been renamed) business was sold to the conglom-
erate British Aerospace, better known for jet fighters and weaponry
than turning out iconic hangovers from the era of peace and love.

The little car still had its eccentric loyalists in Britain and
Europe. Frayed-at-the-edges Minis chugged on as shopping cars
or teenage rites-of-passage mobiles, more often than not donated
by Mum to son or daughter as an eighteenth-birthday present

217

(Mum acquired a sensible Fiat or a VW as a replacement as her own rite of passage into middle age; she may not have been entirely happy).

Mini was still huge in Japan, where affluent car-buying young adults (male and female) prized small motor cars as a place within which to sexually experiment beyond the constraints of the tiny familial living space. Doing it in a Mini brought an extra edge apparently.

In Britain, strangely perhaps, demand for 'hot' Minis revived in the late 'eighties among a loyal circle of both diehards and new, mostly male, young fans. Production continued meanwhile of those girlie-oriented limited editions. The Cooper wheeze of 1961 had catapulted the housewives' car to the heart of fashionable society. Thirty years later, in a brand-crowded world of consumer abundance, could the same trick be played again? Could Mini, the still-just-about-lovable urban runabout, go to the high-fashion ball one more time?

'Historic' rallying in lovingly preserved Coopers meanwhile had kept the 'sixties thrill of Monte victories alive. Pleas by enthusiasts to reinstate a proper Cooper version had long gone unconsidered. But something strange had happened on the other side of the world. In Japan the madly expanding bubble (and soon to deflate) economy of the 'eighties had sucked in a wave of luxury imports – including boatloads of Minis – considered chicly British like Scotch whisky, lamb's-wool pullovers and golf, and ideally scaled for the nation's teeming cities. The original Cooper had been wildly fashionable in Japan. Enthusiast clubs had kept the marque loyalty burning bright since the 'sixties, their members revering Issigonis as a kind of magician. Entrepreneurs had found a niche for importing restored original examples from the glory days (the bigger ADO16 cars were also very desirable, especially the Vanden Plas Princess version). BL began a trickle of new-build Mini imports again in 1982 with modifications to conform to local emissions legislation.

Old Minis never die: They simply fade away. A Countryman finds its last rusting place.

Soon around 3,000 Minis a year were being landed by a concessionaire called Japan England Motors. In 1986 the Tokyo-based president of Austin Rover Japan, Cedric Talbot, approached John Cooper to ask whether it was possible to put an MG Metro engine into a Mini.

Ironically, Cooper had been a Honda concessionaire since 1986, but had nevertheless kept the engineering side of the business very much alive. Technically it was feasible but Austin Rover management were not so keen, citing problems with getting type approval for a 'new' Cooper in the UK and Japan.

John Cooper meanwhile fitted a Mini Mayfair with an MG Metro engine and sent it to Japan, where it was worshipped like a god descending from the heavens. A request to make a thousand more followed but the Musgrove management regime refused to sanction such a diversion from the core business.

An entrepreneurial Tokyo-based journalist published a special Cooper magazine that sold out 50,000 copies, and he himself suggested to John Cooper that if they could not get the car, they could at least have a tuning kit. Mr Cooper obliged and was soon exporting a kit comprising a modified cylinder head, twin carburettors, performance air filters and exhaust system, boosting the 998cc Mini from 40 to 64 bhp. The kit was enshrined in an elaborate box that could fit on a Mini's back seat. The Japanese were enraptured. Two Mini special editions meanwhile were produced for the Japanese market, quaintly subtitled the 'Brighton' and the 'Belfast'. Nobody is quite sure why.

That spring of 1989, John Cooper Garages produced a number of worked-over Mini 30 Anniversary models for the UK market, with an engine Mr Cooper described 'as recalling some of the flavour of the Cooper S'. The birthday meanwhile served to spread immense renewed goodwill over the car. One hundred and twenty thousand fans from all over the world turned up at Silverstone for the party. The organisers (and Rover management) were stunned. Rover sales executive Kevin Morley remembered: 'I was walking along with Paddy Hopkirk and there we met these two Japanese guys who had brought their Cooper all the way from Japan just for this event. The car had white bonnet stripes, Paddy had a black felt pen and signed one. One guy almost fainted . . .'

The newly renamed Rover Group and John Cooper Garages began talking to each other properly at last and soon the JCG conversion kits were available for fitting to 998cc Minis from Rover dealers with full factory warranty. John Cooper and his son Michael met with Rover management to discuss the next step. John Cooper suggested putting the 1275cc engine in the Mini. There were again mutterings about type approval and noise but these problems were soon resolved. Rover Special Products (RSP) handled the development of the new car with input from the Coopers, father and son.

> The special-products boys were a bit worried about starting production of a thirty-year-old car [John Cooper told *Mini* magazine in 1991], they wanted the sunroof and a bit of bull on it to help sales. They said, 'We can put some white stripes on the bonnet' and I said, 'Lovely.' Then they said, 'Would you sign them?' I said, 'That's a bit Promenade Percy, isn't it?' But they thought it right because it's really a 1960s car.

The Mini Cooper RSP (Rover Special Products) was officially launched in July 1990. The cars for Japan were fitted with a different exhaust catalyser and air conditioning (for those Tokyo summers), plus lots of little local-market tweaks. After some deep marketing thought they were branded as 'Rover Mini Coopers' apparently because the Japanese had no perception of Rover being old and woody, whereas 'Mini' was enough to convey the idea that the machine in question was 'liberating, fun and anti-establishment'.

In Britain it just looked old. The reborn Cooper got mixed notices. Some of the new generation of reviewers just didn't see the point in reviving something that dated back three decades. The veteran writer L J K Setright praised 'the staunch independence that makes the Mini as refreshing as it always was, and makes it impossible for the others to bear comparison with it'. The market spoke. There were enough nostalgists and new fans out there for this brave exercise in raising the dead to work. Soon around a third of all Minis sold were Coopers, with production running at 1,000 a month.

The Thatcher epoch was juddering to an end. All that class-war anguish of the first half of the 'eighties was nothing compared with the frustrated ambition of former minister Michael Heseltine (publisher of Mini-loving *Town* magazine back in 1961–2), who challenged her for the party leadership in November 1990.

The Mini in contrast had survived up to now by keeping its head down, existing at the outer margins of what the increasingly embattled Prime Minister was now calling the 'great car economy'. She had coined the phrase in March of that year at an 'environmental' awards ceremony in London; the fact she was there at all was a sign of changing times. The Prime Minister's words were very interesting in the Mini context. She said:

> The great encouragement is that the consumer is urging us to think in new ways, and insisting that they do not like products which heavily pollute the atmosphere, by the fact that they buy things which are ozone friendly, or want catalytic converters on cars, or they want more efficient engines, and so on. We are not going to do without a great car economy; much of our economy would collapse if we did without that; but we are going to have to find more economical ways of using fuel – more economical engines or more economical use of the cars.

It echoed those pleas for automotive thrift made in the mid-'fifties that had led directly to the Mini. Was it patriotic to guzzle or to sip? Sipping was good. Mrs Thatcher's statement was a recognition that the march to autopia was not without cost, even if it seemed unstoppable. But did these born-again conspicuous thrifters that she identifed – urging new ways of thinking on government and industry – actually exist? It looked around 1990 as if what they really wanted was bigger and greedier cars. What they clearly did not want was cars Made in Britain.

The government policies of the previous decade – deregulation of public transport and a new wave of road projects – had led both to a renewed surge in traffic levels and, for the first time, a vocal 'anti-car' movement. Without an oil-price spike or economic crisis to do the downsizing they would resort to taking to the trees or tunnels in bypass-blocking protest.

But the planners must plan on. The old days of 'predict and provide' were not nearly up to it. The 1989 National Road Traffic forecast predicted a 142 per cent growth in traffic levels by 2025. The government responded with the White Paper 'Roads for Prosperity' – with over 500 schemes costing £23 billion – although it was recognised that, whatever road-construction policy was adopted, congestion must increase.

The great plan of course was to atrophy as politics changed and environmentalist voices grew louder. The change of mood did little however to scale back the march of the new generation of 'luxury' four-wheel drives (begun in the UK with the Range Rover of 1969) and the rise of the gas-guzzling SUV in the US. The whole urban 4 x 4 phenomenon had been boosted immeasurably meanwhile by such 'eighties icons as the Suzuki SJ410, which was coveted in its day by the kind of young modernists who a quarter of a century earlier had bought Minis. The trouble was they liked them so much they wanted bigger and bigger versions. Minimalism had become giganticism. It was a cultural turnaround on an extraordinary scale.

So at the outset of the 'nineties there was a new political soundbite in the air, 'sustainable mobility', even if that phrase wasn't exactly on everyone's lips. As far as automakers were concerned, people carriers and sport utes were on a roll. Big cars made maxi-profits. The four-wheel-drive school run had become commonplace without anyone really noticing. But for those car buyers who weren't tempted by the new-wave mastodons, the living fossil from Longbridge seemed modern and practical again. The undead Cooper looked especially so. The amazing thing was, it still existed.

What Car's review of the production Cooper drooled over its ability to 'nip through gaps and squeeze into parking spaces with steering so quick and precise you wonder what has gone wrong with other cars in the intervening decades. Even that bus-like driving position is tolerable once you have adapted.' It described it as 'an extremely relevant car as the roads head toward thrombosis'. It could have been written in 1961.

Mr Atkinson meanwhile, while deriding the remade Cooper as 'tacky' (in *CAR* magazine, November 1991), couldn't get enough of the Mini's basic concept: 'generally all its joyful wieldiness can be attributed to its smallness . . . after a trip in the Mini, getting into a small hatchback is like climbing inside a tank. The huge, bloated, heavy extravagance of it all seems like madness', wrote the comedian.

In March 1991 John Cooper Garages began selling the first of several 'S' packs – to tweak the reborn, go-faster Mini even further. It was sold through Rover dealers. The kit itself was actually manufactured by Janspeed Engineering, which had been founded by the Hungarian exile Jan Odor, who had left Downton Engineering in 1962. The kit consisted of a modified cylinder head, new exhaust system, and twin 1.25-inch SU carburettors. Power was boosted to 77 bhp. *Autocar and Motor* magazine tested one in May 1991. It turned in very similar performance to the 1275S that *Autocar* had tested back in 1964. Top speed was 97 mph and 0–60 mph was reached in eleven seconds.

The magazine raked over all the car's usual faults. It was noisy. It was cramped, uncomfortable, lacking in refinement and 'over the top with its plethora of badges'.

> The Mini Cooper S fails as a car for the nineties [said the review sternly], by today's standards, it's not even particularly quick and, of course, it's astronomically expensive. Are there any other cars out there with sporting pretensions that only have four speeds?
>
> But in one respect at least the Mini succeeds brilliantly. It's a magnificent car to drive, responsive in

a way that nothing for a comparable price can equal, never mind surpass. You don't take the Cooper S to work, you drive it, and if you've forgotten the fun that can be had from driving then you need a car like this to remind you.

The formula seemed to work. The 'woman's car' was made masculine again. The reborn Cooper S was go-fast heaven for a new generation of not-so-boyish racers. The average age of buyers fell by ten years (to a comfortably mature thirty-nine). But resurrecting the Cooper did much more: it reminded anyone who cared vaguely about motor cars that the Mini was still alive. For those who cared a little more it had the 'halo effect' of sprinkling stardust on a now-less-than-lustrous brand. Mini owners were smiling again.

There were more variations on the Mini theme. ERA Specialist Vehicles of Dunstable 'semi-officially' put the 94bhp engine, transmission and brakes from the Metro Turbo plus thirteen-inch alloy wheels into a beefed-up body shell as the 'ERA Mini Turbo'. It could do 0–60 mph in 9.9 seconds and reach 101.7 mph. Costing almost £12,000 it was big in Japan where Mini frenzy was unabated. Some 400 were built between 1989 and 1991.

The German Rover dealer LAMM Autohaus commissioned the famous Karmann bodybuilding firm to do a cabriolet (an echo of the Crayford convertible Mini of 1963). The body was stiffened and big wheel-arch extensions fitted, with a posh interior, and the soft top stowing in a big bag at the back. It cost a hefty £12,250 in the UK but it sold out. In spite of its financial problems, Rover replied with an in-house version with Karmann-made body shells and final assembly at Longbridge. It went on sale in 1993 and would sputter on in low-volume production until almost the end of the decade.

The image of the reborn baby sports saloon was hugely boosted in January 1994 when four new-generation Mini Coopers were entered in the Monte Carlo Rally. Paddy Hopkirk managed to finish fifty-ninth, but the heart-thumping nostalgia and media interest in the thirty-five-year-old design campaigning again in the Col de Turini was overwhelming. Inevitably yet another special edition (200 vehicles with Dunlop Sport tyres, a battery of twin spot and fog lamps, and Monte decals) hit the showrooms.

What was all this really about? Why pimp the old girl around like this? The Mini's makers were not just out to sell cars. They were looking to sell the whole company. British Aerospace as stewards of the Rover car company had been going through financial woes of their own. Their flirtation with volume-car production was proving short-lived. A buyer was being sought, and the assets were being polished up to look as enticing as possible. MG and Land Rover looked a bit sexy. Who knows, the good old Mini name might still be worth something.

The car industry was globalising rapidly. Notions of what made a car from a distinct locus, British, German, Japanese, were becoming meaningless. In Munich, Bavaria, as the German economy strained post-reunification, the BMW company was looking at how to survive on a production base of less than a million cars a year. That wasn't big enough. They could diversify up, down and sideways, into super-luxe or sport utilities – into small cars even. Meanwhile the global auto industry might be coming more and more homogeneous – but the type of vehicles on offer was getting more and more fractured.

As so often in the past, the USA in the last decade of the twentieth century was setting the social if not the technological pace of change in consumer aspirations. Western Europe and Japan were not far behind. A historian of the period succinctly described an 'increasingly fragmented and individualistic society' in which 'people sought meaning no longer in collective fantasies of progress and power but in individual expressions of leisure lifestyles'. This 'gave rise to an increasing differenti-ation of the auto market into niches dominated by lifestyle vehi-cles'. By which he meant all those soccer-mom minivans, multi-purpose vehicles, neo-muscle-cars and above all the SUV, which from the mid-'nineties onwards had come to dominate both the automotive landscape of America and Detroit's corpo-rate bottom line. The profit per unit on a tarted-up truck was fabulous. By 1999 Ford's Michigan Truck Plant (making the Explorer and upmarket Lincoln Navigator plus the F-150 pickup) was declared to be the most profitable factory of any industry in the world. In this baroque replay of the late 'fifties, both engineers and 'stylists' spent their time rearranging old tech-nologies into fantastical lifestyle packages.

Latching on to the (initially unlooked-for) rise of the SUV, automakers went back to the days of the deep motivational analysts to find ways of selling even more. Research found they were bought by people who were 'insecure, vain, self-centred, and self-absorbed, who are frequently nervous about their marriages, and who lack confidence in their driving skills'. There seemed to be plenty of such. And there was more. The French-born anthropologist and 'car shrink' G. Clotaire Rapaille pronounced on the reasons for the SUV's appeal – where 'every-thing surrounding you should be round and soft . . . there should be air bags everywhere'. Being 'high up' made drivers feel more in control, of course it did, while multiple cupholders provided a childhood feeling of being safely surrounded by comforting maternal liquids. Women loved these mobile wombs.

BMW had plans for such a vehicle. It would eventually emerge in 1999, styled in California and put together in South Carolina as the X5. And it had plenty of cupholders. But a small car was the very opposite. Could it be a player in this fragmented 'lifestyle' market? Even more so, could it break the old industry maxim that mini-cars made mini-profits? BMW were prepared to find out.

Since the early 'nineties, the company had been working on a small car codenamed the E1 aimed at the US market, where minimum emissions rather than minimum size were at a premium. In outline it had an aluminium and plastic body and an electric motor. Another concept, the Z13, configured on a central driving position with a set-back passenger seat on each side, a rear-mounted 1000cc petrol engine and continuously variable transmission, was unveiled at the 1993 Geneva motor show. Such machines represented high-risk, high-cost development from within. Growing the company that way would take too long.

BMW's *de facto* owners, the Quandt family, were obsessed with retaining independence, and that meant acquiring a ready-made mass producer. Headed by the company's youthful, goatee-bearded, cigar-loving newly appointed CEO, Bernd Pischetsrieder, the company was looking for a takeover prospect, one that could boost volume significantly without compromising the brand's quality image.

Herr Pischetsrieder was an auto-industry wunderkind. 'Unexpected, unconventional, brilliant', is how *Automobile Industries* magazine described the BMW boss. There was a poignant personal connection. His grandmother was Alec Issigonis's aunt. The great designer had shown him round Longbridge as a teenager.

Rover looked like the ideal target for the mighty BMW – with volume coming from the Longbridge and Cowley legacy plus niche brands with which to do clever things in Land Rover, MG, Riley even. And pottering away in Brum there was 'Mini', an automotive coelacanth, a living fossil, but a brand that manifestly still inspired global affection. Maybe it could be successfully reinvented.

BAe were keen to sell and flirted with potential rival suitors until the very eve of the sale. The Honda connection (which had effectively saved the company's bacon) was discarded without sentiment.

On 1 February 1994 Bernd Pischetsrieder announced the deal. Rover was safe in BMW's hands, he assured anyone who would listen, with big investment in plant and new-model development heading towards Longbridge, Cowley and the rest of the company.

Herr Pischetsrieder had already made it quite clear to the UK government that there would be no closures, and certainly not of mighty Longbridge. And he wanted a British CEO to run Rover. The group managing director, John Towers, was promoted to be the company's chief executive.

At first the Anglo-German romance went as sweetly as Victoria and Albert. Herr Pischetsrieder was clearly a sentimentalist – he hinted that he would like to resurrect some of the company's long-lost marques, most notably Riley to take on Jag and perhaps Austin-Healey to spearhead the British company's return to the US.

It was all about emphasising 'Britishness' while distancing Rover from BMW. The existing UK-made cars were flatteringly depicted in company literature, photographed against craggy Scottish landscapes. Mini squeezed into the picture. But how long could it stagger on? Would it just fade away, or would it be replaced with something that was recognisably a resurrection of the original?

'Retro' cars were certainly fashionable. Those Japanese postmodern ironists had led the way in 1987–9 with the Nissan Micra-based BE-I, Pao and Figaro. The US-born, Pasadena Art Center-trained designer J. Mays, working at VW's design studio in Simi Valley, California, had developed Volkswagen Concept One (the 'New Beetle'), revealed to rave reviews in 1994 (the Germans didn't like it much, however). He would soon be made head of design at mighty Ford.

Herr Pischetsrieder shrewdly sensed the mood. He let it be known that he considered 1999, the Mini's forthcoming fortieth birthday, an ideal date for a 'replacement' to be unveiled. The new Mini, he began to hint, should take as big a step forward in design as Sir Alec Issigonis's 1959 original. It could be an electric or a hybrid. Meanwhile the existing Mini would continue in production.

In April 1995 *Autocar* got a bit of a scoop. Under the headline 'Baby Come Back' it revealed that a team of Rover designers and engineers had been 'researching a core concept' since the beginning of the year. 'Any radical thinking will be applied to making the new car spacious, light and economical, rather than involving complex mechanical design', the magazine claimed.

'The shape is certain to use some of the original car's styling cues – round headlights, a recognisable grille, simple, rounded body sections and the celebrated wheel-at-each-corner layout. Rover will try to recreate the cheeky, friendly nature acknowledged to be one of the Mini's enduring qualities,' so the magazine reported.

'Rover was firmly in charge of the Mini concept and design', it was said, but the accompanying illustrations, it would turn out, showed something conceived a long way from the west Midlands.

Dr Alex Moulton, John Cooper and the now eighty-three-year-old Jack Daniels had been consulted, so a certain continuity with the glory pioneering days seemed assured. It looked as if the engine would be a three-cylinder version of the K-series. A Cooper version was in mind; of course it was.

The new car would be branded as the Mini, according to Wolfgang Reitzle, BMW's powerful technical chief. And it would be 'all-British in design and manufacture'. Gordon Sked, Rover's director of design since 1989, had full control of the project, it was declared. The next-generation Mini would be made at Longbridge, Birmingham.

So that was it. At last, at last, a national icon was to be reborn – under German control, it was true, but still wrapped in the Union flag. Designed in Britain, made in Britain. It would not turn out quite like that.

John Towers, Rover's chief executive, waded in, glowing with optimism, foreseeing a world market for 500,000 Mini-sized cars beyond the year 2000 – estimating that the proposed new Rover-Mini could take about 150,000 of that, against then-current sales of just 20,000 a year. The once-mould-breaking design was now competing in a much more complex market with rival minicars from Mercedes-Benz, General Motors and Volkswagen under development.

To Bernd Pischetsrieder, this was why the next-generation Mini must be special: 'There's no point in doing a new Mini if it's just another small car,' he declared. The Mini must not become a supermini. But the new car would be bigger, because safety rules now demanded crushable structures, and 'drivers' needs have changed'. 'It's not just legislation,' said Wolfgang Reitzle, 'customers want more equipment.'

They certainly would not have put up with Issigonis's utilitarian strictures of 1959 that drivers should be uncomfortable to stay awake and not be surrounded with 'domestic appliances' such as radios. Drivers of the new millennium, whisper it softly, were also likely to be considerably fatter.

Car magazine asked Pischetsrieder how the new Mini was getting on. 'Slowly because there are a lot of other things to get on with,' he replied. 'But there will be a new Mini and the intention is to make it as trendsetting and radical as the first Mini.' No need to worry, then.

All too soon, however, the romance was getting scratchy. By 1996 some of BMW's senior executives were questioning why Rover was consuming so much and returning so little. After a deepening series of rows, John Towers chose to exit with a £500,000 payoff to be replaced first by Wolfgang Reitzle, then by Walter Hasselkus, a long-time company man and self-proclaimed Anglophile. He had had built up the beloved-by-yuppies BMW brand in Britain as chief UK-based salesman in the early Thatcher years.

When he ventured to the RAC Club on Pall Mall to meet the press on his new appointment he was treated by journalists as if Rover was a triumphant British success ruined by don't-mention-the-war Germans. He bore it all in good grace.

BMW's research was showing (a little late – perhaps they could have worked this out before the takeover) that Rover's existing products had no chance of poaching sales from its classier competitors. Pischetsrieder's idea of pitching Rover as a 'cheap Jaguar' was doomed.

The brand was not up to it. The cars were perceived as little more than re-badged Hondas (the relationship with the Japanese auto giant had begun with a simple licensing deal with the Triumph Acclaim in 1979 and progressed to a 20 per cent share swap in 1990 and joint design and production of new models) – good, but not good enough. But without the Honda connection Rover would surely have expired years before. There was already a kind of plan within Rover to offer the Honda Today, a long-established kei car, rebadged as the 'new Mini'. That would have been pretty much an outright surrender. It was quickly stifled by the new regime.

Under BMW tutelage, a mid-size project codenamed R30 was conceived. Although the early design phase of the car was carried out in Gaydon, it soon moved to Germany when plans became more advanced. Having been put into production alongside the new Mini at a revitalised Longbridge, it was to be hoped that the R30 would firmly establish Rover as a global player in the small-medium class (to be sold as the Rover 55). It was also the car that would guarantee the survival of car production at Birmingham, with an anticipated production rate of 250,000 per year. Development and tooling costs were an estimated £2 billion.

But Pischetsrieder's approach was increasingly questioned within BMW's Munich headquarters. Wolfgang Reitzle was coming to the conclusion that Rover was unsaveable, and in fact had been so all along. The 1994 marriage had been a sham. The only way to survive in any form was to close one of the two UK factories and concentrate on the new-generation Mini and a BMW '2-Series' – possibly based on the R30 – at already slimmed-down Cowley.

But while Pischetsrieder was in charge, neither British factory would close. He seemed to have every intention of standing by the promise that he had made to the UK government in 1994. That year Rover had sold 362,876 cars worldwide and its share of the UK car market was about 12 per cent. But with a strengthening pound sterling (30 per cent up against the Deutsche Mark in three years), in order to maintain sales of any sort in continental Europe, Rover were forced to discount to the point that cars were being sold at a loss. In summer 1998, domestic sales 'fell off a cliff', while now-cheaper imports motored on unstoppably. By the following year Rover's market share would be less than 5 per cent, with 60,000 unsold cars parked on disused airfields. The UK operation was gobbling up cash, its embattled local management behaving ever more neurotically, ever less able to act on its own. Developing new models invited jokes about the *Titanic* and deckchairs.

BMW's own cashflow was healthy but it did not possess bottomless coffers. By the last year of the century, Rover losses would hit £780m, prompting the German press to call it 'the English patient'. The patient was dying on the operating table.

Pischetsrieder, looking over his shoulder as moustachioed sceptic-in-chief Wolfgang Reitzle sought to administer a mercy killing, thrashed around to find a magic cure. One result was collaboration with Chrysler in the USA with the announcement in 1997 of a joint engine plant to be built in Brazil, making 1.4- and 1.6-litre engines for use in the new Mini and Chrysler Neon cars. Hopes for a closer union were dashed when, in May 1998, Mercedes-Benz swooped in to buy Chrysler from beneath its rival's nose to form the giant $55 billion DaimlerChrysler Corp.

There were no alternatives left. BMW's share price was crumbling. The Rover workforce was cut. Longbridge went on four-day working. The English patient would take the Bavarian Motor Works down with it. The latest corporate plan for the British subsidary that revolved around the new-generation Mini, the R30, the Range Rover and the retro-styled 'executive' Rover 75 (which would be launched in 1999) looked barely viable. A smash-up was looming.

CHAPTER 28

Second Coming

The MINI is the most successful British revival since Margaret Thatcher privatized the rail system. Join that revival by finding a MINI Cooper dealer . . .

MINI selling copy, USA, 2008

There was hope, and it was Mini-shaped. Those reassuring post-takeover announcements had not been just hot air. BMW management knew perfectly well the potential of the Mini 'brand'. It was all about 'lifestyle cars' not 'runabouts'. And they were surprised that the people who actually owned it seemed not to care. 'They found no emotion there,' recorded one German observer of the misalliance. 'Rover's attitude was "When we can't keep it legal, we're going to let it run down . . ."'

Modern classics like the Porsche 911 and VW Golf had gone through multiple makeovers. It was accidents of history that had kept the little car in production so spookily unchanged. But like a Hollywood silent-film star living in seclusion, only its most fervent fans still bothered to seek the Mini out. But their passion was total. BMW's management groaned under cranky demands that the ancestral heritage be revered and nothing changed. Mini modernists had become arch-conservatives.

Of course it should have been revamped years ago. In the first post-nuptial corporate flush, the discovery that there was indeed some sort of live Mini replacement programme was a reason for surprise as well as celebration. Work in the early 'nineties under

Rover design chief Gordon Sked had sought to replace both the Mini and Metro in an innovative small-car package that would employ a three-cylinder version of the K-series engine and a hydragas suspension system.

The first result was called the 'Minky' – a three-seater with a central driving position. A 'mule' (a prototype built with new mechanicals under a cobbled-together body) was built.

Three designers, David Saddington, David Woodhouse and Oliver le Grice, were involved in the transition-regime design work. The new BMW bosses beamed *bonhomie*. There was money for a proper development programme for a brand-new car. It was codenamed R59. Bernd Pischetsrieder even drove veteran designer Alex Moulton's hydragas-sprung 1966 Mini Cooper and is reported to have been impressed. But what was the new Mini to be, an economy car, a performance car or a fashion icon? Could it be all three?

What emerged were three distinct designs. The Evolution from David Saddington was a four-seater with a transverse K-series engine. The Revolution, with a similar mechanical package, was described as 'looking like a typical small European hatchback'. The Spiritual, shaped by le Grice, had hydragas suspension and full four-seat capability.

Faced with modern safety legislation, the Spiritual pushed its three-cylinder 800cc petrol engine longitudinally and almost horizontally under the rear seats ahead of the transmission. Weight was 700 kg, it turned in 90 mpg, had low emissions and 100mph performance. The Spiritual was outstandingly space-efficient and had room up front for crumple zones and crash protection and had a 'wheel at each corner' in a package only a little bigger than the 1959 car.

It all looked terrific but who was actually in charge? A new Mini was the biggest challenge and creative opportunity in global automotive design. Everyone would have an opinion. BMW had huge styling and product-engineering resources, both in Munich and in the US, since acquiring the DesignWorks studio in Newbury Park, southern California in 1995 (which didn't just do cars but all sorts of other stuff).

In spite of reassurances that the design process would be all-British, a replacement Mini was just too tempting for an ambitious auto designer to pass on. The little machine was the Big One, the Mona Lisa of motor cars. In November 1995 *Autocar* magazine declared the Mini to be the car of the century. It would be voted 'Number One Classic Car of All Time' by *Classic & Sports Car* magazine a year later and European car of the century by a jury of 126 auto experts from thirty-two countries in a poll run in 1999. The Mini took second place behind the Model T Ford for 'Global Car of the Century' – by 742 points to 617. They also voted Giorgetto Giugiaro the most important auto designer of the century and Ferdinand Porsche the most significant automotive engineer.

Thus it was that concepts for a new car were simultaneously emerging in Bavaria as well as in the English Midlands. The Munich version was not a descendant of the car for parsimonious housewives, but a performance machine, a Mini Cooper for the new millennium. Economy and environmental footprint were secondary. Wolfgang Reitzle liked what he was being shown.

Meanwhile behind the scenes at BMW there were furious rows about shackling such a high-value project to a shaggy, unGermanic car that 'let in water and smelled of petrol'.

On 17 October 1995 the Brit-made proposals were put up against the US–German ones (plus one Italian). The Spiritual was also shown in a longer wheelbase, four-door version (the Spiritual Too), looking as radical and innovative as the ADO15 and ADO16 had been almost four decades earlier. The grand shoot-out took place at Gaydon, the newly built BMIH museum that was the site of a spanking-new Rover design and engineering research facility. A fabulous ragbag of historic automotive machinery from the Longbridge and Cowley glory years greeted the solemn executives as they trooped inside.

The stakes were high: rival small-car designs were coming thick and fast, led by the Mercedes-Benz A-class, the Audi A2 and the Ford Ka, before the impact of the Smart was even considered.

The shade of Sir Leonard Lord and his admonition to Issigonis of almost four decades before to 'build the bloody thing' hovered over the proceedings. But just for an instant. This time the English patient could only communicate in a croak. Two models emerged as front runners, the Spiritual and a design from a BMW staffer since 1991, the talented, cigar-smoking Frank Stephenson, who had worked on the corporation's foray into the luxury, off-road market with the X5. Born in Morocco to US parents eight weeks after the launch of the original Mini-Minor, Mr Stephenson's stellar career had thus far followed the globalising auto industry. He had studied car design at Pasadena, California, worked for GM in Michigan, then Ford Werke in Cologne (plus the Ford subsidiary Ghia of Turin) before arriving at booming Beamer in 1991. He would soon be joined by another American, Chris Bangle, as design supremo, who would dramatically (too much so for some) sculpt a new generation of BMWs.

For months to come the design authority swung in the balance: Rover on top, then BMW. Work on the Spiritual ticked over before sputtering out. Rover's nominal design boss, Geoff Upex, put Saddington, the Spiritual's advocate, in charge, with Stephenson reporting to him, but with the American actually in charge of how the final result would look. Mr Bangle declared at the time, 'we think it unfair to put the new Mini in the shadow of the old one'. Which meant that his idea of a replacement might not necessarily be a machine two people wide by two people deep set within a ten-foot-long cube.

In May 1996 the entire project was briefly handed back to Rover. It was renamed R50 and it got a new director called Chris Lee. His comparatively small operation in the Midlands was to be backed by a (much larger) 'shadow' in Munich with lots of shuffling to and fro between the teams. It was a recipe for disaster.

No one had told Alex Moulton that he was no longer required. His second Mini-based prototype, the hydragas-sprung 'Minky II' (a 'hot-cross bun' Mini, cut in four then slightly enlarged in width and length to accommodate a K-series engine and an end-on, five-speed gearbox), was actually running when it was axed in September 1996. It was driven all the way to a BMW test facility in southern Europe; then its Rover sponsors were told to keep out of sight.

The Chrysler joint-venture deal on the Brazil-built engine was contracted meanwhile. That would be the power plant for the new car, which now seemed almost certain to emerge under the hand of the BMW-based design initiative. The Gaydon team were sidelined. An internal memo poured scorn on the E50 as it was now known (in line with BMW coding) as having been 'styled first and packaged second'. It was 'too average a concept' and most damningly 'too serious to have a sense of humour'. The Bavarians had missed the whole essence of Mini-ness.

Relations between the Midlands and Munich became so frosty that Bernd Pischetsrieder had to intervene by hiring a consultant firm called Unicorn to arbitrate between the two. Their advice apparently was that Rover should stop trying to understand BMW's culture and just start doing what they were told. Which is effectively what happened.

Journalists sniffed around. As information leaked, Mini purists feared the worst. The turbulent relationship was getting more and more politically charged as a New Labour government took power. May 1997 seemed like a sea change; a British institution whose glory days in the 'sixties had been followed by years of stodgy oblivion was back in a shiny, made-over 'New' package. Could the same trick be played with another shabby-looking leftover from the fab decade?

Mini concepts were proliferating. At the beginning of 1997, timed for the Monte Carlo Rally, a Mini 'anniversary concept vehicle' had been unveiled – thirty years since the glory days. It was a good-looking little thing, according to those who saw it, tube-framed, an MGF-engined two-seater with recognisable Mini provenance if all gone a bit bulbous. It featured a solid band of wraparound glazing that separated the waistline from the roof, and was styled by thirty-three-year-old Adriaan van Hooydonk, a BMW staffer since 1992 (he would become President of DesignWorks 2001–4). On 9 January the ACV30 stormed round the Monaco Grand Prix circuit in company with three rallying Coopers from the glory days, in a triumphant publicity coup. It would end up in the Museum of Modern Art in New York.

The Spiritual and Spiritual Too (with four doors) were shown at the Geneva Motor Show in March 1997. *Autocar* magazine dedicated a jumbo feature to them as representing the small car's 'big future', egged on by BMW in an ill-concealed bid to upstage the début of the Mercedes A-Class.

In fact they represented a much bolder step into the automotive future, too much so perhaps. Mini purists were getting jittery.

Geoff Upex, the man who seemed to hold the Mini design patrimony in trust, told the magazine: 'We hear a great deal from concerned Mini enthusiasts around the world how we should go forward. We want to show them, first with ACV30 and now with the Spiritual car that we understand the value of what we have and the future of the Mini is safe in our hands.'

What was bubbling to the top of the heap was Frank Stephenson's Munich-made concept. It was transverse-engined and front-wheel-drive. It had key Mini-derived styling cues, the floating roof line above a straight-through waistline, the distinctive windscreen angle, an echo on the bonnet-shut line of the defining Mini front-wing seam, round headlamps, a smiley grille. The wheels were huge compared to the original (at Reitzle's insistence, apparently) and the driving position was straight-legged and laid-back rather than the hunched 'bus driver's' poise of Mini legend.

The interior also had a sort of Mini provenance with an exposed aluminium-coloured dash, an outsize central instrument binnacle, lots of plasticky bits and an ironic row of rocker switches. It wasn't exactly less-is-more austerity but you could see where it was coming from.

At the September 1997 Frankfurt Motor Show Bernd Pischetsrieder and UK Rover boss Walter Hasselkus stood smiling side by side on a lavishly appointed Rover stand. On the eve of the show's opening the 'new' Mini had made a shock appearance badged as a 'Cooper', driving out of a giant paper parcel into the exhibition hall for a few minutes before being chased into the street and back on to the car transporter by a flock of paparazzi and TV crews.

Mini World magazine assumed it was the work of Dave Saddington, 'who was also responsible for the Spiritual seen at Geneva last year'. Nobody from BMW-Rover disabused them. John Cooper was on hand to tell the BBC: 'It's a Mini, the shape is one you would recognise instantly, if a little big bigger, and I'm sure it drives like one too. I'm convinced Sir Alec Issigonis would have been very proud.'

But amid the excitement there was gloom. Herr Hasselkus could not express himself optimistic about Rover breaking even by 2000, indeed at any time. And the 'Mini' so briefly on display was nothing of the sort. It had been put together in summer 1997 with glass-fibre panels taken straight off the clay styling model, fitted on a cut-down Fiat Punto chassis. Nevertheless it conveyed a message. The world thought a new Mini was imminent. It wasn't.

CHAPTER 29

Are We Nearly There Yet?

Mini road rage 2
I'd say most people like the Mini. I'm sure we all get smiles,
waves and/or flashes the majority of the time. There is also
a lot of hatred towards our little mates and I don't know
why . . . you hear them calling out 'You ain't got any money
that's why you have a rubbish old car'; and 'It's like a sardine
tin'; also 'get a proper car like mine'. . .

Mini forum, 2008

Which meant the original still motored on. It had to, to keep
the brand alive. It was amazing really, the car could still be kept
street-legal. Side-impact beams were fitted in doors, a driver's
air bag (from the MGF sports car) and pre-tensioners on seat
belts. On the current forward schedule of EU legislation, the car
could go on being sold until 2002 if demand was still there.

With fuel injection, higher final drive and sound-deadening
this late-late Mini could cruise at motorway speeds more econom-
ically and with far less fuss than ever before. Automatic transmission was dropped, the suppliers could no longer go on
providing boxes in such tiny quantities. There was a new badge,
a winged Mini (based on the old Austin Flying A or so it is said,
although Morris Minor owners would point to the boot badging
of early cars as the inspiration). Rover marketing folk babbled
on cheerfully about Mini brand values – 'energy, escapism, excitement, individuality, innovation'. A lot of them wanted to escape
themselves.

But what was this twilight Mini really? British reviewers were baffled. 'Its dynamics are prehistoric but still great fun,' said one. 'The Mini has to be written off as a car from another era but as an object of basic desire it's still up there with the best of them.' And by now it wasn't particularly cheap. The Mini's boho-bourgeois charms, if not those of their owners, were fading meanwhile. Mini mums (it had never been much good for getting kids in the back) had all but disappeared. The car for the school run had become a people mover or a gigantic four-by-four.

Rover marketeers clutched at something they called 'middle children' – thirty-something men and women who were 'intent on combining the adrenaline-charged excesses of youth culture with the comforts of middle age'. A direct-mail campaign was aimed at 'affluent trend-setters in urban areas', while Rover took the, then, innovative step of launching a website. It had plenty of retro stuff on it, but it was pointed out by marketing commentators that pushing the swinging 'sixties too much might backfire with potential buyers who weren't even anywhere near being born at the time.

There were more limited editions: 1997 saw the 'Paul Smith Mini' (300 for UK and 1,500 for Japan) finished in an austere blue with black leather seats and lots of little designerly tweaks such as bonnet and boot insides in shouty citrus green, like a suit lining. The Japanese loved it.

A new Mini was coming. Everyone knew it. But by now Rover was floundering. The exchange rate was still punitive. BMW's shareholders, led by the Quandt family, demanded results that just could not be delivered. Bernd Pischetsrieder temporarily halted development of both the mid-size R30 and the R50 Mini replacement.

The Rover 75 seemed like the final throw. Its production economics were more viable due to its level of (cheaper) imported content. The factory in which it was to be built (Cowley, now starkly renamed BMW Oxford) had been transformed, while previous owners, British Aerospace, had long before sold off chunks of surplus land for redevelopment. Pischetsrieder's fate rested on the new model, which was being dubbed the 'Last Chance Saloon', in the German press. If it failed, the pro-Reitzle faction would demand his resignation. Without Pischetsrieder, Longbridge would close. The R30, which was still frozen, would not go ahead. And the new Mini? Well, that was anyone's guess.

In June 1998 it was officially indicated that it would be a brand on its own – neither Rover nor BMW but Mini. It would have a dedicated dealer network in Europe and the United States (where its re-entry to the market after a thirty-year absence was being considered as a component of the business plan). Japan would be handled separately.

Marketing experts and psychologists waded in. Academics portentously outlined the problem in 1997, suggesting that the Mini's attraction was not primarily 'at the product level' – that is, do you like this car here before you in the showroom? – but at an 'iconically intangible level' as if it were a kind of romantic mystery. They concluded that 'since this appeal is historically based it is not possible to re-engineer or duplicate', but the attraction would remain while there was demand for that piece of history and the associations that it embodied. A bit like the Royal Family.

Further academic research (based on focus groups drawn from UK classic Mini clubs and car enthusiasts working in the motor trade) revealed that 'the Mini's distinct and unique history associated the brand with celebrity and chic owners of the "trendy" 1960s, such as Twiggy and the Beatles, *The Italian Job* film, Michael Caine, John Cooper Racing and the brand's success in motor sport'. Well, that was a statement of the obvious.

The brand's image was described as 'sporty', 'fashionable', 'cool' – and this was largely a result of the car's handling, which was frequently described as like a 'go kart'. The car's aesthetics were described as 'stylish', 'cheeky', 'small', 'cute', 'different', 'modern' and 'classic'. The car's ability to be customised was also an important part of its appeal. Nobody was asked whether they wanted a means of efficient transport at low cost and low-environmental impact.

Some owners described how owning a Mini 'kept them young, because of its youthful and always fashionable image'; like Granddad in a pair of Levi 501 jeans. The brand's British origins were also a key element of the Mini 'personality'.

So what was BMW meant to do with this sort of stuff? The Bavarian prestige automaker was not going to make a shopping car for housewives. Its ambition was to create a new segment for premium small cars. The chassis, suspension, steering and powertrain engineering would have to be exceptional – to make the best-handling front-drive car in the world. And Mini had to be a long-term success, not just an in-and-out retro fad. It had to do by design what BMC had done entirely by accident in 1960–1 when the yours-for-£100-down baby became the height of fashion (with some timely help from Messrs Cooper and Richmond) and stayed so for years to come.

All that heritage was good but it also introduced huge complications. The reborn Mini would have to be consistent with the spirit of the original, but distinct enough in its own right – and also work globally. The target market wanted a car with 'attitude' but the older British enthusiast wanted something that spoke to the memory of the original. Keeping such Mini fogies on-side required great sensitivity and a certain economy with the truth.

After a briefing on BMW's emerging marketing plans it was reported in British newspapers in summer 1998 that: 'The revitalised and restyled Mini . . . is being promoted as a must-have fashion item for the next millennium . . . Advertising campaigns will use Mary Quant and the Monkees to conjure up the appropriate degree of nostalgia.' It sounded absolutely ghastly.

And it was also publicly stated that 'the new model has been designed by Rover and will, like its ancestor, be built at the Longbridge car plant in Birmingham'. Actually that was not the case at all. BMW were dissembling. At corporate headquarters things were getting pretty desperate.

The launch of the Rover 75 was brought forward. The début at the Birmingham International Motor Show in November 1998 turned into a public opportunity for the increasingly turbulent Bernd Pischetsrieder to rail against the British government's timidity towards the Euro currency and to question whether Longbridge had a future. Two weeks later, Walter Hasselkus resigned, saying he was going because of spiralling losses. He was replaced by Prof. Dr Werner Sämann as chairman and CEO, Rover Group.

The unions agreed to an austerity package of wage freezes and job losses to keep any jobs at all. Pischetsrieder asked for a £200 million state subsidy. The Labour government's answer was no.

This was all very undignified. BMW was being humiliated. Who was the author of this disaster? On 5 February 1999 the supervisory board (with executive power over the main operating board) met in Munich, chaired by Eberhard von Kuenheim, Pischetsrieder's predecessor as chief executive, and architect of the Bavarian company's triumphant rise since the 'sixties. He had backed the move to buy Rover four years earlier.

Pischetsrieder was asked to present his recovery plan for the company. Von Kuenheim rejected it. Pischetsrieder resigned. When the board spilt as to whether his arch-rival Wolfgang Reitzle should take over the job, he too resigned. BMW's production chief, Joachim Milberg, was the last man standing and was appointed boss; and he quickly surprised everybody with his ruthless assessment that Rover had to go at virtually any cost. Land Rover would be sold to Ford along with the research-and-development centre at Gaydon in the Midlands and, ironically perhaps, the British Motor Industry

Heritage Centre on the same site, heavy with Nuffield, Austin and BMC legacy.

BMW's board meanwhile held crisis talks behind closed doors while Rover management talked to no one, especially their own workforce.

The new Milberg regime quickly moved to cut Rover out of the Mini-replacement project altogether. Its first director, a BMW staffer called Dr Heinrich Petra, was put back in charge. In June 1999, of the scores of UK development engineers that had worked on the car for the previous three years, only two decided to go to Munich. Fans and potential customers were not surprisingly kept in the dark as to what was really going on. There had been a glimpse of the new car at the summer 1999 fortieth-birthday party at Silverstone. After the dance of the seven veils at Frankfurt two years earlier the purists got into even more of a tizz.

They would have been appalled to know what was really going on at Rover, where, in early 2000, BMW executives suddenly demanded that all Mini development computer files be hurriedly downloaded on to BMW Research and Engineering Centre hard drives. According to a dissident Rover engineer called Robin Hall: 'BMW had finished the assembly building at Longbridge and wanted to ramp up production for a January 2001 on-sale date. It all looked fantastic when we went to a pep talk in February 2000 explaining what they were going to do. The old dyed-in-the-wool Rover people were sceptical but I was taken in.'

On 15 March came the reality. BMW was bailing out, with a deal under negotiation to sell Longbridge to something called Alchemy Partners, an asset-stripping vehicle that had been prowling round for months. Land Rover and the Gaydon site would be sold to Ford. The Alchemy deal collapsed a month later in a row over who would be funding pensions and redundancies.

On 9 May 2000, BMW sold off the rump of Rover for a nominal £10 to Phoenix Vehicle Holdings, a consortium put together by the former Rover boss John Towers. Union officials would reveal that, almost up to the end, Prof. Werner Sämann, the last BMW-Rover UK head, was dismissing the Phoenix consortium 'as a boy-scout operation that stood no chance of succeeding'. Nevertheless it did succeed.

The deal was generally praised in the British press as going to the only potential bidder that was proposing to retain high-volume car production and full employment at Longbridge. The sweetener in return from BMW was made up of a £427 million interest-free loan and stocks of cars that PVH might sell. At its annual general meeting a week later one BMW shareholder described the 1994 deal to buy Rover as the worst investment decision in German history.

Conspiracy theorists claimed subsequently that Towers tried to hang on to the Mini by claiming it would only work as a premium-priced product produced by an independent small-scale niche producer such as Phoenix. But BMW would be keeping the Mini (now branded as 'MINI'), thank you very much, and the factory at Cowley. Rumours that production of the new Mini would be switched to Germany or somewhere else were quickly denied. A decision to sell in America had yet to be taken.

The rump MG Rover company was allowed to continue building the old Mini at Longbridge for a few months more, the range now consisting of four versions: the Mini Classic Seven, the Mini Classic Cooper, the Mini Classic Cooper Sport and the Mini Knightsbridge. Loyal Mini customers were sent a direct mail in the shape of a box of tissues with a letter suggesting that, while this was a sad occasion, they should wipe their eyes and console themselves by buying one of the last Minis to be manufactured. *Autocar* reported that the executive in charge of the twilight production operation had 'squeezed the necessary cash out of the BMW board' to upgrade the build quality. 'They will be the last version of the current car after forty-one years and I don't want them falling apart in people's garages. These are cars that owners will treasure and the quality must reflect that.' So Wolfgang Vollath told the magazine. 'We've added a washer that should have been installed twenty years ago.'

Mini twilight: The reborn Cooper was the jewel in the Mini crown when BMW took over the sprawling Rover mess – and the Bavarian company invested strategically for the brand in boosting build quality – even though the end was near.

The life-support machine was about to be turned off. The *Financial Times* was unsentimental: 'It does not feel like a terrible loss. Indeed we should all be happy to see the back of what has become a terrible little car . . . A Mini is uncomfortable to get into, uncomfortable to drive and uncomfortable to get out of. It has a weedy throttle, woolly steering and wooden brakes. There is very little space in the front, the back or the boot and it is not even cheap any more.'

The end was near. The wraps formally came off the born-again Mini on Thursday 28 September 2000 at the Paris Auto Salon, where three prototypes were displayed to general excitement. The entire BMW management was present at the show to introduce the car, including Joachim Milberg and finance chief Dr Helmut Panke. Frank Stephenson answered eager questioners, insisting that MINI had 'the genes and many of the characteristics of its predecessor, but is larger, more powerful, more muscular and more exciting'. He would say that.

Six days later, on 4 October 2000, the clattering train at Longbridge was stilled. Crowds began to gather around the antiquated production line, where, so it was rumoured, they still made Minis. A voice from the past boomed from loudspeakers: 'On days like these when skies are blue and fields are green . . . I look around and think about what might have been'. . . older inhabitants would have recognised the voice of Matt Monro. Where was that from? It was the main title theme from *The Italian Job*, a film made three decades before. It still had quite a little following.

That's all folks: The last classic Mini from the Longbridge line drives off into history, October 2000.

Then moments later production-line supervisor Geoff Powell drove the last of 5,378,776 Minis, a Cooper Sport 500, off the production line with 'sixties veteran singer Lulu in the passenger seat. It was all so last-century.

Many Mini personalities were there to see it but John Cooper was too ill to attend. Jack Daniels, aged eighty-eight, said:

> It's a sad day to lose an old friend . . . It's the end of the vehicle but I have always realised for some time that it was inevitable.
>
> We knew the Mini had a finite life. It was going to die three to four years ago. Rover, with due credit, managed to keep it going, but they can't go any further.

John Sheppard said: 'I came from Alvis with Alec in 1957 . . . [He] always told us the car had elegance – not style.' A beaming Paddy Hopkirk said: 'It was a wonderful car, it became part of the nation.' Besides saying 'Fab' quite a lot, Lulu said: 'It reminds me how sweet it was to have a Mini. It brings back a lot of memories of times when things were fun.'

The newly appointed Rover MG chief executive, Kevin Howe, said: 'We are paying tribute to a piece of motoring legend that's been a piece of the nation's heart.'

John Cooper died on Christmas Eve 2000. He had been awarded the CBE in the previous year's New Year's Honours List for services to the motor industry. Jack Daniels died on 27 November 2004, aged ninety-two. 'Issigonis was very much a designer rather than an engineer. His ideas were phenomenal but it took people like Jack Daniels to turn them into reality,' said a contemporary quoted in his obituary. 'Without people such as him the Mini wouldn't have happened.' Daniels had been guest of honour at all sorts of Mini rallies and had travelled to Japan to be hailed by Mini enthusiasts.

Ah yes, those Mini enthusiasts. They were becoming a bit of

a bore. BMW had reassured them all along that the great heritage was safe in their hands. Now, with MINI about to be launched, how would the old guard receive the English-made, German–US styled, Brazilian-engined world car?

And how would a downsized BMW work in America where the Austin-Morris 850 Mini-adventures of the 'sixties were completely forgotten by all except a tiny California-based, English car cognoscenti? Who had ever heard of a Mini? Only the intervention in early 2000 of Scots-born BMW boss Tom Purves, had convinced the Munich management that they should launch the 'small' car in North America at all – and not too long after its European debut. He predicted a sale of 15–20,000 MINIs per year, a tenth of the planned output at Cowley-Oxford.

But meanwhile the new MINI had to work in Mini-heritage-steeped Britain to stay true to the provenance. If it flopped at 'home' how could it play away? Its real-life sales debut was near.

Mini sexpot: The model Mini Moris clad in Agent Provocateur lingerie poses with a MINI Clubman (done up as a bondage-themed police car) at the 2008 Vienna 'Life Ball' in support of AIDS charities. It was held just at the time the global banking system went all wobbly and the cultural cycle was swinging back to pre-PC 'sixties sauciness. From the demure Miss Austin (Mandy Rice-Davies) posing in the back of a Countryman in 1960 to Miss Moris and a Clubman, the Mini has seen it all.

CHAPTER 30

MINI

Forget designing pretty cars. That's completely irrelevant.
A wonderful challenge presents itself to young designers
today – to make a high-efficiency vehicle that will transport four in comfort, has the lowest-possible carbon footprint, is of minimum size and weight and is made of
recyclable materials. That is what a new generation Mini
is really all about.

Dr Alex Moulton, 2008

The MINI suits today so well – global warming, credit
squeeze, the price of oil. And crowded streets, traffic and
tight parking helps – but sentimentality comes into it. The
MINI Cooper is the perfect London car. The mini skirt is
perfect for London legs.

Mary Quant, 2008

At last, on Saturday 7 July 2001, the new MINI went on sale in
Britain – two months ahead of its scheduled launch on the continent of Europe. It would go on sale in North America in March
2002. In the UK the basic MINI One was £10,300; and the MINI
Cooper, £11,600.

There was whiff of 1959 about it all, even if the economic
and cultural landscape of Britain had been utterly transformed.
How would the new MINI be perceived? This time the market
research and advertising had been as sophisticated as money
could buy. The ad agency WCRS had £10 million for the UK

launch. Who would they go for? Thrifty young families? Minimalist modernists? Did MINI exude macho swagger or girlie-car fashion accessory? How gay was it?

It turned out to be a bit of everything. The endearing 'it's a Mini adventure' sales-promotion wheeze was designed to 'present the humour, surprise and quirkiness' of the product, so it was said. It was supposed to be genderless and classless. Pushy estate agents thought it was just the thing.

But MINI's North American ad agency noted in internal research that it had to be a man's car before anything else. 'Women are comfortable driving a guy car, men wince at the thought of being seen in a chick-mobile,' they stated, citing as evidence 'the rise and fall of the new Beetle – as more and more women choose the Bug, fewer and and fewer men do'. MINI in fact would be a hot contender in several subsequent gay car of the year shoot-outs (to be beaten sequentially by the Audi TT).

A little after the UK launch, a forty-seven-year-old German-born graduate of the Royal College of Art, Gert Volker Hildebrand, arrived in Munich as head of MINI design (Frank Stephenson was soon off to Ferrari). He would have distinct ideas about the MINI's gender identity.

Asked what he and his team were going to work on now that the new MINI range was substantially out there (the One, the Cooper and Cooper S), he said: 'Nothing . . . You see, this is the ideal job. Like the old Mini, the new MINI will last another forty years so we have nothing to do.'

In fact there was lots to do. Herr Hildebrand clearly recognised the power of what had been before. His mission was to 'serve the product and the brand, and that has a certain potential and a certain form language', so he told an interviewer. 'It is not my job to create . . . the MINI design [as] my own monument.' That is, although he did not say so, what Alec Issigonis had done over four decades before.

He would explain some of the product-design philosophy in a symposium held in London later. There were strong echoes of the Freudian consumer psychology of the 'fifties that had so appalled the British cultural establishment of the day. But this time his audience was fascinated.

Herr Hildebrand outlined his sensual approach to automotive design, how smell and touch (and the 'taste' of the road) are crucial in making the machine attractive. He cited the work of the California installation artist, Andrea Zittel, originator of the 'Escape Vehicle, a line of snugly appointed mini mobile homes just big enough for a single occupant', as an inspiration.

A car was an 'emotional sculpture', he said, which could subtly incorporate aspects of the human body archetype – 'man, woman and child'. A particular challenge of remaking the Mini was, he said, the need to 'inspire both male and female desire', explaining that the car included a 'cascading male outline' to appeal to women, as well as 'a slight wedge shape to show that it moves forward' (a male response trigger, presumably). There was also a certain amount, as he put it, 'of chrome and Britishness'. But what was most important, he said, was its 'facial expression' – formed by the 'line of the bonnet, radiator grille and front headlamps'. Would women want to mother it – or have a torrid affair with their MINI?

On his reckoning, in the case of the new Mini, 0.01 per cent of the cost went into the design, but design was cited as the main reason for buying by 80 per cent of customers.

How would those whiskery, Anglocentric, Mini retro-design themes play in the global market that MINI was aimed at? Was the fact it was made in Cowley, Oxfordshire, England, of any relevance whatsoever? What did thirty-somethings in Minnesota, Mainz or Maidenhead care about Mary Quant, Alice Pollock, Biba or the Beatles? Should they even be reminded of any of it? It was all such an awfully long time ago.

'People look at the old Mini with rose-tinted spectacles, but they don't want to go back,' Emma Scammell, the UK marketing executive in charge of the 2001 launch, said perceptively at the time. 'We believe that it would be very lazy and cynical of us to borrow that heritage – which is not for us to own or to keep.' Well, that was a disarmingly frank statement on behalf of the German company. Perhaps by now the heritage wasn't quite so fab anyway.

On the other hand, the Mini had a fan base and enthusiast following unlike any other. That was true all over the world. It was abundantly clear that Mini lovers were not docile consumers. They had a deep emotional stake in the 'brand' and in its continuation – of which the Bavarian Motor Works just happened to hold the current stewardship. They were nerdy but they were loyal. And they were everywhere.

The International Mini Meet, for example, had begun as a jolly camping weekend in Germany in 1978 – and had just got bigger and bigger. The annual London-to-Brighton Mini run (which began in 1985, organized by the London and Surrey Mini Club) had become the biggest one-make car event in the world. Those Mini clubs represented the tabernacles of the true faith. How they responded to the new car would surely be crucial to its wider acceptance.

It was not surprising therefore that the secretaries of Mini clubs across the country were invited to Longbridge for the UK launch. It was a shrewd move by BMW – to defuse the loyalists by inviting them into the enemy camp.

> There was a big meal in a Birmingham hotel, lots of food and drink, maybe a hundred or more people there [as one of them recalled]. Some club secretaries were downright hostile, others were much more open-minded. There it was, under sheets. When they came off, I thought: Wow, that's not too bad . . .

> I came back to tell the members about the *Big Change*. 'We'll never have one of those' was the general mood. 'It's a nice car but it's not a Mini' . . .

How would the new car be judged in Britain's traditional motor-industry heartland? The *Coventry Evening Telegraph* expressed itself 'sceptical about BMW's ability to create a modern Mini that would compare with Sir Alec Issigonis's original ground-breaking little car which soldiered on for 40 years. Now I've driven the new MINI, I have to admit BMW has created a superb little successor.'

The *Birmingham Post*, voice of the now Mini-less city, reported:

> Not since the swinging 'sixties has so much interest been shown in a new MINI. The 21st century version, which came on the market at the weekend, has seen crowds of people converging on showrooms to catch a glimpse of the new incarnation of a motoring legend. More than 1,000 orders were taken on Saturday alone, adding to the 4,000 advance orders made since the model was first announced by BMW last autumn . . . The frenzy is in marked contrast to the day in 1959 when the first Mini . . . trundled off the production line virtually unnoticed.

But the UK motoring press had reservations. Even in Cooper form, the new car failed to impress *Autocar*, which thought the 'portly' car's 'sprinting ability slots it into warm-hatch territory . . . Sure, the MINI has enough performance to make it fun, but it's no GTi, at least not in a straight line.'

Then there were the outright dissenters. Lord Snowdon was quoted as saying: 'I can't bear it, it's huge.' The most distinguished anti was perhaps Dr Alex Moulton, the boffinish creator of wondrous suspensions and bicycles, the holder of legendary garden parties, who still could sway the British cultural establishment (if they still cared about such things as automotive design) against how Mini had morphed into MINI.

His recent disagreements with BMW management (but not so much his feud with the elderly Sir Alec, whose post-mortem reputation he was keen to protect) had perhaps conditioned his view. It was pretty damning. As he told *Mini World* at the time:

> It's enormous . . . The [original] Mini was the best-packaged car of all time; this is an example of how not to do it. The interior space is not much bigger than the old Mini, but it's huge on the outside (nearly 12ft long, while the original was ten) and weighs the same as the Austin Maxi! The crash protection has been taken too far. I mean, what do you want . . . an armoured car?

Eight years later his opinion had not changed. The MINI was a 'wicked thing . . . terribly indulgent and far too big', he said, pacing his drawing office in his Jacobean mansion, 'but well made and well engineered', he had to concede.

Actually the upscaling was around 55 centimetres (22 in.) longer, 30 centimetres (12 in.) wider and the kerb weight was 1,050 kg (2,315 lb) rather than the 650 kg (1,433 lb) of the original. But rear legroom and luggage space was indeed less, not more.

The termination of the Minky and the rejection of hydragas for the suspension clearly still rankled. 'The suspension of the [BMW] Mini Cooper is set far too stiff, giving a most uncomfortable ride,' Alex Moulton told *Mini World*. 'To be honest, it's an irrelevance in so far that it has no part in the Mini story . . .' And he'd added this: 'I think [Alec] Issigonis would deplore the new car.'

His view was taken up by the ultra-purists. The use of the

Mini name was a 'travesty', they said. The fifteen-inch wheels threw away the whole point of a go-kart turned into a practical means of transport. It was the 'bloated impostor'. It was the 'BINI' – built by the Teutonic occupiers of Stalag Oxford. It was the 'faux-Mini, a camp parody of the Metro development hack'.

'It's a mongrel of a car, built by the Germans who own the name, powered by the Brazilians, designed by an American and bolted together by English production-line workers,' said an on-line MINI hater.

An American Mini owner (1969 Cooper S Mk 2) was quoted as saying: 'The Mini has ceased production but somehow the name has been scrounged from the dead. They are nothing but grave robbers . . .'

Minidom split. There were those who poured scorn while others hailed the new MINI as a worthy successor. Indeed it was the only way the concept could have gone forward within modern safety, emissions and manufacturing regulatory regimes. As BMW executives explained: 'It had to grow a bit for safety reasons . . . and comfort. We asked ourselves, how would the Mini have grown if it had not been frozen in time? People are taller (and fatter) . . . safety, comfort, equipment, all need more space.' The company had also taken all that after-market customising stuff from the great legacy to heart. All sorts of custom trim and paint jobs could be factory-enabled. BMW called it, somewhat uncomfortably, 'youification'.

Some Mini clubs banned MINI owners from membership. Notts About Mini club held a referendum that decided: 'Owners of the small BMW will be allowed to join provided they own a classic, and that the small BMW is not brought to club meets, events and shows.' The A's of Herts Mini club decided to admit MINIs – having staged a mock funeral complete with hearse and cortège through the streets of Stevenage and Letchworth the day the Mini died.

Mini was no more but there was life in the old girl yet. Mini purists cheered loudly in 2001 when Matt Damon, playing the amnesiac Jason Bourne in the action movie *The Bourne Identity*, escaped from mysterious tormentors alongside scowling Marie Kreutz (played by German actress Franka Potente) in her agreeably battered red Mini (with replacement front wing in black primer). It was payback for all that Bond spurning of the English fabmobile.

'What the hell is that?' exclaims Alexander Conklin, the villainous CIA man, when he first sees the little car in an icy Swiss alley on the US embassy's security CCTV. He might well ask. Then, after a cosily snowbound Mini drive from Zurich to Paris, the boyish hero flings it around the French capital ('it pulls a bit to ze right', the Germanic Marie warns when he takes the wheel for the first time – in an exquisite, driverly touch that still makes the neck hairs of Mini fans bristle) to escape the bungling police. In those blazing ten minutes of Mini action, Bourne buried Bean for ever.

Five cars were used up in the filming until, in the on-screen action, the elusive Mini is finally (darn) abandoned in an underground garage after a chase in which few of the Paris locations actually connect to each other. But who cares. 'You know you can never go back to that car,' Bourne tells Marie in a moment of Mini heartbreak. Meanwhile Bourne fans can spot lots of Minis in the background, generally being as chic as ever in Paris traffic. It was an echo of those glory days so long before when the French capital fell for the BMC baby (it would also feature in all sorts of Francophone art films of the 'sixties and 'seventies, too obscure as yet for deep Mini analysis).

But a Mini was chosen for its totemic outing in Bourne as being consciously retro, apparently. 'It was the kind of car that her [Franka Potente's] character, a gypsy, could have,' the film's producer Frank Marshall told *USA Today*. 'It's got to be at least 20 to 25 years since that model was made. So it was an old car but it was also a hip car,' he said.

Shows what Mr Marshall knew – the Mini was still in production less than two years earlier. But it *was* hip.

Would Americans think the MINI was hip? In the year following its March 2002 launch, 24,000 early adopters across the USA voted with their wallets. Coopers and Cooper S's were big news.

Manhattan was the top-performing franchise. 'MINI sightings are increasingly common, even outside the early Mini enclaves of the West Village and Park Slope,' reported the *New York Times*. 'Smallness is a relatively foreign concept to American car culture,' the newspaper continued. 'And it is true that driving in the MINI makes SUVs look like monster trucks. But the boxy, slick, toy-like car can fit into parking spaces previously unseen. And it can dart in and out of tight traffic.' It could have been a report from soon-to-be-swinging London around 1961–2.

The top complaint in an independent 2003 quality survey among American owners was that the cupholders (yes, the MINI had two) were too small – 'only enough for a regular soda'. MINI sent nearly every US buyer a complimentary mug that actually fitted. A clever accessory company devised a Big Gulp version.

In October 2004 there was the first big design stretch under Gert Hildebrand's stewardship when the MINI convertible (with lots of body-shell stiffening) was launched at the Paris Auto Salon, available in One, Cooper and Cooper S versions. It was an instant hit.

The made-over MINI Mk II appeared in September 2006 after much more than just a mid-life facelift. Every exterior panel was different and the car was 60 mm longer but it came in marginally lighter. The Brazil-made BMW-Chrysler engine had been supplanted by a 1.6-litre unit made at Hams Hall, Birmingham. On 3 April 2007, the one-millionth MINI rolled out of the Oxford plant after six years of production – it had taken a month longer than it took the Issigonis Mini to reach the same total in March 1965.

As that milestone was reached, the MINI Cooper D was

launched, 'the cleanest car the BMW group has ever built', with exemplary carbon-dioxide and particulate-emission figures and excellent fuel economy from a 1.6-litre turbocharged diesel engine. The green but go-fast MINI was hailed as a statement of intent on how BMW and the wider motor industry should be heading.

It had taken just a year for the Issigonis baby to stretch into the estate variants it had launched in October 1960. Over four decades later an early Traveller had been lent by an American enthusiast to the BMW DesignWorks design shop in California, whose trendy inhabitants had apparently gone mad for it. But would a tribute 'woody' MINI emerge as a result?

An extended-wheelbase 'estate' MINI, the R55, had been in development since soon after the orginal MINI's production début. What to call it? The 'Traveller' and 'Countryman' names had copyright problems – and it turned out that the somewhat tainted Clubman name was owned by Honda in Japan. It was applied to a motorcycle. Knowing a stretched version was coming, Mini ironists had suggested a torrent of names on a US automotive website before the official launch. They included the 'Extendo', 'Stretch', 'Trunkster', 'Colossus', 'Royale', 'Beyond', 'Affair', 'Issigonis', 'Pubman', 'U-Boat', 'Englishman', 'Hopkirk', 'Churchill', 'Oxford', 'Big', 'Function' – and 'BMW 0.7 Series'. All were corkers. In the end it was 'Clubman'.

When it finally went on sale in the UK in September 2007, BMW haters dubbed it the 'Clubfoot – an absurd and largely pointless variant of the goitred fraud'. A lot of people rather liked it. It had long been rumoured that MINI would appear in a 'Moke' version or even as a sport ute, something that had Mini purists spluttering in disbelief. 'That's really a joke . . . You've got to be kidding . . . MINI and SUV just don't mesh . . . a MINI 4 x 4? What a joke' were typical blog posts. The project had been given the codename 'Colorado' before the cultural mood turned against automotive frontier muscularity.

The 'cute-ute' MINI was supposed to be immune to the black

looks that greeted drivers of more profligate urban off-roaders. The protoype 4 x 4 MINI 'Crossover' (as it emerged) was shown at the Paris Auto Salon in October 2008. It was 'the biggest Mini yet'. Was that a good thing? It was almost the size of a Ford Focus. Cars always get bigger. But there was another twist.

In summer 2008, veteran rally driver Paddy Hopkirk was at the MINI factory, Oxford, when he noticed some curious vehicles with blanked-off fuel-tank filler flaps. Nor was there much under the bonnet. Shsssh!

The mystery would soon be solved. The existence of E-MINI was revealed in the summer – a MINI powered, as it was announced, by a '150 kW (204 hp) electric motor fed by a high-performance rechargeable lithium-ion battery, transferring its power to the front wheels via a single-stage helical gearbox nearly without a sound and entirely free of emissions'.

MINI Switch-on: The E-MINI hit the freeways of California, New Jersey and New York in late 2008 in a controlled experiment by BMW in a bid to get a practical electric car into the marketplace in line with US legislation. But was it a genuine technological step-change or an expedient boost of the company's eco credentials? MINI meanwhile proved the ideal brand to show the BMW Group as a whole was serious about green-engineering.

E-MINI was a two-seater, the rear cabin space taken up by those rechargeable batteries made up of 5,088 cells. The car had been developed not as an eco-fad but in direct response to California's zero-emissions vehicle programme, which required nearly 60,000 plug-in cars to be sold in the state between 2012 and 2014. Five hundred would be made available to 'select retail and corporate customers' in the states of California, New York and New Jersey on a 'pioneering mission' to test all-electric vehicles in a practical environment, BMW announced. The Oxford-made hull would be fitted out with drivetrain and batteries in Bavaria then shipped to the US. There was a catch. 'Only lockable garages or similar buildings will qualify as homebases and power stations for the MINI E,' it was stated.

There were lots of subtle branding tricks – like a logo of a stylised power plug in the shape of an 'E' and numbering 0–500 on the car's silvery flanks as if the cars were a limited edition of fine-art prints. Such caprices ensured that MINI E drivers could say, 'look at me, I'm rich and saving the planet at the same time'. They were the classic early adopters, the fearless few who would embrace the new technology and be proud. As BMW said: 'The MINI E is a trendsetter – and this also applies to the customers driving these automobiles within the scope of the pilot project. Together, they are charting the course towards a new form of mobility . . .' It could have been 1959, except the Mini beta testers of the Macmillan years had not signed up to be guinea pigs for a new era in transportation. But that is effectively what they were.

And the actual machine itself? According to BMW:

> Thanks to the electric drive's intrinsic properties, the MINI E has an impressive degree of elasticity. The engine's thrilling, instantaneous pickup enables extremely spontaneous bursts of speed. Since the vehicle's suspension has been fine-tuned to the car's

weight distribution, the MINI E possesses the brand's trademark agility when thrown into bends and rapid changes of direction and boasts outstanding road holding capabilities in city traffic.

The MINI E was launched at the LA motor show in late November 2008, a surreal affair full of hybrids, electrics and alternative future automotive concepts – while executives from the three giant US automakers Ford, Chrysler and General Motors failed to attend. They were in Washington, DC, pleading for a $25 billion government bail-out of the motor industry as it teetered on the edge of bankruptcy. Some commentators said it had been culturally bankrupt for years.

The centenary of Sir Alec Issigonis's birth in 2006 was marked by special events all over the world. The biggest tribute of all perhaps was a new wave of small cars from Europe and Japan that reopened the Mini designer's book on packaging vehicles with maximum internal space and minimum footprint. The Fiat 500, spectacularly launched in Italy in summer 2007, was a very fashionable hit – with Mini-style front-wheel drive but plenty of stylistic tributes to Dante Giacosa's tiny rear-engined triumph of fifty years before (if weighing almost twice as much). Fiat designer Roberto Giolito did the fundamentals of Europe's first big retro-car statement post the MINI, while the busy Frank Stephenson had an input on the styling.

In autumn 2008 Toyota (for whom the octogenarian Alex Moulton had acted as a consultant) launched the IQ, the 'world's smallest four-seat car', a front-wheel-drive, urban warrior (but more powerful than a kei car). The IQ was the same length as the 1959 Mini but its spectacularly un-cute styling was unburdened by ghosts of the automotive past.

Volkswagen's Up!, originally trailed as the 'spiritual successor to the original Beetle', emerged in prototype form in 2008 with front-wheel drive. Beyond that a VW microcar was slated, codenamed the 'Chico', a three-door hatch with promised astonishing fuel efficiency and ultra-low emissions. And there were persistent industry rumours that BMW was exploring the potential of a sub-mini, an 'Isetta' from the bubble boom, reborn after over fifty years.

As MINI approached its ninth birthday in the spring of 2009 and Mini its fiftieth, the war between the classic die-hards and fans of the 'small BMW performance car' was effectively over. The Mini, at last, really did belong to history – as its creator, himself always striving to create an even more innovative replacement – had expected it to do. It was a twentieth-century classic to be revered as such – while BMW had proved a practical, indulgent, respectful, intuitive and constantly innovative (in both marketing and technical terms) inheritor of the patrimony. Issigonis was half-Greek, half-Bavarian. Perhaps it needs an outsider to make a British icon.

MINI had proved a stunning market success around the world. Sales had far outstripped original expectations. Would MINI last as long? In snow-bound Munich, as car assembly lines shuddered to a halt amid global economic turmoil, Gert Hildebrand, the man in charge of future MINI design, thought that it had every chance. He outlined a future where the 'mass motoring' age (where the BMC baby had come in) was effectively ending – where the business of communicating would be increasingly done electronically – and cars became part of leisure and lifestyle. That is where MINI was so strong. But the future engineering challenge was the same, he said, 'to take the basic idea of Issigonis – the biggest amount of passenger room on the smallest footprint,' and make it work.

'You should visit BMW World,' he said, the fabulous super-showroom outside the factory that strangely resembles a Bond-villain's movie hideaway.

'Where's MINI world?' this visitor asked.

'It is everywhere,' he replied. 'MINI world is in the streets.' And he was right.

Mini Timeline

1906
Alexander Arnold Constantine Issigonis born in Smyrna, Ottoman empire

1922–3
Issigonis and his mother move to England

1925
Issigonis starts an engineering course at Battersea Technical College, London

1943
Issigonis and small team develop Morris Mosquito prototype at Cowley

1945
Clement Attlee's Labour Party wins general election
Council of Industrial Design formed and mounts Britain Can Make It Exhibition
British civil car production restarts – manufacturers are told, 'export or die'

1948
October first post-war Motor Show, launch of Morris Minor

1950
Petrol rationing ends

1951

3 May – Festival of Britain opens

27 October – Churchill becomes Prime Minister

1952

Nuffield (Morris) and Austin merge to become the British Motor Corporation

Issigonis quits for Alvis

1954

Jack Daniels completes experimental front-wheel-drive Morris Minor

1955

Issigonis returns to the BMC

1956

August–November – Suez Crisis. Petrol rationing in UK. Leonard Lord orders Issigonis to create a small, fuel-efficient car

1957

22 February – First run of prototype XC9003

19 July – Leonard Lord takes test run; production approved

20 July – Harold Macmillans's 'never had it so good' speech

1958

Intensive testing of ADO15 at Chalgrove, Oxfordshire

Design work begins on 'buckboard' military miniature

1959

March – The first Morris Mini-Minor comes off the pre-production line.

May – Mini production starts.

26 August – Austin Se7en and Morris Mini-Minor in basic and de-luxe versions go on sale.

September – RAF test V-bomber and prototype 'Moke' compatibility in bizarre experiment

8 October – Conservative government re-elected

2 November – First section of M1 is opened

September – First works Mini competes in an international event, Viking Rally, finishes 51st overall

November – Mini wins the Mobil economy run, 61.7 mpg over 1,000 miles

1960

January – Downton Engineering offer Mini performance modification for £39

Wolseley Hornet and Riley Elf introduced

1961

17 July – press launch of Mini Cooper: the 1071 S introduced with 70 hp, along with the 997 Cooper with 55 hp

All Minis except 850 get remote gearboxes

Early version of the Pill is introduced in UK for married women only

Austin Se7en becomes Austin Mini

December – 500,000th Mini completed

December – *Autocar* reviews Downton Engineering's 'mini-ton bomb'

1962

21 September – Ford Consul Cortina launched

1963

14 January – British application to the European Economic Community fails

March–June – Profumo Affair: details of the War Minister's affair two years earlier seep into the press

27 March – Beeching Report published

4 May – John Cooper seriously injured in Twini Mini prototype crash on Kingston by-pass

October – Beatlemania begins

November – Prof. Colin Buchanan's *Traffic in Towns* published

1964

January – Cooper S wins first of three Monte Carlo rallies

Hopkirk and Liddon drive on to stage of *Sunday Night at the London Palladium*

Three new Cooper models introduced: 970 and 1275 Cooper S and 998 Cooper. 1071S and 997 Coopers discontinued

Introduction of hydrolastic suspension

15 October – Labour government elected under Harold Wilson

1965

January – Timo Mäkinen wins the Monte Carlo Rally in Cooper S

Millionth Mini produced

Summer – miniskirts become UK high-street fashion

November – Italian-built Innocenti Mini 850 introduced

Fiat-backed Autobianchi Primula launched, using transverse engine driving the front wheels

November – Ralph Nader's *Unsafe at Any Speed* published

Mini-Moke launched in Austin and Morris badged versions

December – UK maximum speed limit of 70 mph introduced

1966

January – 'Stolen' Monte Carlo Rally victory

March – Innocenti Mini Cooper (998cc)

15 April – *Time* Magazine profiles 'Swinging London'

30 July – England beat West Germany 4–2 to win World Cup

Riley & Wolseley models get wind-up windows

BMC & Pressed Steel merge with Jaguar Cars, forming British Motor Holdings (BMH)

1967

January – Aaltonen wins the Monte Carlo Rally in Mini Cooper S

9 October – Road Safety Act introduces breathalyser

The Mini Mk I replaced by the Mk II with bigger rear lights and a larger rear windscreen

December – Beatles *Magical Mystery Tour* features 'psychedelic' Mini

1968

January – Mini Cooper S comes third in the Monte Carlo Rally

BMH merges with the Leyland Motor Corporation, to form British Leyland Motor Corporation (BLMC)

March – Mini production stops at Cowley

October – UK Moke production ends

1969

Mini replacement Project 9X shelved

Mini Clubman introduced. Last Mk II 1275 Cooper S and 998 Coopers built, replaced by Mini 1275 GT; rubber-cone suspension reintroduced to all models

Mk II Countryman and Traveller discontinued

2-millionth Mini built

All models get wind-up windows

27 August – Alec Issigonis knighted

Mini Coopers star in *The Italian Job*

Fiat 128 launched, using transverse engine driving front wheels

1970

18 June – Conservative government elected

Exernal door hinges moved out of sight

Range Rover 'luxury' 4 x 4 launched and Morris Minor production ends

1971

1275 Cooper S Mk III discontinued

Best year for Mini sales: 318,475 built

Issigonis retires. Continues at Longbridge as a consultant

Fiat 128 launched, first true 'supermini'

1972

17 February – 15,007,034th VW Beetle off line, beats Ford
  Model T's previous production record

Mini 1275 GT receives 8″ disc brakes and 12″ wheels

1973

1 January – Britain joins the European Economic
  Community

October – OPEC oil-price shock

1974

10 October – general election gives Harold Wilson and Labour
  a small majority

1975

BLMC nationalised to become British Leyland Ltd

3 November – first North Sea oil comes ashore

1976

May – Mini 1000 Special Limited Edition

1977

Punk rock

Leyland cars split up into Austin Morris (volume-car business)
  and Jaguar Rover Triumph (upmarket)

16 September – singer Marc Bolan killed as passenger in Mini
  1275GT

1978

Mini given transitory UK sales and marketing boost

1979

January – Winter of Discontent

3 May – Conservative government elected under Margaret Thatcher

Mini 850 City Saloon, last of the 850s

Iranian revolution; second oil-price shock

1980

August Clubman and 1275 GT discontinued

Austin Mini-Metro launched; Mini production continues

1981

December – Mini Van and Pickup discontinued

Australian Moke production ends

1982

Mini 1000 City E Saloon (until 1988) new economy model

British Leyland renamed the Austin Rover Group

1983

January – seatbelts in cars made compulsory in Britain

Mini Sprite Limited Edition 1983

Moke production starts in Portugal

1984

May – UK miners' strike begins

May – last of the 10″-wheel Minis leave factory, replaced by 12″ Mini 25 Limited Edition

1985

Mini Ritz Limited Edition

1986

Yuppie boom

Mini Chelsea Limited Edition

Mini Piccadilly Limited Edition

5-millionth Mini is driven off the production line by Noel Edmonds; ARG becomes the Rover Group; production to end in two years' time

1987

Mini Park Lane Limited Edition

Mini Advantage Limited Edition

Wave of Japanese ironic 'retro' cars

1988

British Aerospace Plc buys the Rover Group from the British government; Mini is a 'nice little earner' and reprieved

Mini Red Hot Limited Edition

Mini Jet Black Limited Edition

Mini Designer (Quant) Limited Edition

Mini Sky Limited Edition

Mini Rose Limited Edition

Mini Racing Limited Edition

Mini Flame Limited Edition

9 October – Sir Alec Issigonis dies

1989

Mini 30 celebrations cause huge Mini traffic jam (25,000) crowding into Silverstone racetrack

Moke production in Portugal stops

9 November – protesters begin to dismantle Berlin Wall

Trabants flood west

1990

Mini Racing Green Limited Edition

Studio 2 Limited Edition
Mini Cooper SE (RSP) Limited Edition
22 November – Margaret Thatcher resigns
November – First *Italian Job* rally from UK to Turin to raise
money for UK and Italian charities

1991
January–February – Gulf War
Mini Neon Limited Edition
Mini Cooper 1.3i with fuel-injected engin
Mini Cabriolet from LAMM Autohaus

1992
British Open Classic Limited Edition with factory-fitted
sunroof
Mini Italian Job Limited Edition
Mini Cooper 1.3 Si Limited Edition (John Cooper)
Mini Sprite 1275 c
Mini Mayfair 1275 cc

1993
The 998cc engine discontinued and all Minis receive one of
the two 1.3i-engine versions with either 54 or 63 hp
Mini Cabriolet 1275 cc (until 1996)
Mini Rio Limited Edition
Mini Tahiti Limited Edition

1994
29 January – BMW buys Rover from British Aerospace and
Honda Motor Co. for £800 million
Mini-Cooper Monte Carlo Limited Edition pays tribute to Paddy
Hopkirk's 1964 win
August – Mini-Cooper Grand Prix LE by John Cooper Garages
Dr Alex Moulton, John Cooper and the now-eighty-three-year-old

Jack Daniels brought in by Rover to consult on 'new' Mini
– which will be 'all British' in design and manufacture

1995

June – Mini-Cooper S LE by John Cooper Garages

October – Mini replacement proposals presented to Rover-BMW
management. American Frank Stephenson's design noses
ahead

November – *Autocar* declares the Mini car of the century

1996

Mini Equinox Limited Edition

Mini Cooper 35 Limited Edition

October – Launch of Mini 1.3i and Mini Cooper 1.3i with front-
mounted radiator, multi-point fuel injection system on
engine, steering-wheel air bag, reinforced doors and seatbelt tensioning system on all production Minis

BMW announces deal to build engines for 'new' Mini with
Chrysler in Brazil

1997

January – Mini ACV 30 concept car shown at Monte Carlo Rally

March – UK-designed Spiritual and Spiritual Too Mini replace-
ments shown at Geneva Motor Show.

4 May – general-election landslide win for Labour under Tony
Blair

BMW announces deal to build engines with Chrysler in Brazil

September – 'MINI 2000' concept car shown to excitable press
at Frankfurt motor show

1998

March – Paul Smith LE

June – Stand-alone MINI brand announced

1999

5 February – BMW board in turmoil over Rover fiasco

Hybrid vehicles appear on general sale in the US

Mini 40 Limited Edition

Mini John Cooper LE Limited Edition (John Cooper)

December – BMW cancels the last production run of 3,000 Japan-spec cars insisting that there must be no overlap between what is now known as the classic Mini and the 'new' MINI

2000

9 May – Phoenix consortium signs deal with BMW to take over Rover Cars for £10. BMW retains Mini and Triumph brands

28 September – World debut of 'new' MINI (MINI One and MINI Cooper) at Paris auto salon

4 October – Longbridge Mini production ceases. Last one off production line is registered X411JOP and goes to the Heritage Museum

24 December – death of John Cooper

2001

John Cooper Garages begin developing aftermarket tuning kits for the new MINI

7 July – MINI goes on sale in the UK

Mini Mk II features in *The Bourne Identity*

11 September – terrorist attack destroys World Trade Center in New York

October – MINI Cooper S presented at Tokyo Motor Show

2002

March – MINI Cooper and MINI Cooper S go on sale in the US

2003

20 March – US-led invasion of Iraq begins

2004

October – MINI convertible launched at Paris Salon International de l'Auto (released in 2005 model year) available in One, Cooper and Cooper S versions

27 November – death of Jack Daniels

2006

November – worldwide commemorations of centenary of the birth of Sir Alec Issigonis

November – Mk II MINI launched in Cooper and Cooper S versions

December – BMW Group acquire the rights to the John Cooper Works brand

2007

3 April – 1-millionth MINI from BMW Oxford (Cowley)

Oil price climbs

2008

US car companies plea for government bail-out

November – two-seat E-MINI unveiled at LA auto show

2009

February – 850 agency workers dismissed at BMW Plant Oxford following a 35 per cent slump in MINI sales due to global credit crunch

Countdown begins to Mini's 50th anniversary worldwide celebrations, including Mini United in May and International Mini Meet in August

APPENDIX

50 Mini Facts

1 Alec Issigonis made a prototype small car in between fire-watching at wartime Cowley. It was codenamed the 'Mosquito'; a luxury version was planned called the Wolseley 'Wasp'. It would emerge in 1948 as the Morris Series MM Minor

2 Issigonis drew the first design sketch for his miniature vehicle on a napkin in a restaurant in Davos, Switzerland

3 It was the first car to have a suspension system using rubber instead of steel springs

4 An early codename was Austin Newmarket (a bit like Austin Cambridge, you see – pun intended)

5 Early press reports in 1959 stated that the BMC 'people's car' would have a diagonally mounted engine

6 The informal codename at the factory was 'Sputnik'

7 The first 848cc Mini cost £496 and 19 shillings, including tax

8 Water leaks were endemic in the cars' first winter. Owners wrapped electrical components in plastic bags

9 When told of the leak problems, Issigonis explained 'there was no rain in 1959'

10 When women started buying them Issigonis said 'what could be worse than a suburban housewife with money'

11 Around 15,000 Austin and Morris 850s were exported to the United States before 1968 when federal bumper-height regulations came in

12 The UK government's 'Cars for Cities' report of 1966 recommended the building of aerial urban roadways exclusively

for Mini-sized vehicles and the provision of Mini-sized parking spaces

13 First reviews from design and architecture pundits were critical of the BMC miniature's styling – it looked like a 'pudding'

14 In 1959 the Longbridge assembly line was 220 yards long. There were 57 work stations and each task took 2 mins + 24 secs, making a little over 2 hours to make each car

15 When racing driver Stirling Moss complained on a test drive that the seats were uncomfortable he was told by Issigonis that it was deliberate, to stop people falling asleep

16 Moss got a driving ban in 1961 while testing a Mini for a 'Sunday newspaper'

17 Mini Mk Is had a start button on the floor

18 The chairman of Ford blamed the demise of BMC (absorbed by Leyland in 1968) on the Mini's hopeless production economics – it was estimated that every car was made at a £30 loss

19 Because commercial vehicles were exempt from purchase tax, the Mini Van cost only £360 when launched

20 The Twini Mini of 1964, with an engine at both ends, created a 2.3-litre car with explosive performance. When John Cooper crashed the prototype on a public road, development was suspended

21 The Mini has been made in different forms in Portugal, Australia, New Zealand, Italy, Belgium, South Africa, Chile, Venezuela and Spain

22 Call-girl Christine Keeler drove a Mini

23 As did War Minister John Profumo (a red Mini-Minor), whose dalliance with Miss Keeler, partly conducted within it in the summer of 1961, precipitated a political scandal two years later

24 As did party girl Mandy Rice-Davies, who aged sixteen had been Miss Austin at the 1960 Earl's Court Motor Show and posed with the first Countryman

25 Much-hated Transport Minister Ernest Marples commissioned a special-bodied Mini Cooper hatchback to carry his golf clubs and crates of wine. He told civil servants he had to be seen to be 'up to date'

26 In autumn 1959 RAF Bomber Command tested a stripped-down 'BMC minicar' carried in the bomb bay of a Vickers Valiant nuclear bomber. No operational requirement was forthcoming

27 The British Army and Royal Marines tested the militarised Mini 'Moke' but found its ground clearance inadequate. A twin-engine version was trialled by the US Army

28 The best year for Mini sales was 1971 at 318,475 cars overall

29 Minis were manufactured at the Longbridge and Cowley plants in the UK and later in Australia, Belgium, Chile, Italy, Portugal, South Africa, Spain, Uruguay, Venezuela and Yugoslavia

30 After Paddy Hopkirk and Henry Liddon won the Monte Carlo Rally in a Mini in 1964, the car was flown from Nice airport to appear on the stage of the TV show *Sunday Night at the London Palladium*

31 The enthusiasts' club for the Riley Elf is called 'The Elf Preservation Society'

32 An electric Mini (a Morris Traveller) was built and tested in 1966, with a range of 25 miles – later electric Minis had only marginally improved performance

33 Issigonis experimented with a steam-powered Mini

34 And one with infinitely variable gearing

35 In 1966 suspension pioneer Alex Moulton built a hydragas-sprung Morris Mini Cooper S that was so comfortable he

could 'write reports in the back seat' while his chauffeur propelled him to meetings at high speed

36 Prof. Colin Buchanan, author of the 1963 *Traffic in Towns* report, drove a Jaguar and disliked Minis for causing 'inconsiderate' driving

37 The world record for cramming people into a Mini is 66 – achieved as a TV stunt in 1986

38 Mary Quant created the Mini Designer special edition in 1988

39 In 1991 sales of Minis in Japan were greater than in the UK

40 100,000 owners from all over the world attended the Mini's 40th birthday party

41 In 2003 artist Damien Hirst painted a W-Reg Mini with spots 'for charity', but its display in London by his patron, gallery owner Charles Saatchi, caused a huge row between them

42 The drivers of Minis at Knowsley Safari Park in Merseyside have been chased by confused lions who think they are prey

43 T.Rex singer Marc Bolan died on 16 September 1977 when the Mini 1275GT being driven by his girlfriend Gloria Jones crashed in London

44 In Madonna's song 'American Life', she sings 'I drive my Mini Cooper and I feel super-dooper'

45 The actor Kevin Spacey (who had a Jack Russell terrier named Mini) paid $130,000 at a charity auction for the very last Mini Cooper off the assembly line

46 The Microcar Club of America counts over 150 marques and models as eligible (including Minis)

47 In tribute to the original Mini, the Mazda Suitcase car was designed and built in 1991 as part of a design contest based on the idea 'What if you could get off a plane, get your luggage, and instead of waiting in line for a taxi or shuttle . . . pop open your suitcase and drive off?' It worked

48 Joanne Westlake was the first person to be born in a Mini

49 Among research projects for a replacement Mini was the 'Minky II' of 1996, a 'hot-cross bun' Mini, cut in four then widened and lengthened to accommodate a Rover K-series engine and end-on gearbox

50 In 2007 Future Vehicles Ltd marketed a reworked classic Mini powered by an electric motor for £17.5k+ and BMW launched the two-seat, 95mph-capable E-MINI in 2008 that could go 150 miles between charges

Index

A's of Herts Mini Club, 261
Aaltonen, Rauno, 129, 153–4, 157, 170, 177
Abingdon, 38, 43, 121, 123, 129, 131, 175
About Town magazine, 104
advertising, 28–32, 96
    and market research, 30, 75, 80, 98–9,
        203, 208, 245–6, 255
    and safety, 102–3
Affluent Society, The (Galbraith), 28
Agnelli, Giovanni, 138
Aintree, 89, 128
Al Khalifa, Sheikh Khalifa bin Salman, 151
Alchemy Partners, 248
Alexandra, Princess, 114
Alvis, 66–8, 79, 252
AMC Rambler, 76
Amsterdam Trade Fair, 165
Architectural Review, 72, 92
Arden Racing and Sports Cars, 122
Argosy tracked amphibian, 38
Aston Martin, 80, 163
Atkinson, Rowan, 212, 224
Attlee, Clement, 20, 72
Audi, 191, 238, 256
austerity, 29, 31, 63
Austin, Lord (Herbert), 54, 88
Austin company, 22, 34, 36–7, 43–5, 88,
    178–9, 248
Austin A30, 44, 55
Austin A35, 55–6
Austin A40, 22, 36, 56–7, 69, 74, 86, 92, 97,
    124
Austin A55, 57
Austin Atlantic, 21, 55
Austin Cambridge, 55, 69, 87
Austin Champ, 163–4
Austin Devon, 55
Austin Dorset, 55
Austin Hampshire, 55
Austin Healey, 76, 121, 187, 229
Austin Hereford, 36, 55
Austin Maestro, 207
Austin Maxi, 187, 189–90, 213, 260
Austin Metropolitan, 55, 114
Austin Montego, 207
Austin Princess, 65

Austin Seven, 44, 85–6
Austin Somerset, 55
Austin Westminster, 55, 65
Austin-Rover Group, 207, 217, 219
Australia, 57, 116, 165–6, 205
Authi, 189
Autobahnen, 71
Autobianchi Primula, 191
Autocar magazine, 41, 91, 130, 137, 158, 189,
    205, 224, 230, 237, 240, 249, 259
Automobile Industries magazine, 228
Avengers, The, 167
Avon Rubber, 68

'badge engineering', 45
Bahrain, 151
Balmoral, 50
Bangle, Chris, 238
Banham, Reyner, 63, 107
Barnes Common, 194–5
Baron, The, 167
Bassey, Shirley, 138
Battersea Technical College, 37
BBC, 60, 152, 170, 241
Bean, Mr, 212, 262
Beatles, 116, 152, 156, 214, 245, 257
Beaton, Cecil, 113
Beckett, Terence, 137, 174
Beddard, Doris, 114
Beeching, Richard, 73
Bentley, 36, 96, 115, 122, 126, 131, 151, 163,
    214
Berkeley Bandit, 69
Bernbach, William, 47
Bertoni, Flaminio, 52, 68
Betjeman, John, 35
Biba, 257
Bideford Bay, 38
Birmingham Cathedral, 214
Birmingham–Coventry sewer, 180
Birmingham Motor Show, 14, 247
Birmingham Post, 259
Blenheim Palace, 38
Blow-Up, 167
Blumer, Jimmy, 123
BMC, *see* British Motor Corporation

BMC News, 114, 143
BMW, 13–14, 48, 158, 177
  BMW DesignWorks, 264
  BMW World, 268
  and bubble cars, 48–9
  and MINI development, 235–41, 244–53
  and MINI launch, 255–68
  Rover takeover, 226–34, 247–9
BMW X5, 227, 238
Bolan, Marc, 194–5
Bond, James, 167, 262
Bond Aircraft and Engineering Co., 22
Borgward Goliath, 77
Boulanger, Pierre, 52
Boulting, Roy, 138
Bourne Identity, The, 262
Boyle, Robert, 37–8
Brabham, Jack, 127
Bramley, James, 88
Brands Hatch, 123, 128–9
Brazil, 48, 233, 239
Bristol, 14–15
Bristol Aeroplane Company, 68
British Aerospace, 208, 217, 226, 228, 245
British Army, 164
British Grand Prix, 89
British Leyland Motor Corporation (BL), 8–9,
    179, 188, 190, 102–3, 217
  and dealerships, 186–7, 202
  and *The Italian Job*, 179–80
British Motor Corporation (BMC), 246, 248
  annual report, 134
  and badge engineering, 43–5
  commercial success, 157
  corporate structure, 88
  and export market, 76
  and Jaguar merger, 173, 178
  labour relations, 43, 69, 102, 157, 173
  and Leyland merger, 179
  and marketing, 75, 98–9, 134
  and Mini design and development, 75–82
  and Mini launch, 87–8, 93, 96–100, 104,
    111
  and Mini replacement, 184–5
  and motor sport, 121, 123, 126–7, 129–30,
    153–4, 169–71, 174–5, 177, 187
  products and design, 53–7, 59
  profitability, 173–5
  and Snowdons' wedding, 114
British Motor Holdings, 173, 178
British Motor Industry Heritage Centre, 237,
    247–8
British Railways, 35, 73
British Road Federation, 71–2
British Saloon Car Championships, 193
British Shipbuilders, 208
British Transport and Road Research
    Laboratory, 108, 145
British United Air Ferries, 156
Broadspeed Engineering, 122
bubble cars, 22, 25–6, 47–9, 69–70, 98
Buchanan, Colin, 72–3, 108–9, 111
Buckingham Palace, 114, 165, 186
Buick, 62
Burlington House, 136
Burzi, Ricardo 'Dick', 54–5, 134
Butler Education Act, 135

Cadbury Schweppes, 203
Caine, Michael, 178–81, 245
California, 41, 50, 227, 237–8, 253, 257, 264,
    266
Campaign for Nuclear Disarmament, 103
Campbell, Lindsay, 203
Car and Car Conversions magazine, 163, 190
CAR magazine, 137, 188, 204–5, 212, 224, 231
car radios, 85
car tax, 40, 65
Carli, Renzo, 52
Carlisle, Christabel, 121, 128
Carnaby Street, 54, 115
Carrozzeria Pininfarina, 51–2
Carry on Camping, 167
'Cars for Cities' report, 71, 112
Casson, Sir Hugh, 136
Castrol, 187
catalytic converters, 111, 222
Catch Us If You Can, 167
Chambers, Marcus, 121
Checker, Chubby, 155
Chevrolet, 39, 76
Chongqing Big Science & Technology Co.,
    153, 166
Christiansen, Kay, 149
Chrysler, 233, 239, 267
Churchill, Winston, 23
Citroën 2CV, 49, 52
Citroën Bijou, 93
Citroën DS, 52–4, 68, 170
Citroën Traction Avant, 52, 54
Clark, Roger, 170
class system, 35, 60, 74, 221
  class deference, 103
  class mobility, 115–16
  middle class, 35, 62, 116
  working class, 28, 35, 60, 62–3, 73, 76,
    87, 99–100, 102, 107, 116–17, 137
Classic & Sports Car magazine, 237
Cogan, Alma, 54
Collinson, Tony, 178
Come Dancing, 60
Common Market, 56–7, 131, 173, 177, 200
Communist Party of Great Britain, 43
Compasso d'Oro prize, 50
Conservative Party, 23, 73, 98, 100, 141, 190,
    194, 199
conspicuous consumption, 28–9, 31, 34
conspicuous thrift, 135–8
constant-velocity joints, 68, 79
Consumer Engineering, 31
Consumers' Association, 33
Cooney, Ray, 138
Cooper, John, 124–6, 129–30, 145, 147, 187,
    189, 245–6
  and BMW, 230, 241
  his death, 252
  and last Mini, 252
  and Mini revival, 219–21, 224–5
Cooper, Michael, 220
Cooper, Tommy, 156
Corbett, Harry, 138
Council of Industrial Design, 23, 60
Courrèges, André, 162
Coventry Climax, 124

Coventry Evening Telegraph, 259
Coward, Noël, 114, 178
Cowley, 37–8, 43–4, 66–7, 69, 238
  and BMW, 228–9, 233, 244, 249, 253,
    257, 263, 265
  and Mini development, 82–3
  and Mini launch, 91
  and Mini production, 87–8
  Mini production ends, 188–9
Craig, Wendy, 203
Cuban missile crisis, 134
Cuff, Sue, 193
Curtis, Natalie, 14–16

DAF, 158
Daihatsu Compagno Berlina, 158
Daily Mirror, 98–9, 186
Daily Telegraph, 35, 138
Daimler, 36
DaimlerChrysler, 234
Dallas, Karl F, 161
Damon, Matt, 262
Daniels, William John 'Jack', 38–9, 67, 82,
    89, 230, 252
Datsun, 187, 200, 206
Davies, Marilyn, 142–4
Davos, 113
Dawson, Tony, 210
Day, Graham, 208, 210
Day, Robin, 60
Dean, James, 193
Deeley, Michael, 178–9
Deighton, Len, 163
Design Council, 60, 62, 135
  see also Council of Industrial Design
Design magazine, 92, 112
Detroit, 28–9, 38, 47, 55, 61, 63, 65, 76, 96,
    227
Dichter, Ernest, 30–1, 141
DKW, 158
Dors, Diana, 62
Douglas-Home, Sir Alec, 108, 155
Downing Street, 150
Downton Engineering, 122–3, 125, 129, 163,
    175, 189–90, 224
Duke of Edinburgh, 56, 60
Duke of Kent, 136
Dundalk Engineering, 49
Dunlop, 68, 79–80, 226
Dutch Tulip Rally, 124, 129
Dyson, James, 113

Eagle comic, 137
Earl's Court, 11, 143
  Motor Shows, 23, 40, 53, 93, 142, 151
early adopters, 32, 62
  and Mini, 102, 104, 113, 133, 138
  and MINI, 263
  and performance Minis, 122–3, 127
Easter, Ralph, 157
Economist, 92
Edmonds, Noel, 207
Edwardes, Sir Michael, 203–4
Eisenhower, Dwight D., 71
Ekland, Britt, 151–2
electric cars, 111–12, 265–7
Elizabeth II, Queen, 50, 99, 186

Elsies River plant, 205
Elstree Studios, 149
English Racing Automobiles, 53
environment and pollution, 199, 222–3
  see also traffic congestion
Epstein, Brian, 152
ERA Specialist Vehicles, 225
Evening News, 144

Fairthorpe Atom, 69
Faithfull, Marianne, 152
Farina, Giovanni Battista 'Pinin', 50–2, 54,
    56–7, 69, 75, 86, 169, 185
Farina, Sergio, 52, 86
Fédération Internationale de l'Automobile,
    170
Fend, Fritz, 47
Ferrari, 125–6, 256
Festival of Britain, 23, 60
Fiat, 55, 125, 188, 191, 206, 210, 218
  and *The Italian Job*, 178, 180
Fiat 500, 50, 114, 158, 267
Fiat Punto, 241
Fighting Vehicles Research and Development
    Establishment, 90
Financial Times, 250
'Fish carburettor', 148
Fisher & Ludlow, 87
Fisher-Bendix, 187
Flajole, William, 55
Flockhart, Ron, 116
Fonteyn, Dame Margot, 138
Ford, Henry, 24
Ford, 45, 55, 62, 81, 122, 187, 229, 238,
    267
  and Austin-Rover, 217
  and BMC, 75, 100, 173–4
  and Land Rover, 247–8
  SUV sales, 227
Ford Anglia, 87, 93, 174
Ford Consul, 62, 135
Ford Cortina, 108, 137, 169–70, 186, 188
Ford Edsel, 30
Ford Escort, 187
Ford Falcon, 76, 155
Ford Fiesta, 191
Ford Focus, 265
Ford Galaxy, 131
Ford Ka, 238
Ford Model T, 237
Ford Pilot, 36
Ford Popular, 87, 107
Ford Zephyr, 62, 123
Ford Zodiac, 34
Forman, Freddie, 65
Forsyth, Bruce, 156
four-wheel drives (4 x 4), 223, 265
France, 48–50, 52–4, 60, 79, 84, 101, 131,
    208
Frankfurt Motor Show, 241, 248
front-wheel drive, 79, 169, 191, 213, 240
Fry, Jeremy, 113–14

Gaggia espresso machines, 54
Galbraith, John Kenneth, 27–8, 135
Galvin, Theresa, 71
Gaydon, 232, 237, 239, 247–8

General Motors, 205, 231, 238, 267
Geneva Motor Show, 228, 240–1
Germany, 25, 45–6, 71, 249, 258
Ghia, 238
Giacosa, Dante, 50, 210, 267
gin, 86, 93, 123
Giolito, Roberto, 267
Giugiaro, Giorgetto, 200, 237
Glanville, Sir William, 145
Goodyear, Charles, 67
Goons, 116
Gordini, Amédée, 124
Gosling military vehicle, 164
Grace, Princess, of Monaco, 138
Griffin, Charles, 69, 83

Hagendorf, Dana B, 263
Hahn, Carl H, 47
Hall, Robin, 248
Hamilton, Richard, 61
Hams Hall, 263
Hanks, Reginald, 40
Hardman, PC David, 195
Harlow, 107–8
Harriman, George, 43, 76, 81, 87–8, 125–6,
    130, 134, 154
Harrison, Donald, 39
Harrison, George, 152
Harrow, Dale, 59
Hartwell, Lord, 138
Hasselkus, Walter 231, 241, 247
Haynes, Roy, 186, 188
Heath, Edward, 199
Heinkel bubble cars, 22, 49
Henderson, Bob, 148
Heseltine, Michael, 221
Hidden Persuaders, The (Packard), 96
Hildebrand, Gert Volker, 256–7, 268
Hill, Graham, 122
Hillman Avenger, 113
Hillman Imp, 87, 134, 158
Hillman Minx, 20, 62, 76
Hino Motors, 49
hire-purchase controls, 100, 174
Hispano-Suiza, 115
Honda, 213, 228, 232, 264
Hooydonk, Adriaan van, 240
Hopkirk, Paddy, 7, 21, 91, 119, 179, 213, 220,
    265
    and last Mini, 252
    Monte Carlo successes, 129–31, 153–6,
        169–71, 226
Hornby, Lesley, see Twiggy
Horse under Water (Deighton), 163
Howe, Kevin, 252
hydrostatic transmission, 207

import duty, 23
Innocenti, 57, 189
Insolent Chariots, The, 61
Institute of Contemporary Arts, 61
International Mini Meet, 258
Iranian revolution, 29, 205
Ireland, 49, 57
Isle of Wight festival, 7
Issigonis, Sir Alec, 2, 7–9
    arrogance, 37, 40, 82, 211

and BMW MINI, 228, 230–1, 241, 252,
    256, 259–60, 268
his centenary, 267
his death and funeral, 212–14
feud with Moulton, 185, 210, 260
General Motors praise for, 205
honoured, 183–4, 186
illness and decline, 210
and The Italian Job, 178
and later BL cars, 190, 200, 202
later designs, 206–7
and Lord Snowdon, 8, 113–14, 143
marginalised at BL, 179
and military vehicles, 164
and Mini design and development, 69,
    75–82, 84–5, 104, 238
and Mini launch, 93, 98, 99–100
and Mini replacement, 184–5, 210
and Mini windows, 134, 183
and Morris Minor, 36–41, 66
and motor sport, 121–2, 124–6, 130, 154–5
his name as trade mark, 133
politics and prejudices, 76–7, 80–, 261
retirement and legacy, 186–8
his return to Longbridge, 66–8
and safety, 85, 102–3, 196–7
and transport of the future, 109, 111
and VW Beetle, 68–9
Italian Job, The, 163, 177–81, 214, 245
Italy, 25, 50, 54, 56–7, 59–60, 62, 189

Jagger, Mick, 152, 214
Jaguar, 23, 36, 76, 111, 137, 173, 203, 205,
    217, 229, 232
Jaguar E-type, 115, 147, 151
Janspeed Engineering, 123, 224
Japan, 131, 191, 200, 205, 210, 226
    and kei cars, 49, 112
    and Mini revival, 218–21, 244–5, 252
Jay, Douglas, 46
Job, Reg, 39
Jones, Gloria, 194–5
Jowett, 36, 41
Julienne, Rémy, 179–80

Karmann, 225
Keeler, Christine, 141–2, 144
Kekkonen, President, 138
Kennedy Martin, Troy, 177–8
King's Road, 115–16, 161, 164–5, 189
Kingham, Chris, 67
Kirby, Kathy, 156
Koto, Holden R, 44
Kuenheim, Eberhard von, 247

Labour Party, 20, 33, 137
    New Labour, 239, 247
Lagonda, 36
Lambretta scooters, 57, 99
LAMM Autohaus, 225
Lampredi, Aurelio, 125
Lancia, 54
Land Rover, 23, 163, 165, 217, 226, 228
    sold to Ford, 247–8
Lane, Carla, 203
Le Figaro, 101
le Grice, Oliver, 236

Lee, Chris, 238
Lefèbvre, André, 52–3
Lennon, John, 152
Levassor, Emile, 213
Liddon, Henry, 131, 154, 177
Lightweight Special, 37
Lincoln Continental, 151
Live and Let Die, 167
Lockheed brakes, 125
Locomobile steam car, 67
Loewy, Raymond, 29, 44, 55, 62
Lollobrigida, Gina, 52
London
    post-war, 20, 72
    traffic congestion and parking, 107–9
    swinging, 161–2, 175
London and Surrey Mini Club, 258
London Palladium, 156, 171, 178
London-to-Brighton Mini run, 258
Longbridge, 9, 43–4, 54–6, 217, 238
    and BMW, 228–30, 232–4, 245, 247–9, 251
    and British Leyland, 178–9
    and Issigonis' retirement, 188
    labour relations, 43, 69, 173, 202, 207
    and Metro production, 206
    and Mini Coopers, 125–7, 145
    and Mini design, 77–82, 104
    and Mini launch, 95–6
    and Mini production, 84, 87–8, 189
    Mini production ends, 13
    and Moke production, 165
    new factory opens, 22, 25
    return of Issigonis, 66–8
    Snowdons visit, 114
    Thatcher visits, 206
Longman, Richard, 193
Loos, Adolf, 82
Lord, Sir Leonard, 25–6, 37, 43–4, 53, 55–6, 66
    and Mini development, 68–70, 76–7, 83–4, 238
    and Mini marketing, 87, 97–8
Los Angeles Motor Show, 267
Love, John, 129
Lucas, 78, 81
Lulu, 13, 204, 252

M1 motorway, 73–4, 196
McCartney, Paul, 152
McLaren, Bruce, 127
Macmillan, Harold, 33, 73, 108, 116, 141, 150, 266
McQueen, Steve, 127–9
Magical Mystery Tour, 152
Magistretti, Vico, 50
Magnificent Seven, The, 127
Mäkinen, Timo, 154, 157, 170
Man in a Suitcase, 167
Margaret, Princess, 8, 114, 143, 149, 152, 165
Marina, Princess, 114
Marples, Ernest, 73, 93, 108, 112, 145
Marshall, Frank, 262–3
Maudling, Reginald, 142
Maugham, W. Somerset, 123
Mays, J, 229
Mercedes-Benz, 155, 231, 233
Mercedes-Benz A class, 238, 240
Messel, Oliver, 113

Messerschmitt bubble cars, 22, 47–8
Metro, 206–7, 210, 219, 225, 236
MG, 13, 41, 43, 76, 121, 217, 226, 228
MG Midget, 21, 36
Michelotti, Giovanni, 54
microcars, 23, 69
Milberg, Joachim, 247–8, 251
Milligan, Spike, 204
Millinder, Margaret, 114
Mills, Hayley, 138
Mini
    1275GT, 189, 193–5
    badge branding, 86–9, 117, 134, 243
    birthdays, 16, 214, 220, 248, 268
    body shell, 81, 84, 213
    Clubman, 188, 190, 196, 199
    colours, 89
    commercial success, 157–8
    design and development, 75–82
    engine, 77–9, 82, 84–5, 87, 213
    estate versions, 117, 134, 188
    and female demographic, 208–9
    front-wheel drive, 79–80, 213
    gearbox, 79, 87
    'gearless', 9, 206
    handling and acceleration, 102–3
    internal layout, 85–6
    last Mini, 252
    launch, 88–92
    limited and special editions, 205–6, 211–12, 220
    Lord Snowdon and, 114, 127, 136
    marketing, 87–90, 203–4, 209
    and MINI launch, 249–52
    modifications, 147–9
    and motor sport, 119–33, 193, 245, *see also* Mini Cooper
    and parking, 107, 112
    popularity, 102–5, 113–17
    press reviews, 91–2, 101–2
    price and profitability, 87–8, 91, 99, 174, 181, 187, 189, 206, 208
    production approved, 84
    production ends, 13–14, 188–9
    production numbers, 1, 92, 102, 117, 133, 185, 207, 210, 214, 252, 263
    prototypes, 8, 80–4, 86
    replacement model, 184–5
    reprieved, 204–5, 208
    revival, 218–21, 223–5
    safety, 85, 102–3, 122, 196–7, 208
    sales, 95–100, 113, 117, 133–4, 190
    and sex, 161–2, 218
    speedometer, 85
    steam-powered, 207
    suspension, 79–80, 85, 87, 169
    and swinging sixties, 141–5
    on television, 152, 156, 167
    Vanden Plas Princess, 218
    vans, 117, 134
    water ingress problem, 84, 95
    wheels, 79–80, 174
    windows, 85–6, 134, 183
    see also Mini Cooper
MINI, 2, 14–15, 27
    dimensions, 260
    early development, 235–41

electric drive model, 265–7
gender identity, 256
launch, 249–53, 255–68
marketing, 255–8
production numbers, 263
variants, 264–5
Mini clubs, 258, 261
Mini Cooper, 7, 109, 113, 115, 119, 145, 158, 186
fashionable owners, 150–2, 162–3
and *The Italian Job*, 178, 180
and Mini revival, 218–21, 223–5
and motor sport, 124–33, 153–7, 169–71, 174–5, 177–8, 240
production ends, 189, 199, 204
'Mini crams', 134
Mini Miglia National Rally, 129
Mini Racing (Carlisle), 121
Mini World magazine, 208, 221, 260
minicabs, 117
minicars, 22–3, 25–6
Minilite magnesium wheels, 122
miniskirts, 115, 162
Ministry of Supply, 38–9
Ministry of Town and Country Planning, 72
Ministry of Transport, 71
Minnow GT, 147–8
Mitchell, Nancy, 101, 155
Mixed Blessing – the Motor in Britain (Buchanan), 73
Mobil economy run, 102
Moke, 153, 164–7
Monkees, 246
Monro, Matt, 13, 251
Montague, Lord, of Beaulieu, 75
Monte Carlo Rally, 124, 129, 154–7, 169–71, 174–5, 177–8, 218, 226, 240
Monza, 125
Moonraker, 167
Moore, Roger, 167
Morley, Kevin, 220
Morley, Lewis, 142
Morris, Ken, 180
Morris, Marcus, 137
Morris company, 37, 43, 45, 178–9, 217
Morris Engines, 87, 125
Morris 10, 38, 116
Morris 1100, 169, 213
Morris Eight, 40
Morris Marina, 190
Morris Minor, 7, 9, 23, 26, 54, 88, 96, 123
badge, 243
design and development, 36–41, 44–5
experimental models, 66–9
export sales, 47, 55, 76
Lord Snowdon and, 114
production numbers, 117
production peak, 70
profitability, 75–6
seats, 80
and small-car design, 213–14
wheels, 79
Morris Oxford, 36, 69
Moskvitch, 93
Mosquito prototype, 39–40
Moss, Pat, 124, 129
Moss, Stirling, 85, 103, 128

MOT test, 35–6, 74
Motor magazine, 25, 36, 69, 92, 137, 189, 224
Motor Sport magazine, 147, 153
motor trade
and BL, 186–7, 202
car dealerships, 35, 45, 75, 91, 96, 98
second-hand, 21
motorways, 36, 72–4
Moulton, Alex, 37, 126, 205, 255, 267
and bicycles, 135–6
and BMW, 230, 239, 260
feud with Issigonis, 185, 210, 260
and MINI, 259–60
and Mini launch, 91, 96, 104
his modified Mini Cooper, 109, 236
and rubber suspension, 67–9, 79
and safety fetures, 102–3
Moulton bicycles, 135–6
Munich, 48, 71, 236–7, 239–40, 256
Musgrove, Harold, 207, 219

Nader, Ralph, 28, 102, 135, 196
Nairn, Ian, 72
Nerus, 122
New Jersey, 47, 266
New York, 263, 266
Museum of Modern Art, 240
New Zealand, 57, 205
Newbury Park, 237
Nissan, 158, 187, 229
Noble, Paula, 138
Northavon Mini club, 13–16
Notts About Mini Club, 261
NSU, 93, 158, 191
Nuffield, Lord (William Morris), 37, 39–40, 43, 45
Nuffield group, 40–1, 43–4, 88, 164, 248

Oak, A V, 39, 66
Odor, Jan, 123, 224
oil-price shocks, 29, 112, 190–1, 199–200, 205
Oselli Engineering, 122
Oulton Park, 128, 131

Packard, Vance, 96, 135
Palmer, Gerald, 36, 41, 44, 66
Panhard, 213
Panke, Helmut, 251
Paradise, Filmer, M, 186
Paramount Studios, 178
Paris, 101, 131, 170
Paris Auto Salon, 52–4, 68, 250, 265
Paris Match, 52
parking meters, 73, 107
Payne, Dorothy, 114
Persuaders, The, 167
'Petite', 69
Petra, Heinrich, 248
petrol rationing, 19–20, 36, 57, 69
Peugeot, 54, 191
Phoenix Vehicle Holdings, 248–9
Pininfarina, *see* Farina, Giovanni Battista 'Pinin'
Pischetsrieder, Bernd, 228–9, 231–3, 236, 239, 241, 244–5, 247
planned obsolescence, 31
Plymouth Valiant, 76

Pollock, Alice, 257
Pomeroy, Laurence, 53, 85, 91, 100, 196
Ponti, Gio, 50
pop culture, 61
Popular Mechanics magazine, 62
Porsche, Ferdinand, 237
Porsche, 193, 235
Portugal, 166
Potente, Franka, 262
Powell, Geoff, 13, 252
Pressed Steel, 173
Prince of Wales, 163
Prisoner, The, 167
Profumo, John, 104, 141–2
public transport, 222
purchase tax, 105, 117
Purves, Tom, 253

Quandt family, 228, 244
Quant, Mary, 20, 63, 65, 115, 135, 162, 199,
    212, 246, 255, 257
Queen, The, magazine, 115–17, 141

RAC Club, 232
RAC Rally, 153
Racing Car Show, 145
Radford coachbuilders, 151–2
RAF Bomber Command, 164
Range Rover, 223, 234
Rapaille, G. Clotaire, 227
Reitzle, Wolfgang, 230–3, 237, 240, 245, 247
Reliant Regal, 22, 212
Renault, 49, 93, 114, 191, 206
Renault Dauphine, 49–50, 76, 80, 99, 116–17,
    124, 135
Reynolds, Bruce, 65
Rice-Davies, Mandy, 142–3, 147
Richardson, Tony, 113
Richmond, Bunty, 123, 190
Richmond, Daniel, 122–3, 129–30, 147, 179,
    187, 190, 246
Riley, 41, 43–5, 88, 217, 228–9
Riley Elf, 134, 188
Road and Track magazine, 101
road building, 71–4, 107, 199–200, 222–3
road safety, 28, 85, 102–3, 196–7
Road Traffic Acts, 73, 107
Robinson, Derek ('Red Robbo'), 202
Rolls-Royce, 36, 76, 104, 114, 122, 149, 151–2
Rootes, Lord, 45
Rootes company, 62, 87, 91
Rotork, 113
Rover, 133, 217
    and BMW takeover, 226–34, 247–9
    and Mini replacement, 235–41, 243–4,
        247–9
    and Mini revival, 220, 224–5
Rover 75, 234, 244, 247
Rover 90, 36, 103
Royal Academy of Arts, 136
Royal Electrical and Mechanical Engineers, 45
Royal Navy, 37–8, 164`
Royal Society, 183
rubber, vulcanised, 67–8
Russell, Sir Gordon, 62
Ryder Report, 202

Saab, 49, 77
Saddington, David, 236, 238, 241
Saint, The, 167
Salvadori, Roy, 127
Sämann, Werner, 13, 247, 249
Scammell, Emma, 258
Scratchwood service area, 74
seat belts, 35, 85, 103, 145
Sellers, Peter, 149–51, 214
Setright, L J K, 188, 221
Sex Discrimination Act, 204
Shand, Camilla, 163
Sheppard, John, 67, 210, 252
Shot in the Dark, A, 149
Shrimpton, Jean, 11
Silverstone, 119, 214, 220, 248
Sked, Gordon, 230, 236
Skoda, 186
Small Car and Mini Owner, 137, 147, 149,
    157–8, 196
Smart Car, 238
Smeed, R J, 108
Smith, Paul, 244
Smith, Sidney, 84
Smyrna, 36–7
Snowdon, Lord (Tony Armstrong-Jones), 8,
        103, 143, 165, 206, 214
    and Mini, 113–14, 127, 136
    and MINI, 259
South Africa, 57, 205
Soviet Union, 84, 155, 164
Spain, 84, 189
speed limits, 36, 196
Speedwell Performance Conversions, 122
Spence, Sir Basil, 104
Spencer, Lady Diana, 206
Spencer Moulton, 68
Sputnik I, 84
Spy Who Loved Me, The, 167
Standard-Triumph, 54–5
Standard Vanguard, 36, 54
Starr, Ringo, 152
steel production, 21
steering, rack-and-pinion, 38, 40
Stephenson, Frank, 238, 240, 251, 256,
    267
Stokes, Donald, 179, 185–7, 189, 202
Strategy of Desire, The (Dichter), 30, 141
Studebaker Lark, 76
Subaru 450, 158
subtopias, 72
Suez Crisis, 19, 25, 36, 43, 57, 69, 191
Sunbeam Alpine, 76, 116
Sunday Mirror, 142
Sunday Telegraph, 109
Sunday Times, 214
superminis, 190–1
suspension
    hydragas, 109, 236, 239, 260
    hydrolastic, 169
    independent, 38, 40
    McPherson struts, 185
    rubber, 66–8, 79–80, 85, 185
    torsion bar, 38–9
SUVs, 223, 263–4
Suzuki SJ410, 223
Swift, Ernestine, 186

Talbot, Cedric, 219
Tarbuck, Jimmy, 171
Taurus Performance Tuning, 122
Tech Dell, 122
teenagers, 63
Thatcher, Margaret, 9, 135, 206–7, 210, 217, 221–2, 231, 235
Theory of the Leisure Class (Veblen), 28
Thomas, Miles, 39–40
Thoroughbred & Classic Cars magazine, 8
Times, The, 91
Toivonen, Pauli, 170
Tomalin, Nicholas, 116, 135
Tortoise self-propelled gun, 38
Toth, George, 123
Tothill, Peter, 82
Tour de France, 131, 153
'Tourette', 69
Towers, John, 229, 231, 248–9
Town magazine, 116, 135–7, 193, 221
Townsend, Peter, 114
Toyota, 158, 267
Trade Motors Federation, 20
trade unions, 43, 207, 247–8
Trades Union Congress, 72
traffic congestion, 71–4, 107–9, 111–12, 222–3
traffic wardens, 73, 108
transverse engine, 79, 85, 169, 191, 213, 240
Tripp, Sir Alker, 72
Triumph, 21, 76, 179, 205, 217
Triumph Acclaim, 232
Triumph Herald, 54, 93, 102
Trojan, 49
Turin, 50–1, 56, 81, 86, 103, 238
and *The Italian Job*, 178, 180
Turnbull, George, 179
Turner, Stuart, 129, 131, 154, 170, 187
Twiggy (Lesley Hornby), 21–2, 204, 209, 214, 245

Unicorn consultancy, 239
Unipower, 79
United States of America
and British car exports, 46–7, 57
and British design, 61–3
car ownership, 24, 27–31, 108–9
and discrete car design, 38
and European cars, 50, 76
and marketing, 28–32, 80–1, 96, 99–100, 104, 133, 135, 227
and Mini, 101–2, 181, 196, 205
and MINI, 245, 249, 253, 256, 263
and road safety, 196

and SUV craze, 226–7
and VW sales, 46, 76
Upex, Geoff, 238, 240
US Army, 165
USA Today, 262
Ustinov, Sir Peter, 212

V W Derrington, 122
V&A Museum, 23
Vauxhall, 34, 55, 62
Veblen, Thorstein, 28
Viking Rally, 124
Viz comic, 195
Vogue magazine, 8, 101, 155
Volkswagen, 218, 229, 231, 267–8
Volkswagen Beetle, 22, 45–7, 68, 76, 114, 135, 147, 158, 256
Volkswagen Golf, 200, 213, 235
Volkswagen Polo, 191, 206
Vollath, Wolfgang, 250
Volvo, 135

Walker, George, 62
War Lover, The, 128
War Office, 38
Ward, Stephen, 144
WCRS advertising agency, 255
Webster, Harry, 179
Welbeck Motors, 117
welfare state, 62
Westminster Abbey, 114
What Car magazine, 223
Which? magazine, 33, 135, 196
Whitmore, Sir John, 128
Widcombe Manor, 113
Williams, T L, 22
Wilson, Harold, 137, 174, 199
Windsor Great Park, 99
Wisdom, Norman, 138
Wodehouse, P G, 8
Wolfe, Tom, 161–2
Wolfsburg, 45, 47
Wolseley, 36, 39, 43–5, 57, 87, 217
Wolseley Hornet, 134, 188
women, 30–1, 80–1, 90, 203–4, 208–9, 227, 256–7
Woodgate, Crispian, 11
Woodhouse, David, 236
World Cup football, 174

Yimkin Engineering, 122
Yorkshire Post, 22
You Only Live Twice, 167
Young, Michael, 33

Zittel, Andrea, 257

Picture Credits

© jalopnik.com
265

© Original ad from the Miguel Plano collection
10 (original David Sparrow), *110, 120, 125, 195, 201, 209*

© Mirrorpix
140, 176

© PA Photos
144, 149

© Pictorial Press Ltd / Alamy
168

© Popperfoto / Getty Images
150

© Science & Society Picture Library
33

© Snowdon / VOGUE, Camera Press London
viii

© TopFoto
89, 211

© *Town* magazine, 1962, cartoon by Trog
136

© E.J. Wing
115